LanCom
Language & Communication

대치동 기적의 중학영어 영단어 1800 2단계

발행일	2025년 10월 20일 1쇄 발행
지은이	더 좋은 교육연구소
발행인	손건
편집기획	김상배, 장수경
마케팅	최관호, 김재명
디자인	보스코
제작	최승용
인쇄	선경프린테크
발행처	랭컴
주소	서울시 영등포구 영등포동 4가 146-5
등록번호	312-2006-00060
도서구입문의	전화 02-2636-0895 팩스 02-2636-0896

ISBN 979-11-7142-093-3 13740

국제학교 학생들만큼 영어를 잘하게 만들어주는, 세상에 없던 대한민국 유일의 주니어용 쉐도잉 & 딕테이션 영단어 교재

대치동, 기적의 중학영어 영단어 1800

하루 20단어, 20문장씩
이미지로 연상하고 듣고 따라하면서 학습하는
가장 확실하고, 놀라운 실력향상 프로그램

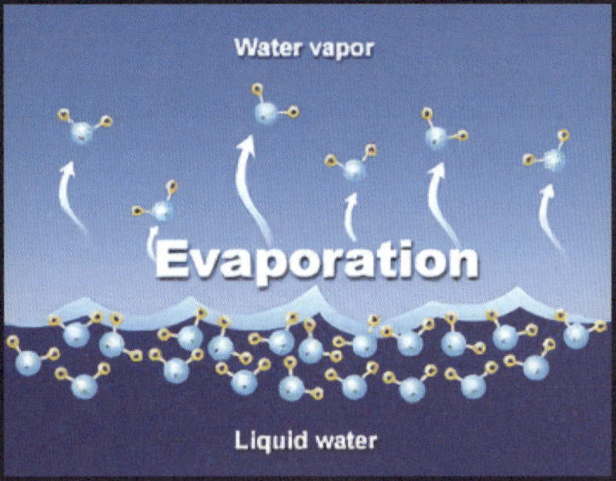

AI 학습자료와 인강

세상에 없던 대한민국 유일의 주니어용 쉐도잉 & 딕테이션 영단어 교재

VOCABULARY LEVEL 2
AGE 7-15

정말, 놀라운 대치동 기적의 중학영어 3 STEP 반복 훈련법이 적용된 주니어 필수교재!

LanCom
Language & Communication

국제학교 학생들만큼 영어를 잘하게 만들어 주는, 대치동 기적의 3 STEP 학습법과 훈련법이 적용된
대치동 기적의 속진선행 영재교육 프로그램 안내

대치동 기적의 영재교육 속진선행 PROGRAM

대상 / 단계	속진선행 영재교육	수월성 선행교육	평준화 현행교육
고등 대기고 3단계 8권	초등 5, 6학년 때 완성	중학 1, 2, 3학년 때 완성	고등 1, 2, 3학년 때 완성
중학 대기중 3단계 8권	초등 3, 4학년 때 완성	초등 4, 5, 6학년 때 완성	중학 1, 2, 3학년 때 완성
초등 대기초 6단계 14권	초등 1, 2학년 때 완성	초등 1, 2, 3학년 때 완성	초등 1, 2, 3, 4, 5, 6학년 때 완성

*대치동 기적의 초등영어, 중학영어, 고등영어 시리즈는 대치동 기적의 속진선행 영재교육 PROGRAM에서 사용하는 핵심 교재입니다.

*대치동 기적의 초등영어, 중학영어, 고등영어 시리즈의 핵심 공부법은 QR 찍고 따라하기 입니다. QR 찍고 따라만 해도 기적이 일어납니다!

*대치동 기적의 초등영어, 중학영어, 고등영어의 내용은 인생에서 언젠가 한 번은 완성해야 할 피할 수 없는 영어 학습의 필수 과정입니다. 따라서 최대한 어린 시기에 빨리 완성해야 합니다. 부모가 아이의 언어학습을 미루면 결국 아이는 언어습득을 포기하게 되거나 늦은 시기에 시작한 대가를 치르게 될 뿐 이로운 점은 하나도 없습니다.

대치동 기적의 초등영어 LEVEL CHART

Book Level	대기초 영단어 1800	대기초 통문장 1800	내용
총정리 워크북			국제학교 학생들만큼 영어를 잘하게 만들어 주는 대치동 기적의 초등영어 커리큘럼은 총정리 워크북을 포함해 전체 14권 6단계로 구성되어 있습니다. 먼저 대기초 영단어 1단계와 대기초 통문장 1단계를 한 달에 끝내세요. 한 달에 2권씩 6개월 안에 6단계의 대기초 시리즈를 끝냅니다. 이후 바로 대치동 기적의 중학영어 커리큘럼을 순서대로 공부해 나가면 됩니다.
6단계			
5단계			
4단계			
3단계			
2단계			
1단계			

*대치동 기적의 초등영어는 만4세에서 만12세 사이의 학습자를 위한 교재입니다.

국제학교 학생들만큼 영어를 잘하게 만들어 주는, 대치동 기적의 3 STEP 학습법과 훈련법이 적용된
대치동 기적의 초등영어, 중학영어, 고등영어 시리즈 안내

대치동 기적의 중학영어 LEVEL CHART

Book Level	대기중 영단어 1800	대기중 통문장 1800	내용
총정리 워크북			대치동 기적의 중학영어 커리큘럼은 총정리 워크북을 포함해 전체 8권 3단계로 구성되어 있습니다. 먼저 대기중 영단어 1단계와 대기중 통문장 1단계를 한 달에 끝내세요, 한 달에 2권씩 3개월 안에 3단계의 대기중 시리즈를 끝내고 대치동 기적의 고등영어 커리큘럼을 순서대로 공부해 나가면 됩니다.
3단계			
2단계			
1단계			

*국제학교 학생들의 수준이 되기 위해서는 대기중 공부 시기에 사이먼 미국교과서 100에서 900까지를 병행해 완성해야 합니다!

*대치동 기적의 중학영어는 만7세에서 만15세 사이의 학습자를 위한 교재입니다.

대치동 기적의 고등영어 LEVEL CHART

Book Level	대기고 영단어 1800	대기고 통문장 1800	내용
총정리 워크북			대치동 기적의 고등영어 커리큘럼은 총정리 워크북을 포함해 전체 8권 3단계로 구성되어 있습니다. 먼저 대기고 영단어 1단계와 대기고 통문장 1단계를 한 달에 끝내세요, 한 달에 2권씩 3개월 안에 3단계의 대기고 시리즈를 끝내고 본격적인 수능영어 모의고사 문제 풀이를 시작하면 됩니다.
3단계			
2단계			
1단계			

*국제학교 학생들의 수준이 되기 위해서는 대기고 공부 시기에 사이먼 미국교과서 1000에서 1800까지를 병행해 완성해야 합니다!

*대치동 기적의 고등영어는 만10세에서 만18세 사이의 학습자를 위한 교재입니다.

미국 영국 캐나다 호주 독일 프랑스 이탈리아 일본 인도 학생들이 공부하는 세계 최고의 주니어 영어교육 프로그램
사이먼 미국교과서 시리즈 안내

Dr. Simon's Magic English Series LEVEL CHART

Book Level	Subject	USA Grade in School	Typical Age
1800 1700 1600	 Technology Series	**Grade 6** (Non-native Grade 8-9) 대치동 기준 중학 2, 3학년부터	
1500 1400 1300	 Social Science Series	**Grade 5** (Non-native Grade 7-8) 대치동 기준 중학 1, 2학년부터	**Age 10-12** (Non-native Age 13-15)
1200 1100 1000	 Science Series	**Grade 4** (Non-native Grade 6-7) 대치동 기준 초중 6, 1학년부터	
900 800 700	 History Series	**Grade 3** (Non-native Grade 5-6) 대치동 기준 초등 5, 6학년부터	
600 500 400	 Biography Series	**Grade 2** (Non-native Grade 4-5) 대치동 기준 초등 4, 5학년부터	**Age 7-9** (Non-native Age 10-12)
300 200 100	 Literature Series	**Grade 1** (Non-native Grade 3-4) 대치동 기준 초등 3, 4학년부터	

*CORRELATED TO USA CURRENT STATE STANDARDS

*시리즈 전체 18권을 끝내게 되면 TOEFL READING과 LISTENING 섹션의 만점과 대한민국 수능영어 절대 1등급의 영어실력 달성이 가능합니다.

VOCA 100-900		**VOCABULARY BOOK 100-900** 사이먼 미국교과서 **100**에서 **900**까지의 어휘를 총정리한 영영 사전식 단어장 겸 테스트 북
VOCA 1000-1800		**VOCABULARY BOOK 1000-1800** 사이먼 미국교과서 **1000**에서 **1800**까지의 어휘를 총정리한 영영 사전식 단어장 겸 테스트 북

첨단기술 시리즈

기술적인 문해력 향상과 디지털 시민성 개발, 창의적인 문제 해결능력과 혁신력 발전, 직업적인 진로 방향성 인식과 미래 직업 시장에 대한 이해, 윤리적인 기술의 사용과 기술의 사회적 영향에 대한 이해를 목적으로 하는 시리즈

사회과학 시리즈

사회적인 현상과 인간관계에 대한 이해, 세계 문화의 이해와 다양성 인식, 시민의식과 공동체 참여의식 향상, 현재와 미래 사회 변화에 대한 이해, 분쟁의 해결능력과 비판적 사고능력의 발달을 목적으로 하는 시리즈

과학 시리즈

탐구적인 태도와 호기심 개발, 문제 해결능력과 비판적 사고능력 발달, 과학적 사고와 관련된 기술과 지식 습득, 인간의 신체와 자연과 환경에 대한 이해와 지속 가능성 인식, 미래 직업적 가능성과 **STEM** 분야에 대한 이해를 목적으로 하는 시리즈

역사 시리즈

역사인식과 시대상황의 이해, 문화적인 다양성 인정과 세계 시민성 강화, 과거의 실수로부터 배우는 교훈과 상식 습득, 시간과 사건의 원인 · 결과 관계 이해, 역사적인 연속성 속에서 자아 정체성 구축을 목적으로 하는 시리즈

인물전기 시리즈

인류를 이끈 위대한 위인들의 소개, 영감을 주는 역사적 롤 모델의 제시, 도덕적 가치와 성찰의 중요성 인식, 인내와 끈기와 근성의 가치 습득, 역사적인 인물들이 인류사회에 끼친 사회적 영향력 이해를 목적으로 하는 시리즈

문학 시리즈

문학적 지식의 향상과 언어 기술의 개발, 인간의 경험과 감정에 대한 이해, 비판적 사고와 분석력 개발, 창의적인 사고와 상상력 발달을 목적으로 하는 시리즈

5회 반복 표제어 QR　5회 반복 예문 QR

DAY 01

30 days

AI 학습자료와 인강 youpass.co.kr

PREVIEW A 다음 단어의 뜻을 한국어로 써보세요.

- ☐ escalate ____________
- ☐ escape ____________
- ☐ especially ____________
- ☐ essence ____________
- ☐ essential ____________
- ☐ establish ____________
- ☐ estimate ____________
- ☐ ethic ____________
- ☐ ethical ____________
- ☐ ethnic ____________
- ☐ evaluate ____________
- ☐ evaporate ____________
- ☐ eventually ____________
- ☐ evidence ____________
- ☐ evident ____________
- ☐ evil ____________
- ☐ evolve ____________
- ☐ exactly ____________
- ☐ exaggerate ____________
- ☐ examine ____________

PREVIEW B 사진을 보고 알맞은 영어 단어를 **PREVIEW A** 에서 찾아 써보세요.

____

____

____

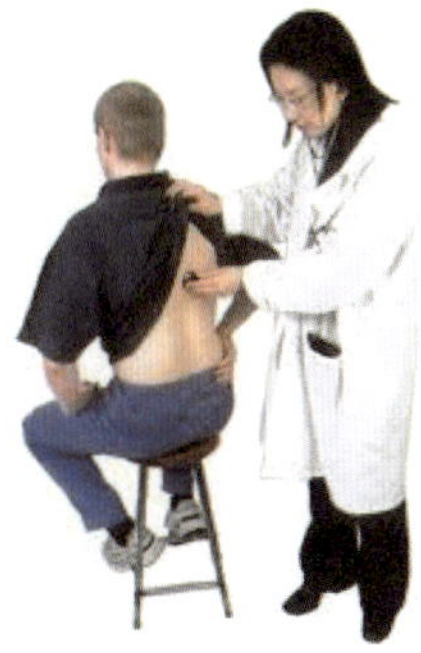
____

0601 □□□

escalate
[ˈeskəleɪt]

v 확대[악화]되다, 증가하다, 고조되다

= intensify, increase, heighten, magnify
+ escalation n 확대, 증대 **escalator n** 에스컬레이터

Q: Will this conflict escalate any further? 이 갈등이 더 고조될까요?

A: ....

0602 □□□

escape
[ɪˈskeɪp]

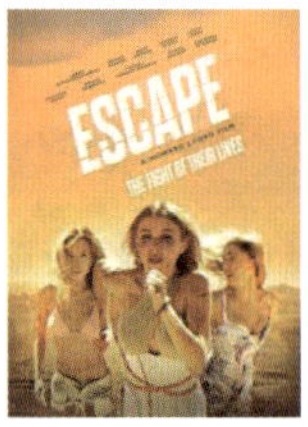

v 탈출하다, 달아나다 **n** 탈출

= flee, run away, evade, get away, breakthrough
+ fire escape (화재 대피용) 비상계단[사다리]

Q: How did they escape the locked room? 그들은 잠긴 방에서 어떻게 탈출했나요?

A: ....

0603 □□□

especially
[ɪˈspeʃəli]

adv 특히

= particularly, notably, specifically, primarily
+ special a 특별한 **especial a** 특별한

Q: Is this especially popular these days? 요즘 이게 특히 인기가 많나요?

A: ....

0604 □□□

essence
[ˈesns]

n 본질, 정수

= core, crux, heart, fundamental nature, spirit
+ essential a 필수적인, 본질적인 **essentially adv** 본질적으로

Q: What's the essence of this whole situation? 이 전체 상황의 본질은 무엇인가요?

A: ....

0605 □□□

essential
[ɪˈsenʃl]

a 필수적인, 본질적인

= vital, crucial, fundamental, indispensable, necessary
+ essence n 본질, 정수 **essentiality n** 본질적임
essentially adv 본질적으로, 근본적으로

Q: What's essential for a successful project?
성공적인 프로젝트에 필수적인 것은 무엇인가요?

A: ....

0606 □□□

establish
[ɪˈstæblɪʃ]

v 설립하다, 확립하다

= set up, found, create, confirm, prove
+ establishment **n** 설립, 시설 **established** **a** 확립된, 인정받는

Q: When did they establish the new guidelines? 새로운 지침을 언제 확립했나요?
A: ....

0607 □□□

estimate
[ˈestɪmət] **n** [ˈestɪmeɪt] **v**

v 평가하다, 추정하다 **n** 견적, 추정치

= guess, assess, approximate, calculate, appraisal
+ estimation **n** 평가, 추정 **estimated** **a** 추정된

Q: Can you estimate the total project cost? 총 프로젝트 비용을 추정할 수 있나요?
A: ....

0608 □□□

ethic
[ˈeθɪk]

n 윤리, 도덕

= moral code, principles, values, morality
+ ethics **n** 윤리학, 윤리 **ethical** **a** 윤리적인

Q: Is a strong work ethic important here? 여기서는 강한 직업윤리가 중요한가요?
A: ....

0609 □□□

ethical
[ˈeθɪkl]

a 윤리적인, 도덕적인

= moral, principled, righteous, conscientious
+ ethic **n** 윤리 **ethics** **n** 윤리학 **ethically** **adv** 윤리적으로

Q: Is this decision really ethical and fair? 이 결정이 정말 윤리적이고 공정한가요?
A: ....

0610 □□□

ethnic
[ˈeθnɪk]

a 민족의, 인종의

= racial, cultural, tribal, ancestral
+ ethnicity **n** 민족성

Q: Have you tried any ethnic foods lately? 최근에 민족 음식을 먹어본 적 있나요?
A: ....

0611 □□□

evaluate
[ɪˈvæljueɪt]

v 평가하다

= assess, appraise, judge, analyze, gauge
+ evaluation **n** 평가 **evaluative** **a** 평가하는

Q: When do you usually evaluate your progress?
보통 언제 진행 상황을 평가하나요?

A: ....

0612 □□□

evaporate
[ɪˈvæpəreɪt]

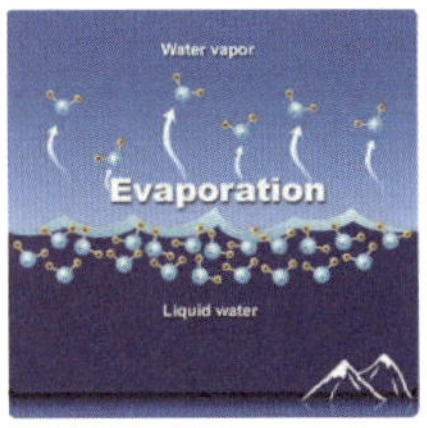

v 증발하다

= vaporize, disappear, vanish, dissipate
+ evaporation **n** 증발

Q: How fast does the water evaporate outside?
밖에서 물이 얼마나 빨리 증발하나요?

A: ....

0613 □□□

eventually
[ɪˈventʃuəli]

adv 결국, 마침내

= ultimately, finally, in the end, in due course
+ eventual **a** 최종적인, 궁극적인 **event** **n** 사건

Q: Will they eventually find a good solution? 그들이 결국 좋은 해결책을 찾을까요?

A: ....

0614 □□□

evidence
[ˈevɪdəns]

n 증거

= proof, data, grounds, indication, testimony
+ evident **a** 분명한 **evidently** **adv** 명백히

Q: Isn't there enough solid evidence so far? 아직 충분한 확실한 증거가 없는 건가요?

A: ....

0615 □□□

evident
[ˈevɪdənt]

a 명백한

= obvious, apparent, clear, manifest, plain
+ evidence **n** 증거 **evidently** **adv** 명백히, 분명히

Q: Was it evident from his body language? 그의 몸짓에서 분명히 드러났나요?

A: ....

0616 □□□

evil
[ˈiːvl]

a 사악한 **n** 악

= **wicked, malicious, malevolent, harmful, vice**
+ **evil-doer** **n** 악한, 악당 **evil eye** 악마의 눈, 저주[독기] 서린 눈초리

Q: Was he really evil in the story? 이야기에서 그가 정말 악했나요?
A: ....

0617 □□□

evolve
[ɪˈvɑːlv]

v 진화하다, 발전하다

= **develop, progress, grow, mature, adapt**
+ **evolution** **n** 진화 **evolutionary** **a** 진화적인

Q: How did this species evolve over time?
이 종은 시간이 지남에 따라 어떻게 진화했나요?
A: ....

0618 □□□

exactly
[ɪgˈzæktli]

adv 정확히

= **precisely, accurately, truly, strictly**
+ **exact** **a** 정확한 **exactness[exactitude]** **n** 정확성

Q: What exactly did she mean by that? 그녀가 정확히 무엇을 의미했나요?
A: ....

0619 □□□

exaggerate
[ɪgˈzædʒəreɪt]

v 과장하다

= **overstate, overdo, magnify, inflate**
+ **exaggeration** **n** 과장

Q: Do people often exaggerate their accomplishments?
사람들이 종종 자신의 업적을 과장하나요?
A: ....

0620 □□□

examine
[ɪgˈzæmɪn]

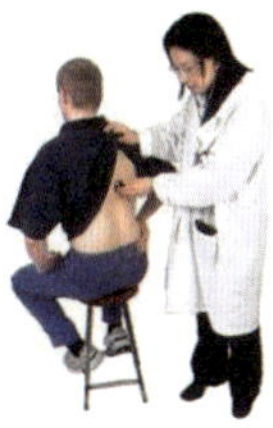

v 조사하다, 검토하다

= **inspect, investigate, analyze, scrutinize, test**
+ **examination** **n** 시험, 조사 **examiner** **n** 시험관 **examined** **a** 조사된

Q: Did the doctor examine you carefully yesterday?
어제 의사가 당신을 주의 깊게 진찰했나요?
A: ....

DAY 01 | DICTATION TEST

5회 반복 예문 QR

DICTATION TEST 예문 QR을 듣고 다음 빈칸에 올바른 단어를 쓰세요.

601. Will this conflict ______________ any further?

602. How did they ______________ the locked room?

603. Is this ______________ popular these days?

604. What's the ______________ of this whole situation?

605. What's ______________ for a successful project?

606. When did they ______________ the new guidelines?

607. Can you ______________ the total project cost?

608. Is a strong work ______________ important here?

609. Is this decision really ______________ and fair?

610. Have you tried any ______________ foods lately?

611. When do you usually ______________ your progress?

612. How fast does the water ______________ outside?

613. Will they ______________ find a good solution?

614. Isn't there enough solid ______________ so far?

615. Was it ______________ from his body language?

616. Was he really ______________ in the story?

617. How did this species ______________ over time?

618. What ______________ did she mean by that?

619. Do people often ______________ their accomplishments?

620. Did the doctor ______________ you carefully yesterday?

5회 반복 표제어 QR　5회 반복 예문 QR

DAY 02
30 days

AI 학습자료와 인강 youpass.co.kr

PREVIEW A 다음 단어의 뜻을 한국어로 써보세요.

□ **exceed** ________	□ **exist** ________
□ **except** ________	□ **existence** ________
□ **excess** ________	□ **exotic** ________
□ **exchange** ________	□ **expand** ________
□ **excitement** ________	□ **expect** ________
□ **exclude** ________	□ **expend** ________
□ **exhaust** ________	□ **expense** ________
□ **exhausted** ________	□ **experience** ________
□ **exhibit** ________	□ **experiment** ________
□ **exhibition** ________	□ **expert** ________

PREVIEW B 사진을 보고 알맞은 영어 단어를 **PREVIEW A** 에서 찾아 써보세요.

____

____

____

____

0621 □□□

exceed
[ɪk'siːd]

v 초과하다

= **surpass, go beyond, outdo, excel**
+ **excessive** **a** 과도한 **excess** **n** 초과

Q: Did the costs exceed our initial budget? 비용이 초기 예산을 초과했나요?

A: ....

0622 □□□

except
[ɪk'sept]

prep ~을 제외하고

= **excluding, apart from, but, other than**
+ **exceptional** **a** 예외적인 **exceptionally** **adv** 예외적으로, 특별히

Q: Is everyone coming except John today? 오늘 존 빼고 다 오나요?

A: ....

0623 □□□

excess
['ekses] **n** [ɪk'ses] **a**

n 초과, 과잉 **a** 과잉의

= **surplus, overflow, redundancy, too much**
+ **excessive** **a** 과도한 **excessively** **adv** 지나치게

Q: Is there excess food after the event? 행사 후에 남는 음식이 있나요?

A: ....

0624 □□□

exchange
[ɪks'tʃeɪndʒ]

v 교환하다 **n** 교환

= **trade, swap, convert, communication, interchange**
+ **exchangeable** **a** 교환 가능한

Q: Can we exchange these items for others?
이 물품들을 다른 것으로 교환할 수 있나요?

A: ....

0625 □□□

excitement
[ɪk'saɪtmənt]

n 흥분

= **thrill, enthusiasm, agitation, exhilaration**
+ **excite** **v** 흥분시키다 **exciting** **a** 신나는 **excited** **a** 흥분한

Q: Was the excitement at the game overwhelming?
경기에서의 흥분이 압도적이었나요?

A: ....

0626 □□□

exclude
[ɪkˈskluːd]

v 제외하다, 배제하다

= omit, bar, prevent, shut out, rule out
+ exclusion n 제외, 배제 exclusive a 독점적인

Q: Did they exclude anyone from the list? 그들이 목록에서 누구를 제외했나요?
A:

0627 □□□

exhaust
[ɪɡˈzɔːst]

v 지치게 하다, 다 써버리다

= tire out, deplete, drain, consume, fumes
+ exhaustion n 고갈, 탈진 exhausting a 힘든, 지치게 하는 exhausted a 지친

Q: Did the long hike exhaust you completely?
긴 하이킹이 당신을 완전히 지치게 했나요?
A:

0628 □□□

exhausted
[ɪɡˈzɔːstɪd]

a 기진맥진한, 소진된

= tired, weary, drained, fatigued, depleted
+ exhaustion n 탈진 exhaust v 지치게 하다, 고갈시키다

Q: Are you feeling exhausted after work today? 오늘 퇴근 후에 지쳤나요?
A:

0629 □□□

exhibit
[ɪɡˈzɪbɪt]

v 전시하다, 보여주다 n 전시품

= display, show, present, manifest, artifact
+ exhibition n 전시회

Q: Did you see the new art exhibit downtown? 시내의 새 미술 전시회를 봤나요?
A:

0630 □□□

exhibition
[ˌeksɪˈbɪʃn]

n 전시회

= display, show, expo, fair, demonstration
+ exhibit v 전시하다 exhibitor n 전시자

Q: Is the exhibition open to the public now? 전시회가 지금 대중에게 개방되나요?
A:

0631 □□□

exist
[ɪɡˈzɪst]

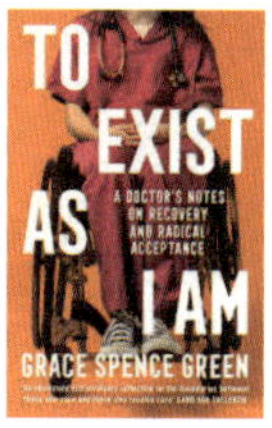

v 존재하다

= **live, be, survive, subsist, occur**
+ **existence** **n** 존재 **existent** **a** 현존하는 **existing** **a** 현존하는

Q: Does life exist on other planets, really? 정말 다른 행성에 생명체가 존재하나요?

A: ....

0632 □□□

existence
[ɪɡˈzɪstəns]

n 존재

= **being, presence, life, reality, survival**
+ **exist** **v** 존재하다

Q: Is the existence of ghosts proven? 유령의 존재가 증명되었나요?

A: ....

0633 □□□

exotic
[ɪɡˈzɑːtɪk]

a 이국적인, 색다른

= **foreign, unusual, unfamiliar, unique, rare**
+ **exoticism** **n** 이국적인 특성

Q: Have you tried any exotic fruits recently?
최근에 이국적인 과일을 먹어본 적 있나요?

A: ....

0634 □□□

expand
[ɪkˈspænd]

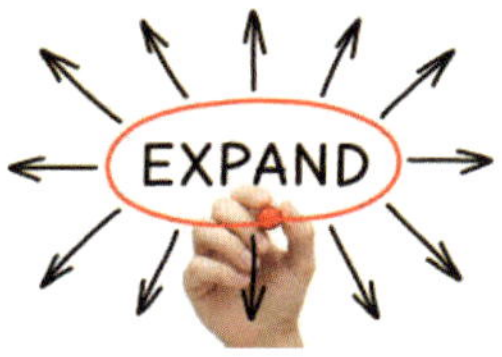

v 확장하다, 팽창하다

= **enlarge, grow, extend, broaden, swell**
+ **expansion** **n** 확장, 팽창 **expansive** **a** 확장적인, 광범위한

Q: Will they expand the business next year? 그들이 내년에 사업을 확장할 건가요?

A: ....

0635 □□□

expect
[ɪkˈspekt]

v 예상하다, 기대하다

= **anticipate, foresee, hope for, require, assume**
+ **expectation** **n** 기대 **expectancy** **n** 예상 **expected** **a** 예상된
unexpected **a** 예상치 못한

Q: What do you expect from the meeting tomorrow?
내일 회의에서 무엇을 기대하나요?

A: ....

0636 □□□

expend
[ɪkˈspend]

v 소비하다, 쓰다

= **spend, consume, use up, exhaust**
+ **expenditure** n 지출 **expense** n 비용

Q: How much energy do you expend daily? 하루에 얼마나 많은 에너지를 소모하나요?

A: ....

0637 □□□

expense
[ɪkˈspens]

n 비용, 지출

= **cost, charge, outlay, expenditure**
+ **expensive** a 비싼 **inexpensive** a 저렴한

Q: Are travel expenses covered by the company?
출장 경비는 회사에서 부담하나요?

A: ....

0638 □□□

experience
[ɪkˈspɪriəns]

n 경험 v 경험하다

= **encounter, knowledge, skill, ordeal, undergo**
+ **experienced** a 경험이 많은

Q: Did you enjoy your experience at the concert? 콘서트 경험이 즐거웠나요?

A: ....

0639 □□□

experiment
[ɪkˈsperɪmənt] n
[ɪkˈsperɪment] v

n 실험 v 실험하다

= **test, trial, research, investigate, try out**
+ **experimentation** n 실험 **experimental** a 실험적인
experimentally adv 실험적으로

Q: Did the experiment produce expected results?
실험이 예상된 결과를 낳았나요?

A: ....

0640 □□□

expert
[ˈekspɜːrt]

n 전문가 a 전문적인

= **specialist, master, professional, skilled, adept**
+ **expertise** n 전문 지식

Q: Is she considered an expert in her field?
그녀는 자기 분야에서 전문가로 여겨지나요?

A: ....

DAY 02 | DICTATION TEST

DICTATION TEST 예문 QR을 듣고 다음 빈칸에 올바른 단어를 쓰세요.

621. Did the costs ______________ our initial budget?

622. Is everyone coming ______________ John today?

623. Is there ______________ food after the event?

624. Can we ______________ these items for others?

625. Was the ______________ at the game overwhelming?

626. Did they ______________ anyone from the list?

627. Did the long hike ______________ you completely?

628. Are you feeling ______________ after work today?

629. Did you see the new art ______________ downtown?

630. Is the ______________ open to the public now?

631. Does life ______________ on other planets, really?

632. Is the ______________ of ghosts proven?

633. Have you tried any ______________ fruits recently?

634. Will they ______________ the business next year?

635. What do you ______________ from the meeting tomorrow?

636. How much energy do you ______________ daily?

637. Are travel ______________ covered by the company?

638. Did you enjoy your ______________ at the concert?

639. Did the ______________ produce expected results?

640. Is she considered an ______________ in her field?

5회 반복 표제어 QR　5회 반복 예문 QR

DAY 03

30 days

AI 학습자료와 인강 youpass.co.kr

PREVIEW A 다음 단어의 뜻을 한국어로 써보세요.

- ☐ explain ______
- ☐ explode ______
- ☐ explore ______
- ☐ export ______
- ☐ expose ______
- ☐ express ______
- ☐ expression ______
- ☐ extend ______
- ☐ extent ______
- ☐ external ______
- ☐ extinct ______
- ☐ extra ______
- ☐ extraordinary ______
- ☐ extreme ______
- ☐ fabric ______
- ☐ facility ______
- ☐ factor ______
- ☐ fade ______
- ☐ failure ______
- ☐ faint ______

PREVIEW B 사진을 보고 알맞은 영어 단어를 **PREVIEW A**에서 찾아 써보세요.

______

______

______

______

0641 ☐☐☐

explain
[ɪkˈspleɪn]

v 설명하다

= clarify, elaborate, describe, account for, interpret
+ explanation **n** 설명 explanatory **a** 설명하는

Q: Can you explain the problem clearly now?
이제 문제를 명확하게 설명해 줄 수 있나요?

A: ....

0642 ☐☐☐

explode
[ɪkˈsploʊd]

v 폭발하다

= burst, detonate, erupt, shatter, blow up
+ explosion **n** 폭발 explosive **a** 폭발성의

Q: Did the bomb explode without any warning?
폭탄이 아무 경고 없이 폭발했나요?

A: ....

0643 ☐☐☐

explore
[ɪkˈsplɔːr]

v 탐험하다, 탐구하다

= investigate, survey, discover, venture into, analyze
+ exploration **n** 탐험 explorer **n** 탐험가 exploratory **a** 탐험적인

Q: Have you explored the city fully? 도시를 완전히 탐험했나요?

A: ....

0644 ☐☐☐

export
[ˈekspɔːrt] **n** [ɪkˈspɔːrt] **v**

v 수출하다 **n** 수출(품)

= send out, ship, trade abroad, overseas trade
+ exporter **n** 수출업자

Q: Does your company export goods internationally?
귀사는 상품을 국제적으로 수출하나요?

A: ....

0645 ☐☐☐

expose
[ɪkˈspoʊz]

v 노출시키다, 폭로하다

= reveal, uncover, disclose, subject to, lay open
+ exposure **n** 노출 exposed **a** 노출된

Q: Will this report expose the hidden facts?
이 보고서가 숨겨진 사실들을 폭로할까요?

A: ....

0646 □□□

express
[ɪkˈspres]

v 표현하다, 나타내다 **a** 특급의

= articulate, convey, communicate, state, rapid
+ expression **n** 표현 expressiveness **n** 표현력 expressive **a** 표현력이 풍부한 expressly **adv** 명백히

Q: How do you express your true feelings? 당신의 진정한 감정을 어떻게 표현하나요?

A: ....

0647 □□□

expression
[ɪkˈspreʃn]

n 표현, 표정

= phrase, look, manifestation, utterance, facial look
+ express **v** 표현하다 expressive **a** 표현력이 풍부한

Q: Is that expression common in your culture?
그 표현이 당신의 문화에서 흔한가요?

A: ....

0648 □□□

extend
[ɪkˈstend]

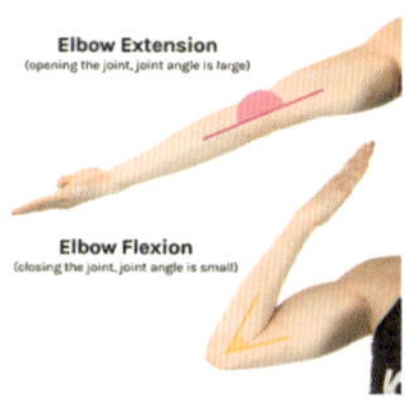

v 연장하다, 확대하다

= lengthen, expand, stretch, offer, prolong
+ extension **n** 연장, 확장 extent **n** 정도, 범위 extensive **a** 광범위한

Q: Can you extend the deadline by one week?
마감 기한을 일주일 연장해 줄 수 있나요?

A: ....

0649 □□□

extent
[ɪkˈstent]

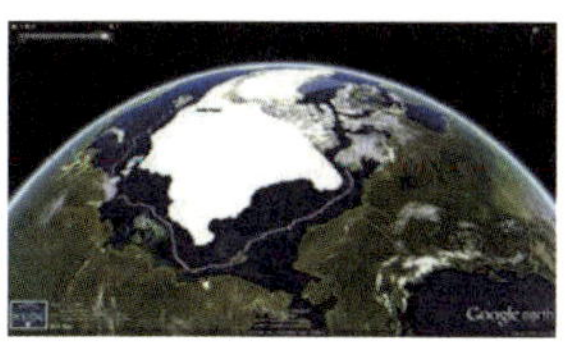

n 정도, 범위

= degree, scope, range, measure, magnitude
+ extend **v** 확장하다

Q: To what extent did the damage affect us?
피해가 우리에게 어느 정도 영향을 미쳤나요?

A: ....

0650 □□□

external
[ɪkˈstɜːrnl]

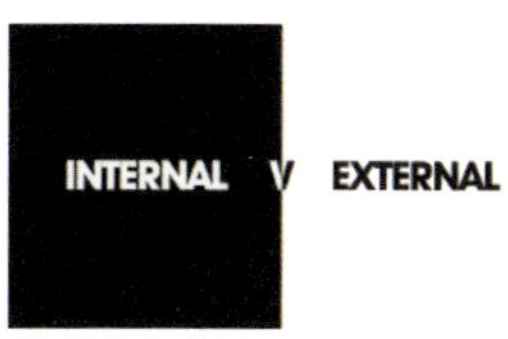

a 외부의

= outer, outside, exterior, superficial
+ externals **n** 외부적인 것들 externally **adv** 외부적으로

Q: Are the external factors affecting the results?
외부 요인이 결과에 영향을 미치나요?

A: ....

0651 □□□

extinct
[ɪkˈstɪŋkt]

a 멸종된

= vanished, defunct, no longer existing
+ extinction n 멸종

Q: Do you know why dinosaurs became extinct? 공룡이 왜 멸종했는지 아나요?
A: ....

0652 □□□

extra
[ˈekstrə]

a 여분의, 추가의 n 추가적인 것

= additional, surplus, supplementary, spare, bonus
+ extra time 연장전(overtime)

Q: Do you need any extra help today? 오늘 추가적인 도움이 필요한가요?
A: ....

0653 □□□

extraordinary
[ɪkˈstrɔːrdəneri]

a 비범한, 놀라운

= remarkable, unusual, exceptional, outstanding, incredible
+ extraordinarily adv 유난히, 비상하게

Q: Was that an extraordinary experience for you?
그것이 당신에게 특별한 경험이었나요?
A: ....

0654 □□□

extreme
[ɪkˈstriːm]

a 극심한, 극단적인 n 극단

= severe, intense, utmost, radical, drastic
+ extremity n 극단, 말단 extremist n 극단주의자 extremely adv 극도로

Q: Have you ever faced extreme weather conditions?
극심한 기상 조건을 겪어본 적 있나요?
A: ....

0655 □□□

fabric
[ˈfæbrɪk]

n 직물, 천

= cloth, material, textile, structure
+ cotton fabric 면직물

Q: Is this fabric suitable for summer clothes? 이 직물이 여름옷에 적합한가요?
A: ....

0656 □□□

facility
[fəˈsɪləti]

n 시설, 기능

= **amenity, convenience, resource, skill, establishment**
+ **facilitate** **a** 용이하게 하다

Q: Is the new facility ready for operation? 새 시설이 운영 준비가 되었나요?

A: ....

0657 □□□

factor
[ˈfæktər]

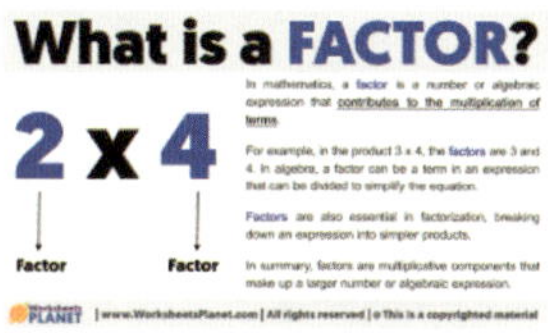

n 요인, 요소

= **element, component, determinant, cause, aspect**
+ **economic factors** 경제적 요인

Q: What's the most important factor in success?
성공에 있어 가장 중요한 요소는 무엇인가요?

A: ....

0658 □□□

fade
[feɪd]

v 희미해지다, 바래다

= **diminish, dwindle, disappear, grow dim, wilt**
+ **fade away** 시름시름 하다[앓다] 죽다

Q: Did the colors fade after washing the clothes?
옷을 세탁한 후 색깔이 바랬나요?

A: ....

0659 □□□

failure
[ˈfeɪljər]

n 실패

= **breakdown, fiasco, downfall, defeat, lack of success**
+ **fail** **v** 실패하다

Q: What caused the failure of the project? 프로젝트 실패의 원인은 무엇이었나요?

A: ....

0660 □□□

faint
[feɪnt]

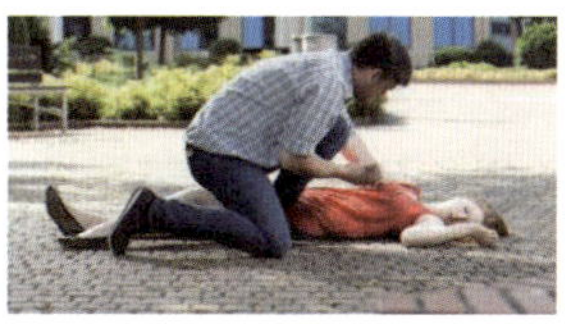

a 희미한, 어렴풋한 **v** 기절하다

= **weak, dim, vague, dizzy, swoon**
+ **faintly** **adv** 희미하게

Q: Did you feel faint after standing too long?
너무 오래 서 있다가 현기증을 느꼈나요?

A: ....

DAY 03 | DICTATION TEST

5회 반복 예문 QR

DICTATION TEST 예문 QR을 듣고 다음 빈칸에 올바른 단어를 쓰세요.

641. Can you ________________ the problem clearly now?
642. Did the bomb ________________ without any warning?
643. Have you ________________ the city fully?
644. Does your company ________________ goods internationally?
645. Will this report ________________ the hidden facts?
646. How do you ________________ your true feelings?
647. Is that ________________ common in your culture?
648. Can you ________________ the deadline by one week?
649. To what ________________ did the damage affect us?
650. Are the ________________ factors affecting the results?
651. Do you know why dinosaurs became ________________?
652. Do you need any ________________ help today?
653. Was that an ________________ experience for you?
654. Have you ever faced ________________ weather conditions?
655. Is this ________________ suitable for summer clothes?
656. Is the new ________________ ready for operation?
657. What's the most important ________________ in success?
658. Did the colors ________________ after washing the clothes?
659. What caused the ________________ of the project?
660. Did you feel ________________ after standing too long?

5회 반복 표제어 QR   5회 반복 예문 QR

DAY 04

30 days

AI 학습자료와 인강 youpass.co.kr

PREVIEW A 다음 단어의 뜻을 한국어로 써보세요.

- ☐ fair ______
- ☐ faith ______
- ☐ fake ______
- ☐ fame ______
- ☐ familiar ______
- ☐ fancy ______
- ☐ fantasy ______
- ☐ fare ______
- ☐ fascinate ______
- ☐ fashionable ______
- ☐ fasten ______
- ☐ fate ______
- ☐ fatigue ______
- ☐ faucet ______
- ☐ fault ______
- ☐ favor ______
- ☐ favorite ______
- ☐ fear ______
- ☐ feast ______
- ☐ feather ______

PREVIEW B 사진을 보고 알맞은 영어 단어를 **PREVIEW A** 에서 찾아 써보세요.

______

______

______

______

0661 □□□

fair
[fer]

a 공정한, 상당한 n 박람회

= just, equitable, impartial, moderate, carnival, market
+ fairness n 공정성 fairly adv 꽤, 공정하게 unfair a 불공평한

Q: Is it fair to judge people so quickly?
사람들을 그렇게 빨리 판단하는 것이 공정한가요?

A:

0662 □□□

faith
[feɪθ]

n 신뢰, 신념

= belief, trust, conviction, confidence, religion
+ faithful a 충실한 faithfully adv 충실히 faithless a 불성실한

Q: Do you have faith in their decision? 그들의 결정에 신뢰가 가나요?

A:

0663 □□□

fake
[feɪk]

a 가짜의 n 가짜

= counterfeit, fraudulent, imitation, bogus, phony
+ fake designer clothing 가짜[짝퉁] 유명 디자이너 의류

Q: How can you tell if something is fake? 어떤 것이 가짜인지 어떻게 알 수 있나요?

A:

0664 □□□

fame
[feɪm]

n 명성

= renown, reputation, prominence, celebrity
+ famous a 유명한

Q: Did she achieve fame after the show? 그녀는 쇼가 끝난 후 명성을 얻었나요?

A:

0665 □□□

familiar
[fəˈmɪliər]

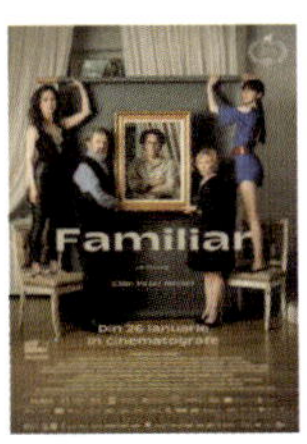

a 익숙한, 친숙한

= well-known, accustomed, common, intimate, acquainted
+ familiarity n 친숙함 familiarize v 익숙하게 하다 familiarly adv 친숙하게

Q: Are you familiar with this area already? 이 지역에 이미 익숙한가요?

A:

0666 □□□

fancy
[ˈfænsi]

a 화려한, 고급의 **v** ~하고 싶어 하다

= elaborate, ornate, imaginative, elaborate, imagine
+ fancily adv 화려하게

Q: Do you fancy going out for dinner tonight? 오늘 저녁 외식하고 싶은가요?

A: ....

0667 □□□

fantasy
[ˈfæntəsi]

n 환상, 공상

= imagination, illusion, dream, hallucination
+ fantastic a 환상적인

Q: Is this movie based on a fantasy story?
이 영화는 판타지 스토리에 기반한 것인가요?

A: ....

0668 □□□

fare
[fer]

n (교통) 요금

= charge, fee, payment, food, manage
+ bus[taxi] fares 버스[택시] 요금

Q: How much is the bus fare to downtown? 시내까지 버스 요금은 얼마인가요?

A: ....

0669 □□□

fascinate
[ˈfæsɪneɪt]

v 매혹시키다

= enthrall, captivate, allure, mesmerize, intrigue
+ fascination n 매혹 **fascinating a** 매혹적인 **fascinated a** 매료된

Q: What topics fascinate you the most? 어떤 주제들이 당신을 가장 매료시키나요?

A: ....

0670 □□□

fashionable
[ˈfæʃnəbl]

a 유행하는, 최신 유행의

= stylish, trendy, chic, in vogue, modish
+ fashion n 유행 **fashionably adv** 유행에 맞게

Q: Is that outfit still fashionable these days? 그 옷은 요즘도 유행인가요?

A: ....

0671 □□□

fasten
[ˈfæsn]

v 고정시키다, 잠그다

= **secure, tie, attach, fix, connect**
+ **fastener** **n** 잠금장치

Q: Did you remember to fasten your seatbelt? 안전벨트 매는 것을 잊지 않았나요?
A: ....

0672 □□□

fate
[feɪt]

n 운명

= **destiny, fortune, lot, predetermination**
+ **fated** **a** 운명 지어진

Q: Do you believe in fate or free will? 운명을 믿나요, 아니면 자유 의지를 믿나요?
A: ....

0673 □□□

fatigue
[fəˈtiːg]

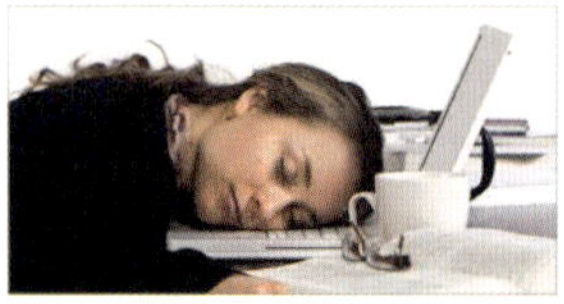

n 피로 **v** 지치게 하다

= **tiredness, exhaustion, weariness, drain, weary**
+ **fatigued** **a** 피곤한 **fatiguing** **a** 피로하게 하는

Q: Are you feeling fatigue after the long trip? 긴 여행 후에 피로를 느끼고 있나요?
A: ....

0674 □□□

faucet
[ˈfɔːsɪt]

n 수도꼭지

= **tap, spigot, spile**
+ **mixing faucet** 온·냉수 혼합 수도꼭지

Q: Is the faucet leaking in the kitchen sink? 부엌 싱크대 수도꼭지가 새고 있나요?
A: ....

0675 □□□

fault
[fɔːlt]

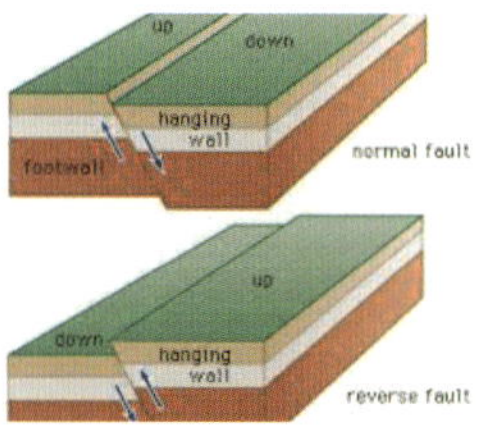

n 잘못, 결점, 단층

= **flaw, defect, mistake, blame, responsibility**
+ **faulty** **a** 결함 있는 **faultless** **a** 결점 없는

Q: Whose fault was the mistake last night? 어젯밤 실수는 누구의 잘못이었나요?
A: ....

0676 □□□

favor
[ˈfeɪvər]

n 호의, 친절 v ~을 지지하다

= preference, kindness, support, endorse, oblige
+ favorite n 가장 좋아하는 것 favorable a 호의적인 favorably adv 호의적으로

Q: Can you do me a favor later today? 오늘 이따가 부탁 하나 들어줄 수 있나요?
A: ....

0677 □□□

favorite
[ˈfeɪvərɪt]

a 가장 좋아하는 n 가장 좋아하는 것

= preferred, beloved, cherished, most liked
+ favor n 호의

Q: What's your favorite type of music? 가장 좋아하는 음악 장르는 무엇인가요?
A: ....

0678 □□□

fear
[fɪr]

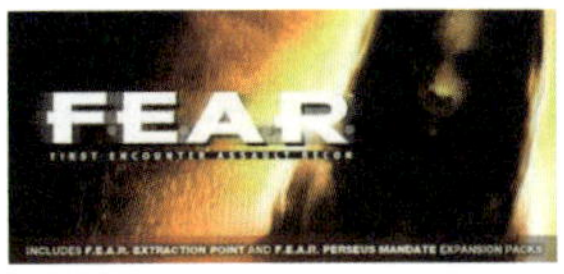

n 두려움 v 두려워하다

= dread, terror, apprehension, fright
+ fearful a 두려워하는 fearless a 두려움 없는 fearfully adv 두렵게

Q: What do you fear the most in life? 인생에서 무엇을 가장 두려워하나요?
A: ....

0679 □□□

feast
[fiːst]

n 잔치, 축제 v 잔치를 벌이다

= banquet, celebration, lavish meal, gorge
+ feast day (기독교의) 축일

Q: Are you ready for the big feast tonight?
오늘 밤 성대한 잔치를 위한 준비는 되었나요?
A: ....

0680 □□□

feather
[ˈfeðər]

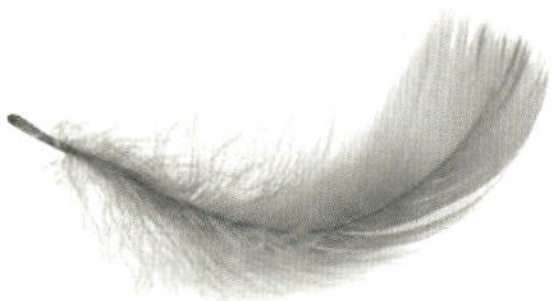

n 깃털

= plume, down, quill
+ feathery a 깃털 같은

Q: Where did you find a feather? 어디서 깃털을 찾았나요?
A: ....

DAY 04 | DICTATION TEST

5회 반복 예문 QR

DICTATION TEST 예문 QR을 듣고 다음 빈칸에 올바른 단어를 쓰세요.

661. Is it ______________ to judge people so quickly?
662. Do you have ______________ in their decision?
663. How can you tell if something is ______________?
664. Did she achieve ______________ after the show?
665. Are you ______________ with this area already?
666. Do you ______________ going out for dinner tonight?
667. Is this movie based on a ______________ story?
668. How much is the bus ______________ to downtown?
669. What topics ______________ you the most?
670. Is that outfit still ______________ these days?
671. Did you remember to ______________ your seatbelt?
672. Do you believe in ______________ or free will?
673. Are you feeling ______________ after the long trip?
674. Is the ______________ leaking in the kitchen sink?
675. Whose ______________ was the mistake last night?
676. Can you do me a ______________ later today?
677. What's your ______________ type of music?
678. What do you ______________ the most in life?
679. Are you ready for the big ______________ tonight?
680. Where did you find a ______________?

5회 반복 표제어 QR　5회 반복 예문 QR

DAY 05

30 days

AI 학습자료와 인강 youpass.co.kr

PREVIEW A 다음 단어의 뜻을 한국어로 써보세요.

- ☐ feature
- ☐ fee
- ☐ feed
- ☐ fellow
- ☐ fiction
- ☐ field
- ☐ figure
- ☐ filter
- ☐ finance
- ☐ financial
- ☐ fine
- ☐ firm
- ☐ fit
- ☐ flame
- ☐ flash
- ☐ flat
- ☐ flavor
- ☐ flesh
- ☐ flexible
- ☐ flight

PREVIEW B 사진을 보고 알맞은 영어 단어를 PREVIEW A 에서 찾아 써보세요.

0681 □□□

feature
[ˈfiːtʃər]

n 특징, 특색, 특종 **v** 특징으로 하다

= characteristic, attribute, trait, aspect, highlight, present
+ featured **a** 특징이 있는

Q: Does this phone feature a high-performance camera?
이 휴대폰은 고성능 카메라를 특징으로 하나요?

A: ....

0682 □□□

fee
[fiː]

n 요금, 수수료

= charge, cost, payment, remuneration
+ membership fees (회원) 회비

Q: How much is the admission fee today? 오늘 입장료는 얼마인가요?

A: ....

0683 □□□

feed
[fiːd]

v 먹이를 주다, 먹이다

= nourish, provide for, consume, supply, give food
+ feeding **n** 수유, 식사

Q: Can you feed the dog before leaving? 떠나기 전에 개에게 먹이를 줄 수 있나요?

A: ....

0684 □□□

fellow
[ˈfeloʊ]

n 동료 **a** 동료의

= companion, comrade, associate, peer, person
+ a fellow of the Royal College of Surgeons 영국 왕립 외과의 협회 회원

Q: Is he your fellow student or colleague?
그는 당신의 동료 학생인가요, 아니면 동료인가요?

A: ....

0685 □□□

fiction
[ˈfɪkʃn]

n 소설, 허구

= novel, story, fantasy, invention, falsehood
+ fictional **a** 허구의

Q: Do you enjoy reading fiction books? 소설책 읽는 것을 즐기나요?

A: ....

0686 □□□

field
[fiːld]

n 들판, 분야, 경기장

= area, domain, discipline, ground, cultivated land
+ field trip 견학 여행, 현장 학습

Q: Which field do you want to specialize in? 어떤 분야를 전문으로 하고 싶나요?

A:

0687 □□□

figure
[ˈfɪgjər]

n 숫자, 인물, 모습 **v** 생각하다, 이해하다

= number, digit, shape, person, compute, represent
+ figurative **a** 비유적인

Q: Can you figure out the answer now? 이제 답을 알아낼 수 있나요?

A:

0688 □□□

filter
[ˈfɪltər]

n 필터, 여과기 **v** 여과하다

= strain, purify, screen, sift, device
+ an air[oil] filter 공기[오일] 필터

Q: Did you remember to change the filter? 필터 교체하는 것을 기억했나요?

A:

0689 □□□

finance
[ˈfaɪnæns] [fɪˈnæns]

n 재정, 금융 **v** 자금을 조달하다

= money management, funds, economics, fund, provide money
+ finances **n** 재정 financier **n** 금융업자 financial **a** 재정적인

Q: Who handles the company's finance department?
회사의 재무부서는 누가 담당하나요?

A:

0690 □□□

financial
[faɪˈnænʃl] [fɪˈnænʃl]

a 재정의, 금융의

= monetary, fiscal, economic, budgetary
+ finance **n** 재정 financially **adv** 재정적으로

Q: Are you aware of your financial status? 당신의 재정 상태를 알고 있나요?

A:

0691 □□□

fine
[faɪn]

a 좋은, 괜찮은, 미세한 **n** 벌금

= excellent, satisfactory, delicate, thin, penalty, punish
+ finely **adv** 곱게, 섬세하게

Q: Is everything going to be fine today? 오늘 모든 것이 괜찮을까요?

A: ……………………

0692 □□□

firm
[fɜːrm]

a 확고한, 단단한 **n** 회사

= strong, stable, unyielding, resolute, company, business
+ firmness **n** 견고함, 단호함 **firmly** **adv** 확고하게

Q: Is this firm known for good service? 이 회사는 좋은 서비스로 유명한가요?

A: ……………………

0693 □□□

fit
[fɪt]

v 맞다, 적합하다 **a** 적합한, 건강한

= suit, match, adaptable, healthy, able, spasm
+ fitness **n** 적합성, 건강 **fitting** **a** 적절한

Q: Does this jacket fit you perfectly? 이 재킷이 당신에게 완벽하게 맞나요?

A: ……………………

0694 □□□

flame
[fleɪm]

n 불꽃

= blaze, fire, glow, passion, burn
+ flaming **a** 불타는 듯한

Q: Did you see the flame in the fireplace? 벽난로의 불꽃을 봤나요?

A: ……………………

0695 □□□

flash
[flæʃ]

n 섬광, 번쩍임 **v** 번쩍이다

= gleam, burst, sparkle, sudden light, brief
+ a flash of hope (번득이는) 희망의 빛

Q: Was the camera flash too bright just now? 방금 카메라 플래시가 너무 밝았나요?

A: ……………………

0696 □□□

flat
[flæt]

a 평평한, 납작한 n 아파트

= level, even, plain, apartment, deflated, dull
+ flatness n 평평함 flatly adv 단호히, 평평하게

Q: Do you live in a flat or a house? 집이 아파트예요, 아니면 단독주택이에요?
A:

0697 □□□

flavor
[ˈfleɪvər]

n 맛, 풍미 v 맛을 내다

= taste, savor, essence, zest, season
+ flavorful a 풍미 있는 flavorless a 맛없는

Q: What's your favorite ice cream flavor? 가장 좋아하는 아이스크림 맛은 무엇인가요?
A:

0698 □□□

flesh
[fleʃ]

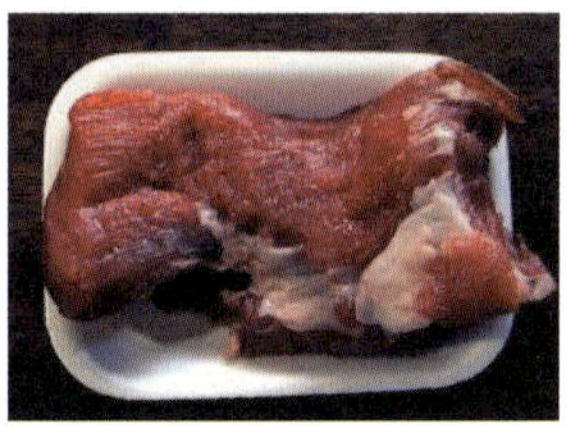

n 살, 육체

= meat, skin, body, pulp
+ fleshy a 살집이 있는

Q: Did the wound affect the flesh deeply? 상처가 살에 깊이 영향을 미쳤나요?
A:

0699 □□□

flexible
[ˈfleksəbl]

a 유연한, 융통성 있는

= adaptable, pliable, versatile, elastic, adjustable
+ flexibility n 유연성

Q: Are you flexible with your working hours? 근무 시간에 유연한가요?
A:

0700 □□□

flight
[flaɪt]

n 비행, 항공편

= journey, trip, escape, ascent, air travel
+ fly v 날다

Q: Is your flight delayed or on time? 당신의 항공편이 지연되나요, 아니면 정시인가요?
A:

DAY 05 | DICTATION TEST

5회 반복 예문 QR

DICTATION TEST 예문 QR을 듣고 다음 빈칸에 올바른 단어를 쓰세요.

681. Does this phone ______________ a high-performance camera?
682. How much is the admission ______________ today?
683. Can you ______________ the dog before leaving?
684. Is he your ______________ student or colleague?
685. Do you enjoy reading ______________ books?
686. Which ______________ do you want to specialize in?
687. Can you ______________ out the answer now?
688. Did you remember to change the ______________?
689. Who handles the company's ______________ department?
690. Are you aware of your ______________ status?
691. Is everything going to be ______________ today?
692. Is this ______________ known for good service?
693. Does this jacket ______________ you perfectly?
694. Did you see the ______________ in the fireplace?
695. Was the camera ______________ too bright just now?
696. Do you live in a ______________ or a house?
697. What's your favorite ice cream ______________?
698. Did the wound affect the ______________ deeply?
699. Are you ______________ with your working hours?
700. Is your ______________ delayed or on time?

5회 반복 표제어 QR 5회 반복 예문 QR

DAY 06

30 days

AI 학습자료와 인강 youpass.co.kr

PREVIEW A 다음 단어의 뜻을 한국어로 써보세요.

□ float ________	□ forecast ________
□ flood ________	□ foreign ________
□ flourish ________	□ foresee ________
□ flow ________	□ forever ________
□ fluid ________	□ forget ________
□ fold ________	□ forgive ________
□ folk ________	□ formal ________
□ following ________	□ format ________
□ forbid ________	□ former ________
□ force ________	□ formula ________

PREVIEW B 사진을 보고 알맞은 영어 단어를 **PREVIEW A** 에서 찾아 써보세요.

____

____

____

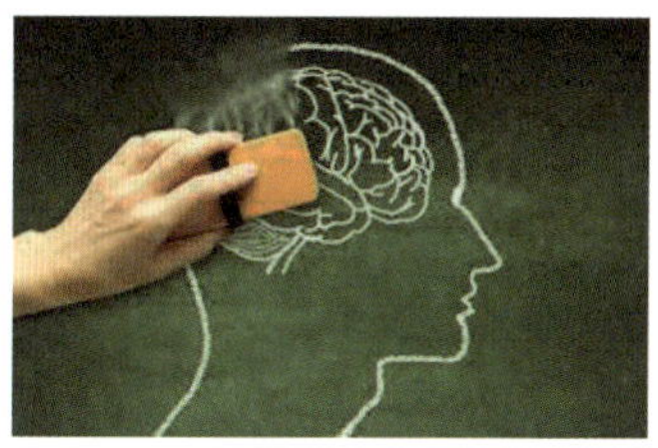
____

0701 □□□

float
[floʊt]

v 뜨다, 떠다니다

= drift, hover, glide, suspend, remain on surface
+ afloat **a** (물에) 뜬, 빚은 안 질 정도의, 도산은 안 당하는

Q: Can this boat float on water easily? 이 배가 물에 쉽게 뜰 수 있나요?

A: ....

0702 □□□

flood
[flʌd]

n 홍수 **v** 범람하다

= deluge, inundation, overflow, submerge, overwhelm
+ flash flood 갑작스런 홍수, 갑자기 불어난 물 **flood tide** 만조, 밀물(**high tide**)

Q: Did the flood cause any damage here? 홍수가 여기에 피해를 입혔나요?

A: ....

0703 □□□

flourish
[ˈflɜːrɪʃ]

v 번창하다, 잘 자라다 **n** 수식, 장식, 과장

= thrive, prosper, bloom, succeed, brandish
+ with a flourish 화려[요란]하게, 성대히

Q: How can small businesses flourish today?
오늘날 소규모 사업체들은 어떻게 번창할 수 있나요?

A: ....

0704 □□□

flow
[floʊ]

n 흐름 **v** 흐르다

= stream, current, movement, progress, gush
+ cash flow 현금 유동성(한 사업체의 수입과 지출의 흐름) **flow chart** 플로 차트, 업무 흐름[절차]도

Q: Is the traffic flow smooth during rush hour?
출퇴근 시간에도 교통 흐름이 원활한가요?

A: ....

0705 □□□

fluid
[ˈfluːɪd]

n 유체, 액체 **a** 유동적인

= liquid, gas, flowing, smooth, changeable
+ fluidity **n** 유동성

Q: Is this fluid safe to drink or not? 이 액체는 마시기에 안전한가요?

A: ....

0706 □□□

fold
[fould]

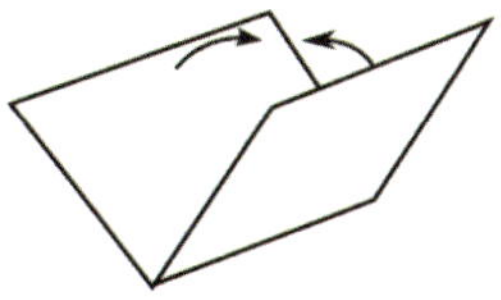

v 접다, 포개다 **n** 접힌 부분

= crease, pleat, bend, collapse, layer
+ fold a letter[tent] 편지를[천막을] 접다

Q: Did you fold the clothes properly before? 전에 옷을 제대로 개어 놓았나요?

A: ....

0707 □□□

folk
[fouk]

n 사람들, 민속 **a** 민속의

= people, common people, traditional, popular
+ folk song 민요, 포크 송

Q: Are these folk songs popular in your country?
이 민요들이 당신 나라에서 인기가 있나요?

A: ....

0708 □□□

following
[ˈfɑːlouɪŋ]

prep ~후에, ~에 따라 **a** 다음의 **n** 추종자들

= subsequent, next, supporters, result of, after
+ follow **v** 따르다 follower **n** 추종자

Q: What happened following the meeting yesterday?
어제 회의 후에 무슨 일이 있었나요?

A: ....

0709 □□□

forbid
[fərˈbɪd]

v 금지하다

= prohibit, ban, disallow, outlaw
+ forbiddance **n** 금지 forbidden **a** 금지된

Q: Did the school forbid using phones during class?
학교에서 수업 중 휴대전화 사용을 금지했나요?

A: ....

0710 □□□

force
[fɔːrs]

n 힘, 군대 **v** 강요하다

= strength, power, might, coercion, compel, exert
+ forceful **a** 강력한 forcefully **adv** 강력하게

Q: Can you force the door open if locked? 문이 잠겼을 때 강제로 열 수 있나요?

A: ....

0711 □□□

forecast
[ˈfɔːrkæst]

n 예보 **v** 예보하다

= predict, project, foretell, prognosis, prediction
+ weather forecast 일기 예보, 기상 통보

Q: What's the weather forecast for tomorrow? 내일 일기예보는 어떤가요?
A:

0712 □□□

foreign
[ˈfɔːrən]

a 외국의

= alien, external, exotic, unfamiliar, overseas
+ foreigner **n** 외국인

Q: Have you ever traveled to a foreign country? 외국에 여행 가본 적 있나요?
A:

0713 □□□

foresee
[fɔːrˈsiː]

FORESEE

v 예견하다, 미리 알다

= anticipate, predict, envision, expect
+ foreseeable **a** 예견할 수 있는

Q: Could you foresee this problem coming early?
이런 문제가 온다는 것을 일찍 알 수 있을까요?
A:

0714 □□□

forever
[fərˈevər]

adv 영원히

= eternally, perpetually, always, endlessly
+ last forever 영원히 계속되다

Q: Do you think love lasts forever really?
사랑이 정말 영원히 지속된다고 생각하나요?
A:

0715 □□□

forget
[fərˈget]

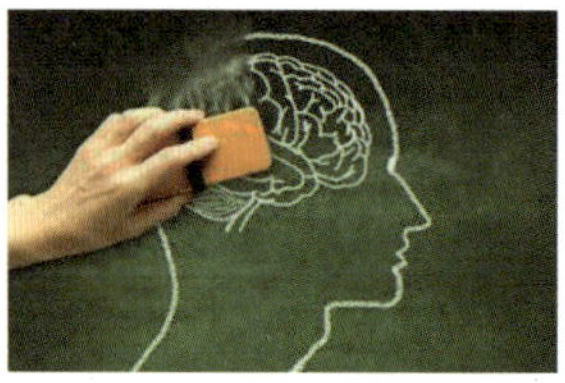

v 잊다

= neglect, overlook, omit, fail to remember
+ forgetfulness **n** 건망증 forgettable **a** 잊을 수 있는
unforgettable **a** 잊을 수 없는

Q: Did you forget to turn off the lights? 불 끄는 것을 잊었나요?
A:

0716 □□□

forgive
[fər'gɪv]

v 용서하다

= pardon, excuse, absolve, condone

+ forgiveness **n** 용서 **forgivable** **a** 용서할 수 있는

Q: Can you forgive someone who lied often?
자주 거짓말한 사람을 용서할 수 있나요?

A:

0717 □□□

formal
['fɔːrml]

a 공식적인, 형식적인

= official, ceremonial, stiff, proper, conventional

+ formality **n** 격식 **formation** **n** 형성 **form** **v** 형성하다 **formally** **adv** 정식으로

Q: Is the event going to be formal or casual?
행사는 공식적인가요, 비공식적인가요?

A:

0718 □□□

format
['fɔːrmæt] **n** [fər'mæt] **v**

n 형식 **v** 형식화하다

= layout, structure, arrangement, organize, standardize

+ data format 데이터의 형식 **print format** (인쇄 장치에 지정하는) 인쇄 양식

Q: In what format should the document be saved?
문서를 어떤 형식으로 저장해야 하나요?

A:

0719 □□□

former
['fɔːrmər]

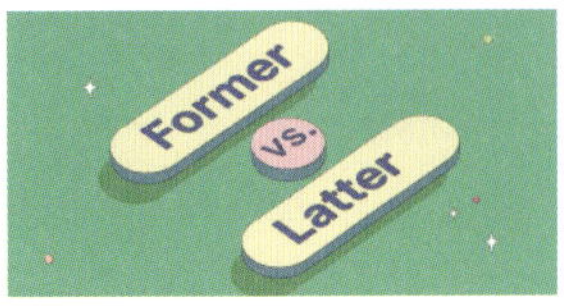

a 이전의, 전자의

= previous, prior, past

+ form **n** 형태 **formerly** **adv** 이전에

Q: Is he your former teacher or current one?
그가 당신의 이전 선생님인가요, 아니면 현재 선생님인가요?

A:

0720 □□□

formula
['fɔːrmjələ]

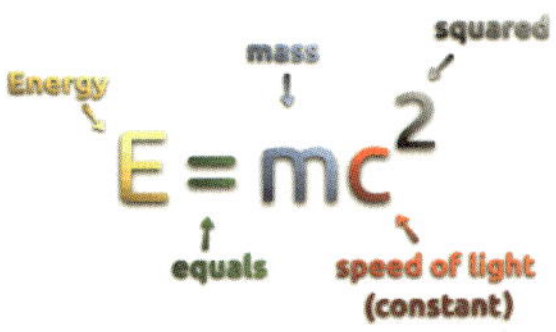

n 공식, 방식

= recipe, prescription, method, rule, chemical representation

+ formulate **a** 공식화하다 **formulation** **n** 공식화

Q: Did you use the right formula in math? 수학에서 올바른 공식을 사용했나요?

A:

DAY 06 | DICTATION TEST

5회 반복 예문 QR

DICTATION TEST 예문 QR을 듣고 다음 빈칸에 올바른 단어를 쓰세요.

701. Can this boat ______________ on water easily?
702. Did the ______________ cause any damage here?
703. How can small businesses ______________ today?
704. Is the traffic ______________ smooth during rush hour?
705. Is this ______________ safe to drink or not?
706. Did you ______________ the clothes properly before?
707. Are these ______________ songs popular in your country?
708. What happened ______________ the meeting yesterday?
709. Did the school ______________ using phones during class?
710. Can you ______________ the door open if locked?
711. What's the weather ______________ for tomorrow?
712. Have you ever traveled to a ______________ country?
713. Could you ______________ this problem coming early?
714. Do you think love lasts ______________ really?
715. Did you ______________ to turn off the lights?
716. Can you ______________ someone who lied often?
717. Is the event going to be ______________ or casual?
718. In what ______________ should the document be saved?
719. Is he your ______________ teacher or current one?
720. Did you use the right ______________ in math?

5회 반복 표제어 QR　　5회 반복 예문 QR

DAY 07

30 days

AI 학습자료와 인강 youpass.co.kr

PREVIEW A 다음 단어의 뜻을 한국어로 써보세요.

- □ fortunate ____________
- □ fortunately ____________
- □ fortune ____________
- □ found ____________
- □ fountain ____________
- □ fragile ____________
- □ frame ____________
- □ frankly ____________
- □ freedom ____________
- □ freezing ____________
- □ frequent ____________
- □ friendship ____________
- □ fright ____________
- □ frighten ____________
- □ frustrate ____________
- □ fuel ____________
- □ fulfill ____________
- □ function ____________
- □ fund ____________
- □ fundamental ____________

PREVIEW B 사진을 보고 알맞은 영어 단어를 **PREVIEW A** 에서 찾아 써보세요.

____

____

____

____

0721 □□□

fortunate
[ˈfɔːrtʃənət]

a 운이 좋은

= lucky, blessed, advantageous, favored
+ fortune n 운, 재산 misfortune n 불운 fortunately adv 다행히

Q: Are you fortunate to have such good friends?
그렇게 좋은 친구들이 있어서 운이 좋다고 생각하나요?

A: ....

0722 □□□

fortunately
[ˈfɔːrtʃənətli]

adv 다행히도, 운 좋게도

= luckily, thankfully, by good fortune, happily
+ fortunate a 운 좋은 fortune n 운

Q: Fortunately, did they arrive on time today?
다행히도 오늘 그들이 제시간에 도착했나요?

A: ....

0723 □□□

fortune
[ˈfɔːrtʃuːn]

n 운, 재산

= luck, fate, wealth, riches, destiny
+ fortunate a 운 좋은 unfortunate a 불운한 misfortune n 불운

Q: Did he make a fortune from that business? 그 사업으로 큰돈을 벌었나요?

A: ....

0724 □□□

found
[faʊnd]

v 설립하다

= establish, create, initiate, originate, discover (past of find)
+ foundation n 기초, 재단 founder n 설립자

Q: When did you found your new startup company?
새로운 스타트업 회사를 언제 설립했나요?

A: ....

0725 □□□

fountain
[ˈfaʊntən]

n 분수

= source, spring, jet, cascade
+ fountain pen 만년필 water fountain 식수대(drinking fountain)

Q: Have you seen the fountain in the city park? 도시 공원에 있는 분수를 봤나요?

A: ....

0726 □□□

fragile
[ˈfrædʒl]

a 깨지기 쉬운, 허약한

= delicate, brittle, flimsy, vulnerable, breakable
+ fragility n 부서지기 쉬움, 취약성

Q: Is this package too fragile to carry around?
이 소포는 들고 다니기엔 너무 깨지기 쉬운가요?

A: ....

0727 □□□

frame
[freɪm]

n 틀, 액자 v 틀에 넣다, 구성하다

= structure, border, casing, context, compose, build
+ framed a 틀에 끼워진

Q: Can you put the picture in the frame properly?
액자에 사진을 제대로 넣을 수 있나요?

A: ....

0728 □□□

frankly
[ˈfræŋkli]

adv 솔직히

= honestly, openly, candidly, to be honest
+ frank a 솔직한 frankness n 솔직함

Q: Can I speak frankly about your performance?
당신의 성과에 대해 솔직하게 말해도 될까요?

A: ....

0729 □□□

freedom
[ˈfriːdəm]

n 자유

= liberty, independence, autonomy, release
+ free a 자유로운 freely adv 자유롭게

Q: Do you value your freedom more than anything?
무엇보다 자유를 중요하게 생각하나요?

A: ....

0730 □□□

freezing
[ˈfriːzɪŋ]

a 몹시 추운

= icy, frigid, chilling, bitterly cold
+ freeze v 얼다, 꼼짝마

Q: Is it freezing outside this morning already? 오늘 아침 벌써 밖이 꽁꽁 얼었나요?

A: ....

0731 □□□

frequent
[ˈfriːkwənt] a [frɪˈkwent] v

a 빈번한, 잦은

= common, regular, recurrent, habitual, often visit
+ frequency n 빈도 frequently adv 자주

Q: Do you make frequent trips abroad these days?
요즘 해외여행을 자주 가나요?

A: ......

0732 □□□

friendship
[ˈfrendʃɪp]

n 우정

= companionship, camaraderie, bond, affection
+ friend n 친구 friendly a 친근한 unfriendly a 불친절한

Q: How important is friendship in your life? 당신 삶에서 우정은 얼마나 중요한가요?

A: ......

0733 □□□

fright
[fraɪt]

n 공포, 두려움

= fear, terror, alarm, dismay
+ frighten v 겁주다 frightening a 무서운 frightened a 겁먹은

Q: Did you get a fright from the sudden noise? 갑작스러운 소음에 놀랐나요?

A: ......

0734 □□□

frighten
[ˈfraɪtn]

v 겁먹게 하다

= scare, alarm, intimidate, terrify
+ fright n 두려움 frightening a 무서운 frightened a 겁먹은

Q: Does the dark forest frighten you at night?
밤에 어두운 숲이 당신을 겁먹게 하나요?

A: ......

0735 □□□

frustrate
[ˈfrʌstreɪt]

v 좌절시키다

= thwart, baffle, hinder, discourage, vex
+ frustration n 좌절, 불만 frustrating a 좌절시키는 frustrated a 좌절한

Q: Does slow internet frustrate you often enough?
느린 인터넷이 당신을 자주 좌절시키나요?

A: ......

0736 □□□

fuel
[ˈfjuːəl]

n 연료 **v** 연료를 공급하다

= energy source, propellant, power, fire up, ignite
+ fossil fuel 화석 연료 **fuel cell** 연료 전지

Q: Is there enough fuel for the long journey? 긴 여정을 위한 연료가 충분한가요?

A: ....

0737 □□□

fulfill
[fʊlˈfɪl]

v 이행하다, 충족시키다

= satisfy, complete, achieve, carry out, realize
+ fulfillment n 성취, 이행

Q: Did you fulfill all your promises on time? 모든 약속을 제시간에 이행했나요?

A: ....

0738 □□□

function
[ˈfʌŋkʃn]

n 기능 **v** 기능하다

= purpose, role, duty, operation, operate, work
+ functional a 기능적인 **functionally adv** 기능적으로

Q: What function does this button actually serve?
이 버튼이 실제로 어떤 기능을 하나요?

A: ....

0739 □□□

fund
[fʌnd]

n 기금, 자금 **v** 자금을 대다

= money, capital, endowment, finance, provide money
+ funding n 자금

Q: Who will fund the new community project here?
여기서 누가 새로운 지역사회 프로젝트에 자금을 댈 건가요?

A: ....

0740 □□□

fundamental
[ˌfʌndəˈmentl]

a 근본적인, 기본적인

= basic, essential, foundational, primary, underlying
+ fundamentals n 기본 원리 **fundamentally adv** 근본적으로

Q: Are these fundamental rules easy to understand?
이 기본 규칙들은 이해하기 쉬운가요?

A: ....

DAY 07 | DICTATION TEST

5회 반복 예문 QR

DICTATION TEST 예문 QR을 듣고 다음 빈칸에 올바른 단어를 쓰세요.

721. Are you ________________ to have such good friends?
722. ________________, did they arrive on time today?
723. Did he make a ________________ from that business?
724. When did you ________________ your new startup company?
725. Have you seen the ________________ in the city park?
726. Is this package too ________________ to carry around?
727. Can you put the picture in the ________________ properly?
728. Can I speak ________________ about your performance?
729. Do you value your ________________ more than anything?
730. Is it ________________ outside this morning already?
731. Do you make ________________ trips abroad these days?
732. How important is ________________ in your life?
733. Did you get a ________________ from the sudden noise?
734. Does the dark forest ________________ you at night?
735. Does slow internet ________________ you often enough?
736. Is there enough ________________ for the long journey?
737. Did you ________________ all your promises on time?
738. What ________________ does this button actually serve?
739. Who will ________________ the new community project here?
740. Are these ________________ rules easy to understand?

5회 반복 표제어 QR 5회 반복 예문 QR

DAY 08
30 days

AI 학습자료와 인강 youpass.co.kr

PREVIEW A 다음 단어의 뜻을 한국어로 써보세요.

☐ furniture ________	☐ generous ________
☐ further ________	☐ genetic ________
☐ furthermore ________	☐ genius ________
☐ gap ________	☐ genuine ________
☐ garage ________	☐ geography ________
☐ gender ________	☐ gesture ________
☐ general ________	☐ glance ________
☐ generally ________	☐ glory ________
☐ generate ________	☐ glow ________
☐ generation ________	☐ govern ________

PREVIEW B 사진을 보고 알맞은 영어 단어를 **PREVIEW A**에서 찾아 써보세요.

 ________

 ________

 ________

 ________

DAY 01 DAY 02 DAY 03 DAY 04 DAY 05 DAY 06 DAY 07 DAY 08 DAY 09 DAY 10 DAY 11 DAY 12 DAY 13 DAY 14 DAY 15 DAY 16 DAY 17 DAY 18 DAY 19 DAY 20 DAY 21 DAY 22 DAY 23 DAY 24 DAY 25 DAY 26 DAY 27 DAY 28 DAY 29 DAY 30

0741 □□□

furniture
[ˈfɜːrnɪtʃər]

n 가구

= furnishings, movable articles, household items
+ a piece of furniture 가구 한 점

Q: Is this furniture suitable for small apartments?
이 가구가 작은 아파트에 적합한가요?

A: ....

0742 □□□

further
[ˈfɜːrðər]

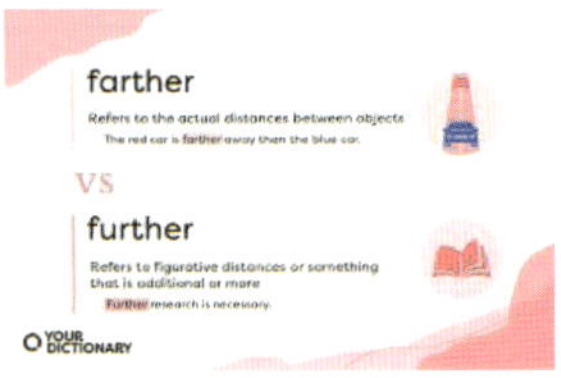

adv 더 멀리, 추가적으로 **a** 더 이상의

= additional, more, deeper, promote, assist
+ furtherance n 발전

Q: Can you explain further what you meant?
무슨 뜻인지 더 자세히 설명해 줄 수 있나요?

A: ....

0743 □□□

furthermore
[ˌfɜːrðərˈmɔːr]

adv 게다가, 더욱이

= moreover, in addition, besides, additionally
+ and furthermore 그 위에, 더욱이, 더군다나

Q: Furthermore, do you think these new regulations will truly benefit the environment?
게다가, 이러한 새로운 규제가 정말로 환경에 도움이 될 것이라고 생각하시나요?

A: ....

0744 □□□

gap
[gæp]

n 틈, 격차

= space, opening, interval, void, disparity
+ the gap between rich and poor 빈부 격차

Q: Is there a big gap between these two ideas?
이 두 아이디어 사이에 큰 차이가 있나요?

A: ....

0745 □□□

garage
[gəˈrɑːʒ] [ˈgærɑːʒ]

n 차고

= workshop, car park, auto shop
+ garage sale (사람이 자기 집 차고에서 하는) 중고 물품 세일 **parking garage** 차고

Q: Do you park your car inside the garage? 차를 차고 안에 주차하나요?

A: ....

0746 □□□

gender
[ˈdʒendər]

n 성별

= sex, male & female, social identity

+ **gendered** **a** 성에 따른

Q: Is gender equality important in your workplace?
직장에서 성 평등이 중요한가요?

A: ....

0747 □□□

general
[ˈdʒenərəl]

a 일반적인, 전반적인 **n** 장군

= widespread, common, universal, overall, commander

+ **generalization** **n** 일반화 **generalize** **v** 일반화하다 **generally** **adv** 일반적으로

Q: What's your general opinion about this topic?
이 주제에 대한 전반적인 의견은 어떤가요?

A: ....

0748 □□□

generally
[ˈdʒenərəli]

adv 일반적으로

= usually, typically, commonly, broadly

+ **general** **a** 일반적인

Q: Generally, do you agree with this policy? 대체적으로 이 정책에 동의하나요?

A: ....

0749 □□□

generate
[ˈdʒenəreɪt]

v 생성하다, 발생시키다

= produce, create, engender, cause, originate

+ **generation** **n** 세대, 발생 **generator** **n** 발전기

Q: Can this machine generate enough electricity?
이 기계가 충분한 전기를 생산할 수 있나요?

A: ....

0750 □□□

generation
[ˌdʒenəˈreɪʃn]

n 세대, 발생

= age group, cohort, progeny, production

+ **generate** **v** 생성하다, 발생시키다 **generator** **n** 발전기

Q: How is the younger generation different today?
오늘날 젊은 세대는 어떻게 다른가요?

A: ....

0751 □□□

generous
[ˈdʒenərəs]

a 관대한, 후한

= liberal, philanthropic, openhanded, bountiful
+ generosity n 관대함 generously adv 관대하게

Q: Are your parents known for being generous?
부모님이 너그러우신 걸로 알려져 있지요?

A:

0752 □□□

genetic
[dʒəˈnetɪk]

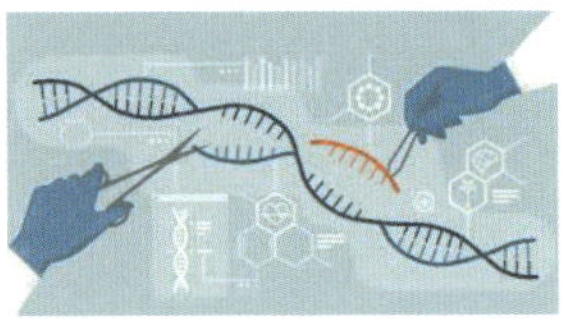

a 유전적인

= hereditary, inherited, biological
+ genetics n 유전학 gene n 유전자 genetically adv 유전적으로

Q: Is genetic testing becoming more popular nowadays?
요즘 유전자 검사가 더 인기를 얻고 있나요?

A:

0753 □□□

genius
[ˈdʒiːniəs]

n 천재

= brilliance, intellect, prodigy, mastermind
+ ingenious a 독창적인

Q: Do you think he's a genius or just lucky?
그가 천재라고 생각하나요, 아니면 단지 운이 좋은 건가요?

A:

0754 □□□

genuine
[ˈdʒenjuɪn]

a 진짜의, 진심 어린

= authentic, real, true, sincere, legitimate
+ genuineness n 진정성 genuinely adv 진정으로

Q: Is her apology sincere and genuine enough?
그녀의 사과가 진심이고 충분히 진정한가요?

A:

0755 □□□

geography
[dʒiˈɑːgrəfi]

n 지리

= topography, landscape, physical features of earth
+ geographic[geographical] a 지리적인 geographically adv 지리적으로

Q: Did you study geography in high school? 고등학교 때 지리학을 공부했나요?

A:

0756 □□□

gesture
[ˈdʒestʃər]

n 몸짓, 제스처 **v** 몸짓을 하다

= **signal, motion, sign, indication**

+ **facial gesture** 표정

Q: Was that gesture meant to be friendly or rude?
그 제스처는 친근함을 의미했나요, 아니면 무례함을 의미했나요?

A: ……………………………………

0757 □□□

glance
[glæns]

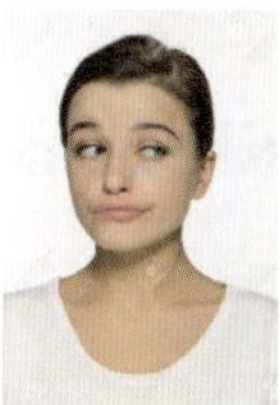

n 흘끗 봄 **v** 흘끗 보다

= **glimpse, quick look, peek, scan**

+ **at first glance** 처음에는[언뜻 보기에는]

Q: Did you take a quick glance at the report? 보고서를 빠르게 훑어봤나요?

A: ……………………………………

0758 □□□

glory
[ˈglɔːri]

n 영광

= **splendor, majesty, fame, honor, renown**

+ **glorious** **a** 영광스러운 **glorify** **v** 찬미하다, 영광을 돌리다

Q: Do you seek glory in your career choices? 직업 선택에서 영광을 추구하나요?

A: ……………………………………

0759 □□□

glow
[gloʊ]

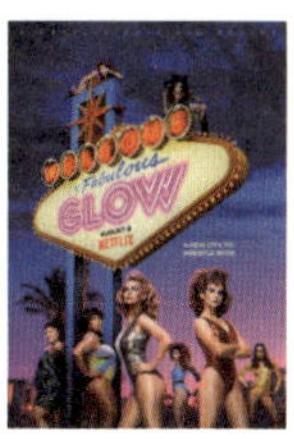

n 빛, 불빛 **v** 빛나다

= **shine, radiate, glimmer, warmth, radiance**

+ **afterglow** **n** (해가 진 후의) 잔광, (기분 좋은) 여운

Q: Does your new skincare routine make your skin glow?
새 스킨케어 루틴이 피부를 빛나게[환하게] 만드나요?

A: ……………………………………

0760 □□□

govern
[ˈgʌvərn]

v 통치하다, 다스리다

= **rule, administer, regulate, control, manage**

+ **government** **n** 정부 **governor** **n** 주지사 **governing** **a** 통치하는

Q: Who will govern the country after the war?
전쟁 후에 누가 나라를 통치할 건가요?

A: ……………………………………

DAY 08 | DICTATION TEST

5회 반복 예문 QR

DICTATION TEST 예문 QR을 듣고 다음 빈칸에 올바른 단어를 쓰세요.

741. Is this ________________ suitable for small apartments?
742. Can you explain ________________ what you meant?
743. ________________, do you think these new regulations will truly benefit the environment?
744. Is there a big ________________ between these two ideas?
745. Do you park your car inside the ________________?
746. Is ________________ equality important in your workplace?
747. What's your ________________ opinion about this topic?
748. ________________, do you agree with this policy?
749. Can this machine ________________ enough electricity?
750. How is the younger ________________ different today?
751. Are your parents known for being ________________?
752. Is ________________ testing becoming more popular nowadays?
753. Do you think he's a ________________ or just lucky?
754. Is her apology sincere and ________________ enough?
755. Did you study ________________ in high school?
756. Was that ________________ meant to be friendly or rude?
757. Did you take a quick ________________ at the report?
758. Do you seek ________________ in your career choices?
759. Does your new skincare routine make your skin ________________?
760. Who will ________________ the country after the war?

5회 반복 표제어 QR　　5회 반복 예문 QR

DAY 09

30 days

AI 학습자료와 인강 youpass.co.kr

PREVIEW A 다음 단어의 뜻을 한국어로 써보세요.

□ government ________	□ grateful ________
□ grab ________	□ grave ________
□ grade ________	□ gravity ________
□ gradual ________	□ grip ________
□ gradually ________	□ grocery ________
□ graduate ________	□ growth ________
□ graduation ________	□ guarantee ________
□ grain ________	□ guard ________
□ grammar ________	□ guest ________
□ grant ________	□ guilty ________

PREVIEW B 사진을 보고 알맞은 영어 단어를 **PREVIEW A**에서 찾아 써보세요.

____

____

____

____

0761 □□□

government
[ˈɡʌvərnmənt]

n 정부, 정권

= administration, regime, state, authority
+ govern **v** 통치하다 governmental **a** 정부의

Q: Does the government support small businesses well?
정부가 중소기업을 잘 지원하나요?

A:

0762 □□□

grab
[ɡræb]

v 붙잡다, 움켜쥐다

= seize, snatch, grasp, capture, take hold of
+ grab a purse 지갑을 낚아채다

Q: Can you grab me a coffee on your way? 오는 길에 커피 한 잔 사다 줄 수 있나요?

A:

0763 □□□

grade
[ɡreɪd]

n 학년, 성적, 등급 **v** 등급을 매기다

= mark, level, rank, quality, evaluate, categorize
+ low-grade **a** 질 낮은, 저질의 high-grade **a** 고급의

Q: What grade did you get on the test? 시험에서 몇 점을 받았나요?

A:

0764 □□□

gradual
[ˈɡrædʒuəl]

a 점진적인

= slow, progressive, steady, gentle
+ gradualness **n** 점진적임 gradually **adv** 점진적으로

Q: Do you think the shift in public opinion will be gradual or sudden?
대중의 의견 변화가 점진적일 것이라고 생각하시나요, 아니면 갑작스러울 것이라고 생각하시나요?

A:

0765 □□□

gradually
[ˈɡrædʒuəli]

adv 점차적으로

= slowly, progressively, steadily, incrementally
+ gradual **a** 점진적인

Q: Will the temperature gradually rise this week?
이번 주에 기온이 점차적으로 오를까요?

A:

0766 □□□

graduate
[ˈgrædʒuət] n [ˈgrædʒueɪt] v

v 졸업하다 n 졸업생

= complete, finish, alumni, degree holder
+ graduation n 졸업

Q: When did you graduate from college? 언제 대학을 졸업했나요?

A: ....

0767 □□□

graduation
[ˌgrædʒuˈeɪʃn]

n 졸업

= commencement, completion ceremony
+ graduate v 졸업하다

Q: Are you attending the graduation ceremony tomorrow?
내일 졸업식에 참석할 건가요?

A: ....

0768 □□□

grain
[greɪn]

n 곡물, 알갱이

= cereal, particle, kernel, texture, smallest amount
+ grainy a 거친, 낟알 같은

Q: Is this grain organic or conventionally grown?
이 곡물은 유기농인가요, 아니면 일반 재배인가요?

A: ....

0769 □□□

grammar
[ˈgræmər]

n 문법

= syntax, linguistics, rules of language
+ grammatical a 문법적인 grammatically adv 문법적으로

Q: Did you check the grammar in your essay? 에세이의 문법을 확인했나요?

A: ....

0770 □□□

grant
[grænt]

v 승인하다, 주다 n 보조금

= bestow, award, allow, concede, subsidy, scholarship
+ grant permission 허가해 주다

Q: Did they grant you permission to proceed?
그들이 계속 진행할 허락을 해주었나요?

A: ....

0771 □□□

grateful
[ˈgreɪtfəl]

a 감사하는

= thankful, appreciative, obliged, indebted
+ gratitude n 감사 gratefully adv 감사하게

Q: Are you grateful for all the help received? 받은 모든 도움에 감사하고 있나요?
A: ....

0772 □□□

grave
[greɪv]

n 무덤 a 심각한

= serious, solemn, somber, tomb, burial site
+ gravity n 중력, 심각성

Q: Is his injury serious or just a grave concern?
그의 부상이 실제로 심각한가요, 아니면 그저 심각한 우려 사항 정도인가요?
A: ....

0773 □□□

gravity
[ˈgrævəti]

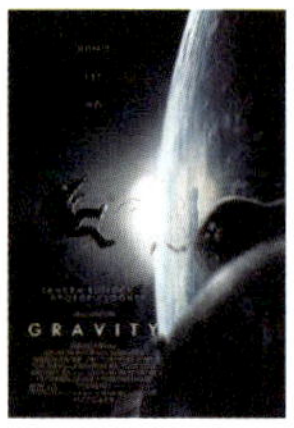

n 중력, 심각성

= seriousness, importance, solemnity, weight, pull
+ grave a 심각한

Q: Do you understand the gravity of the situation?
상황의 심각성을 이해하나요?
A: ....

0774 □□□

grip
[grɪp]

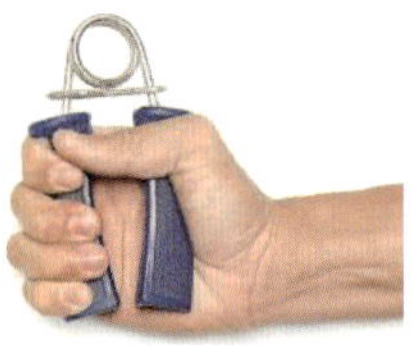

n 꽉 잡음, 통제 v 꽉 잡다

= grasp, hold, control, mastery, seize, clutch
+ hairgrip n (금속제의 가늘고 작은) 머리핀(bobby pin, grip, hairpin)

Q: Does the handle have a good grip on it? 손잡이에 그립감이 좋은가요?
A: ....

0775 □□□

grocery
[ˈgroʊsəri]

n 식료품, 식료품점

= food store, supermarket, provisions
+ grocer n 식료품상인

Q: Did you go grocery shopping this morning? 오늘 아침에 장 보러 갔었나요?
A: ....

0776 □□□

growth
[groʊθ]

n 성장, 증가

= development, increase, expansion, progress, mass
+ grow v 자라다

Q: What factors contribute to economic growth?
경제 성장에 어떤 요인들이 기여하나요?

A: ……

0777 □□□

guarantee
[ˌgærən'tiː]

n 보증 v 보증하다

= assure, promise, warrant, pledge, warranty
+ money-back guarantee 환불 보장

Q: Is there a guarantee on this product warranty?
이 제품 보증서에 보증이 있나요?

A: ……

0778 □□□

guard
[gɑːrd]

n 경비원, 보호 v 지키다, 보호하다

= protect, defend, watch, sentinel, escort
+ guardian n 보호자

Q: Who will guard the building overnight here?
여기서 누가 밤새 건물을 지킬 건가요?

A: ……

0779 □□□

guest
[gest]

n 손님

= visitor, caller, invitee, lodger
+ guest room 손님방

Q: Are the guests arriving earlier than expected?
손님들이 예상보다 일찍 도착하고 있나요?

A: ……

0780 □□□

guilty
['gɪlti]

a 유죄의, 죄책감을 느끼는

= responsible, culpable, liable, regretful, ashamed
+ guilt n 죄책감 guiltily adv 죄책감을 느끼며

Q: Do you feel guilty about what happened? 일어난 일에 대해 죄책감을 느끼나요?

A: ……

DAY 09 | DICTATION TEST

5회 반복 예문 QR

DICTATION TEST 예문 QR을 듣고 다음 빈칸에 올바른 단어를 쓰세요.

761. Does the ________________ support small businesses well?
762. Can you ________________ me a coffee on your way?
763. What ________________ did you get on the test?
764. Do you think the shift in public opinion will be ________________ or sudden?
765. Will the temperature ________________ rise this week?
766. When did you ________________ from college?
767. Are you attending the ________________ ceremony tomorrow?
768. Is this ________________ organic or conventionally grown?
769. Did you check the ________________ in your essay?
770. Did they ________________ you permission to proceed?
771. Are you ________________ for all the help received?
772. Is his injury serious or just a ________________ concern?
773. Do you understand the ________________ of the situation?
774. Does the handle have a good ________________ on it?
775. Did you go ________________ shopping this morning?
776. What factors contribute to economic ________________?
777. Is there a ________________ on this product warranty?
778. Who will ________________ the building overnight here?
779. Are the ________________ arriving earlier than expected?
780. Do you feel ________________ about what happened?

5회 반복 표제어 QR　5회 반복 예문 QR

DAY 10

30 days

AI 학습자료와 인강 youpass.co.kr

PREVIEW A 다음 단어의 뜻을 한국어로 써보세요.

□ habitat ________	□ heaven ________
□ haircut ________	□ height ________
□ handle ________	□ heritage ________
□ happen ________	□ hesitate ________
□ hardly ________	□ hiccup ________
□ harm ________	□ highlight ________
□ harvest ________	□ highly ________
□ haste ________	□ hire ________
□ hatch ________	□ historic ________
□ heal ________	□ historical ________

PREVIEW B 사진을 보고 알맞은 영어 단어를 **PREVIEW A** 에서 찾아 써보세요.

____

____

____

____

0781 □□□

habitat
[ˈhæbɪtæt]

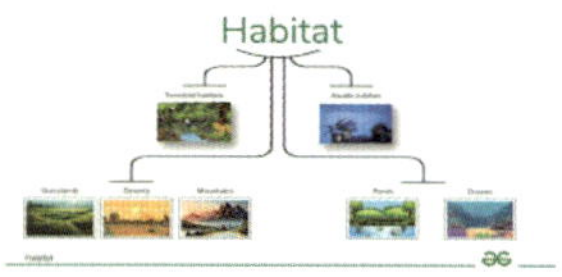

n 서식지

= environment, dwelling, home, natural home
+ habitation **n** 거주, 주거 **the destruction of wildlife habitat** 야생 서식지 파괴

Q: Is this habitat suitable for endangered animals?
이 서식지가 멸종 위기 동물에게 적합한가요?

A: ....

0782 □□□

haircut
[ˈherkʌt]

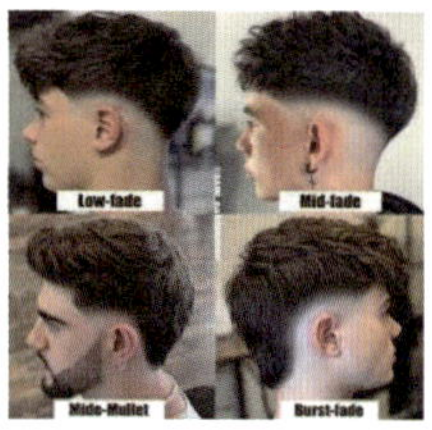

n 이발

= trim, styling, coiffure
+ a trendy haircut 최신 유행 헤어스타일

Q: Did you like your new haircut this time? 이번에 새 헤어스타일 마음에 들었나요?

A: ....

0783 □□□

handle
[ˈhændl]

n 손잡이 **v** 다루다, 처리하다

= manage, deal with, operate, grip, mechanism
+ the handle of a knife 칼자루

Q: Can you handle this situation by yourself? 이 상황을 혼자서 처리할 수 있나요?

A: ....

0784 □□□

happen
[ˈhæpən]

v 발생하다, 일어나다

= occur, take place, transpire, arise, befall
+ happening **n** 사건

Q: What will happen if we miss the deadline? 마감 기한을 놓치면 어떻게 되나요?

A: ....

0785 □□□

hardly
[ˈhɑːrdli]

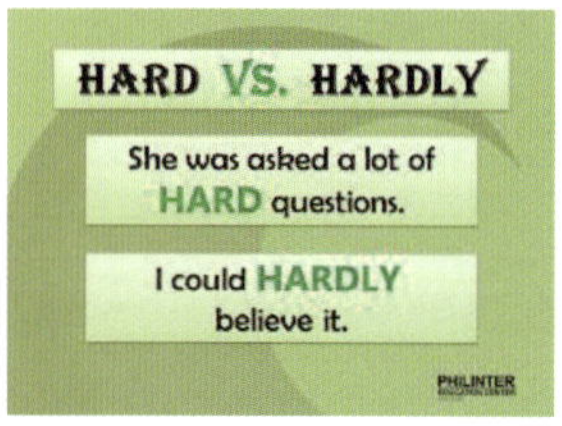

adv 거의 ~않다

= barely, scarcely, almost not, with difficulty
+ hard **a** 어려운, 단단한 **hardness** **n** 단단함

Q: Do you hardly ever eat out during weekdays?
평일에는 거의 외식을 하지 않나요?

A: ....

0786 □□□

harm
[hɑːrm]

n 해악, 손해 v 해치다

= **damage, injure, hurt, detriment, injury**
+ **harmful** a 해로운 **harmless** a 무해한 **harmfully** adv 해롭게 **harmlessly** adv 무해하게

Q: Could this chemical harm your skin somehow?
이 화학 물질이 당신의 피부에 어떤 식으로든 해를 끼칠 수 있나요?

A: ....

0787 □□□

harvest
[ˈhɑːrvɪst]

n 수확 v 수확하다

= **reap, gather, collect, yield, crop**
+ **harvest festival** 추수 감사제(**Thanksgiving**)

Q: When do farmers usually harvest the crops?
농부들은 보통 언제 작물을 수확하나요?

A: ....

0788 □□□

haste
[heɪst]

n 서두름

= **hurry, rush, speed, alacrity**
+ **hasty** a 성급한 **hastily** adv 성급하게

Q: Did you act in haste without thinking clearly?
명확히 생각하지 않고 성급하게 행동했나요?

A: ....

0789 □□□

hatch
[hætʃ]

v 부화하다 n 부화

= **emerge, develop, contrive, opening, brood**
+ **an escape hatch** 탈출구 **a serving hatch** 음식을 내는 창구

Q: When will the eggs hatch this season? 이번 시즌에 알들은 언제 부화할까요?

A: ....

0790 □□□

heal
[hiːl]

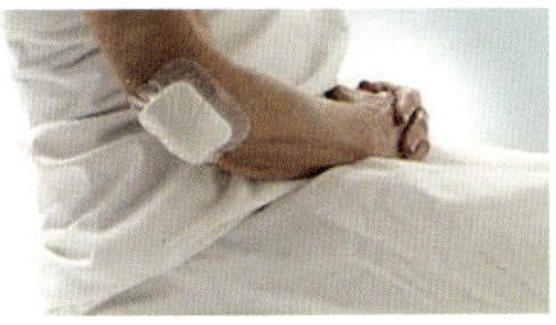

v 치유하다

= **cure, mend, recover, restore, soothe**
+ **healing** n 치유

Q: How long does it take to heal completely? 완전히 치유되는 데 얼마나 걸리나요?

A: ....

0791 □□□

heaven
[ˈhevn]

n 천국, 하늘

= paradise, afterlife, sky, divine realm
+ heavenly **a** 천국의

Q: Do you believe in heaven after death? 죽음 후에 천국을 믿나요?

A: ....

0792 □□□

height
[haɪt]

n 높이, 키

= altitude, elevation, stature, peak, extent
+ high **a** 높은 **heighten** **v** 높이다

Q: What's your height compared to others here?
여기 다른 사람들에 비해 당신의 키는 어떤가요?

A: ....

0793 □□□

heritage
[ˈherɪtɪdʒ]

n 유산

= legacy, inheritance, tradition, patrimony
+ World Heritage Site 세계 문화 유산

Q: Is this festival part of your cultural heritage?
이 축제가 당신의 문화유산의 일부인가요?

A: ....

0794 □□□

hesitate
[ˈhezɪteɪt]

v 망설이다, 주저하다

= pause, waver, falter, delay, scruple
+ hesitation **n** 망설임 **hesitant** **a** 망설이는 **hesitantly** **adv** 망설이며

Q: Did you hesitate before making that decision?
그 결정을 내리기 전에 망설였나요?

A: ....

0795 □□□

hiccup
[ˈhɪkʌp]

n 딸꾹질

= spasm, glitch, temporary problem
+ a loud hiccup 크게 딸꾹 하는 소리

Q: How do you usually stop a hiccup quickly?
딸꾹질을 보통 어떻게 빨리 멈추나요?

A: ....

0796 □□□

highlight
[ˈhaɪlaɪt]

v 강조하다, 형광펜을 치다 **n** 가장 중요한 부분

= **emphasize, stress, feature, accent, best part**

+ **the highlight of his talk** 그의 이야기 중 가장 인상적인 부분

Q: What was the highlight of your vacation?
휴가 중 가장 좋았던 점은 무엇이었나요?

A: ……………………

0797 □□□

highly
[ˈhaɪli]

adv 매우, 대단히

= **very, greatly, extremely, intensely, favorably**

+ **high** **a** 높은

Q: Is she highly recommended by previous clients?
그녀는 이전 고객들에게 강력히 추천받았나요?

A: ……………………

0798 □□□

hire
[ˈhaɪər]

v 고용하다 **n** 고용

= **employ, recruit, lease, rent, engage**

+ **new hire** 신입 사원

Q: When will they hire new staff for summer?
그들은 언제 여름을 위해 새로운 직원을 고용할까요?

A: ……………………

0799 □□□

historic
[hɪˈstɔːrɪk]

a 역사적으로 중요한, 기억할 만한, 기념비적인, 획기적인

= **significant, momentous, memorable, important**

+ **history** **n** 역사 **historical** **a** 역사적인 **historic moment** 역사적인 순간
historic figure 역사적인 인물

Q: Is this building considered historic or modern?
이 건물은 역사적으로 중요한 것으로 간주되나요, 아니면 현대적인 것으로 간주되나요?

A: ……………………

0800 □□□

historical
[hɪˈstɔːrɪkl]

a 역사에 관한, 역사적인, 과거사실에 기반한

= **factual, ancient, past, chronicled, verifiable**

+ **history** **n** 역사 **historically** **adv** 역사적으로 **historic** **a** 역사적으로 중요한
historical sites 여행 중에 방문하는 유적지, 고고학적 발굴지, 유명한 과거의 건물이 남아있는 곳 **historical research** 역사 연구

Q: Did you visit any historical sites on your trip?
여행 중에 어떤 역사적인 장소를 방문했나요?

A: ……………………

DAY 10 | DICTATION TEST

5회 반복 예문 QR

DICTATION TEST 예문 QR을 듣고 다음 빈칸에 올바른 단어를 쓰세요.

781. Is this ________________ suitable for endangered animals?
782. Did you like your new ________________ this time?
783. Can you ________________ this situation by yourself?
784. What will ________________ if we miss the deadline?
785. Do you ________________ ever eat out during weekdays?
786. Could this chemical ________________ your skin somehow?
787. When do farmers usually ________________ the crops?
788. Did you act in ________________ without thinking clearly?
789. When will the eggs ________________ this season?
790. How long does it take to ________________ completely?
791. Do you believe in ________________ after death?
792. What's your ________________ compared to others here?
793. Is this festival part of your cultural ________________?
794. Did you ________________ before making that decision?
795. How do you usually stop a ________________ quickly?
796. What was the ________________ of your vacation?
797. Is she ________________ recommended by previous clients?
798. When will they ________________ new staff for summer?
799. Is this building considered ________________ or modern?
800. Did you visit any ________________ sites on your trip?

5회 반복 표제어 QR 5회 반복 예문 QR

DAY 11

30 days

PREVIEW A 다음 단어의 뜻을 한국어로 써보세요.

□ hollow ______	□ humanity ______
□ holy ______	□ humble ______
□ honor ______	□ humiliate ______
□ horizon ______	□ hunger ______
□ horizontal ______	□ hurricane ______
□ horror ______	□ hybrid ______
□ hospitality ______	□ hypothesis ______
□ host ______	□ ideal ______
□ hostility ______	□ identical ______
□ household ______	□ identify ______

PREVIEW B 사진을 보고 알맞은 영어 단어를 **PREVIEW A** 에서 찾아 써보세요.

______

______

______

______

0801 □□□

hollow
[ˈhɑːloʊ]

a 속이 빈, 텅 빈 n 움푹 들어간 곳

= empty, vacant, cavernous, sunken, meaningless
+ hollowly adv 공허하게

Q: Is the tree trunk hollow or solid inside?
나무줄기 안이 비어있나요 아니면 꽉 차있나요?

A: ……………………………………

0802 □□□

holy
[ˈhoʊli]

a 신성한, 거룩한

= sacred, divine, spiritual, hallowed, devout
+ holiness n 신성함 holy cow 맙소사

Q: Did you visit any holy places on your trip? 여행 중에 성지 방문했나요?

A: ……………………………………

0803 □□□

honor
[ˈɑːnər]

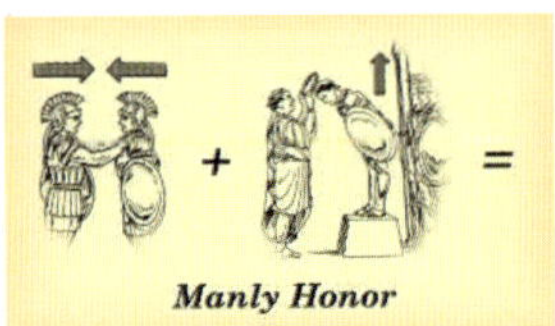

n 명예, 영광 v 존경하다, 영광을 주다

= respect, esteem, prestige, integrity, commend, revere
+ honoree n 수상자 honorable a 명예로운 honored a 영광스러운
honorably adv 명예롭게

Q: Will you honor your promises this time? 이번에는 약속을 지킬 건가요?

A: ……………………………………

0804 □□□

horizon
[həˈraɪzn]

n 수평선, 지평선

= skyline, vista, range, scope, limit
+ horizontal a 수평의

Q: Can you see the horizon clearly from here?
여기서 수평선이 명확하게 보이나요?

A: ……………………………………

0805 □□□

horizontal
[ˌhɔːrɪˈzɑːntl]

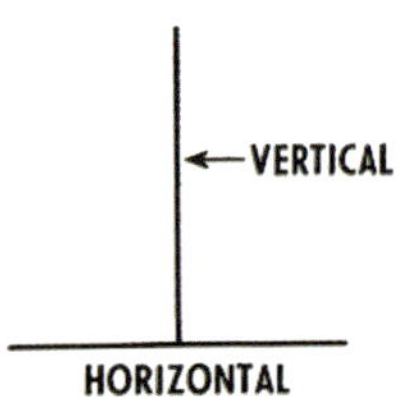

a 수평의

= flat, level, parallel, prone
+ horizon n 수평선 horizontally adv 수평으로

Q: Is the line supposed to be perfectly horizontal?
선이 완벽하게 수평이어야 하나요?

A: ……………………………………

0806 □□□

horror
[ˈhɔːrər]

n 공포, 경악

= terror, dread, fright, revulsion, alarm
+ horrible a 끔찍한 horrifying a 소름 끼치는 horrified a 겁에 질린
horrify v 소름 끼치게 하다

Q: Did the horror movie scare you enough? 공포 영화가 충분히 무서웠나요?

A: ....

0807 □□□

hospitality
[ˌhɑːspɪˈtæləti]

n 환대, 친절, 접객

= welcome, cordiality, friendliness, generosity
+ hospitable a 친절한, 환대하는 hospital n 병원 hospitality industry 접객업

Q: Was the hospitality at the hotel impressive? 호텔의 환대가 인상적이었나요?

A: ....

0808 □□□

host
[hoʊst]

n 주인, 진행자 v 주최하다

= entertainer, presenter, owner, multitude, accommodate, preside
+ hostess n 여주인 hosting n 호스팅 host v 주최하다

Q: Who will host the meeting this afternoon?
오늘 오후 회의는 누가 진행할 건가요?

A: ....

0809 □□□

hostility
[hɑːˈstɪləti]

n 적대감, 적의

= animosity, antagonism, aggression, unfriendliness
+ hostile a 적대적인 hostilely adv 적대적으로

Q: Did you notice any hostility during the debate?
토론 중에 어떤 적대감을 느꼈나요?

A: ....

0810 □□□

household
[ˈhaʊshoʊld]

n 가정, 가구 a 가정의

= domestic, family, home, dwelling
+ the head of the household (집안의) 가장

Q: How many people are in your household now?
현재 당신의 가구에는 몇 명이 있나요?

A: ....

0811 □□□

humanity
[hjuːˈmænəti]

n 인류, 인간성

= humankind, mankind, compassion, benevolence, mortality
+ human **n** 인간 **humanitarian** **n** 인도주의자 **humane** **a** 인도적인
humanize **v** 인간답게 만들다

Q: What can we do to help humanity overall?
인류 전체를 돕기 위해 무엇을 할 수 있을까요?

A: ....

0812 □□□

humble
[ˈhʌmbl]

a 겸손한, 보잘것없는 **v** 겸손하게 하다

= modest, meek, unassuming, lowly, degrade
+ humility **n** 겸손 **humbly** **adv** 겸손하게

Q: Do you consider yourself a humble person?
자신을 겸손한 사람이라고 생각하나요?

A: ....

0813 □□□

humiliate
[hjuːˈmɪlieɪt]

v 굴욕감을 주다

= embarrass, disgrace, mortify, shame, degrade
+ humiliation **n** 굴욕, 창피 **humiliating** **a** 굴욕적인 **humiliated** **a** 굴욕감을 느끼는

Q: Why would someone want to humiliate others?
왜 누군가가 다른 사람들을 모욕하고 싶어 할까요?

A: ....

0814 □□□

hunger
[ˈhʌŋgər]

n 굶주림, 배고픔

= appetite, craving, starvation, desire
+ hungry **a** 배고픈 **hungrily** **adv** 굶주린 듯이

Q: Did you feel hunger after the long walk? 오랜 산책 후에 배고픔을 느꼈나요?

A: ....

0815 □□□

hurricane
[ˈhɜːrɪkeɪn]

n 허리케인

= typhoon, cyclone, tempest, gale
+ a category 5 hurricane 5 등급 허리케인

Q: Is the hurricane expected to hit tonight?
허리케인이 오늘 밤에 강타할 것으로 예상되나요?

A: ....

0816 □□□

hybrid
[ˈhaɪbrɪd]

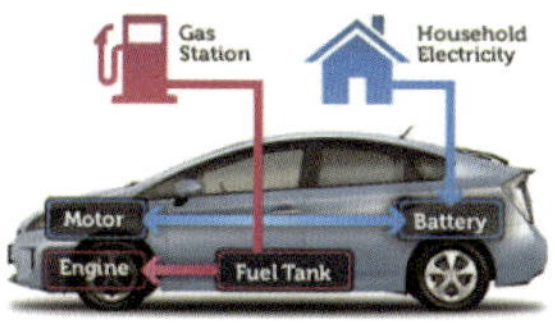

n 혼성물, 잡종 **a** 혼성의

= mixed, blended, composite, crossbreed

+ a hybrid animal 잡종 동물 **hybrid car** 전기와 휘발유를 같이 사용하는 차

Q: Are hybrid cars more popular these days?
요즘 하이브리드 자동차가 더 인기가 많나요?

A: ....

0817 □□□

hypothesis
[haɪˈpɑːθəsɪs]

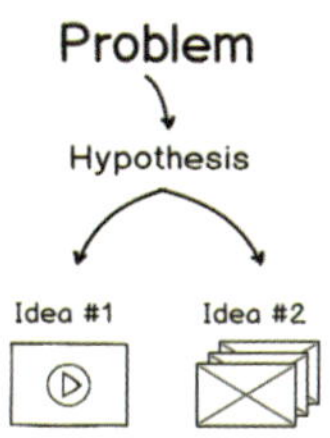

n 가설

= theory, assumption, proposition, conjecture

+ hypothesize v 가설을 세우다 **hypothetical a** 가설의
hypothetically adv 가설에 따라

Q: Can you explain the hypothesis clearly now?
이제 가설을 명확하게 설명해 줄 수 있나요?

A: ....

0818 □□□

ideal
[aɪˈdiːəl]

n 이상 **a** 이상적인

= perfect, exemplary, ultimate, concept, paragon

+ idealism n 이상주의 **idealistic a** 이상주의적인 **idealize v** 이상화하다
ideally adv 이상적으로

Q: What's your ideal vacation destination this year?
올해 이상적인 휴가 목적지는 어디인가요?

A: ....

0819 □□□

identical
[aɪˈdentɪkl]

a 동일한, 똑같은

= same, alike, equivalent, indistinguishable

+ identity n 정체성 **identification n** 신분 확인 **identically adv** 동일하게

Q: Are these two paintings completely identical?
이 두 그림이 완전히 동일한가요?

A: ....

0820 □□□

identify
[aɪˈdentɪfaɪ]

v 확인하다, 식별하다

= recognize, pinpoint, ascertain, name, discover

+ identity n 정체성 **identification n** 신분 확인 **identifiable a** 식별 가능한

Q: Can you identify the person in this photo? 이 사진 속 인물을 식별할 수 있나요?

A: ....

DAY 11 | DICTATION TEST

5회 반복 예문 QR

DICTATION TEST 예문 QR을 듣고 다음 빈칸에 올바른 단어를 쓰세요.

801. Is the tree trunk ________________ or solid inside?
802. Did you visit any ________________ places on your trip?
803. Will you ________________ your promises this time?
804. Can you see the ________________ clearly from here?
805. Is the line supposed to be perfectly ________________?
806. Did the ________________ movie scare you enough?
807. Was the ________________ at the hotel impressive?
808. Who will ________________ the meeting this afternoon?
809. Did you notice any ________________ during the debate?
810. How many people are in your ________________ now?
811. What can we do to help ________________ overall?
812. Do you consider yourself a ________________ person?
813. Why would someone want to ________________ others?
814. Did you feel ________________ after the long walk?
815. Is the ________________ expected to hit tonight?
816. Are ________________ cars more popular these days?
817. Can you explain the ________________ clearly now?
818. What's your ________________ vacation destination this year?
819. Are these two paintings completely ________________?
820. Can you ________________ the person in this photo?

5회 반복 표제어 QR　5회 반복 예문 QR

DAY 12

30 days

AI 학습자료와 인강 youpass.co.kr

PREVIEW A 다음 단어의 뜻을 한국어로 써보세요.

- □ identity ______
- □ idiom ______
- □ idle ______
- □ ignore ______
- □ illegal ______
- □ illustrate ______
- □ imaginary ______
- □ imagination ______
- □ imaginative ______
- □ imagine ______
- □ imitate ______
- □ immediate ______
- □ immediately ______
- □ immigrate ______
- □ immune ______
- □ impact ______
- □ impatient ______
- □ imply ______
- □ import ______
- □ importance ______

PREVIEW B 사진을 보고 알맞은 영어 단어를 **PREVIEW A** 에서 찾아 써보세요.

______

______

______

______

0821 □□□

identity
[aɪˈdentəti]

n 신원, 정체성

= individuality, self, character, recognition, distinctiveness
+ identify v 확인하다, 동일시하다

Q: Can you prove your identity at the entrance?
입구에서 신원을 증명할 수 있나요?

A: ....

0822 □□□

idiom
[ˈɪdiəm]

n 관용구, 숙어

= expression, phrase, saying, peculiar usage
+ idiomatic a 관용적인 idiomatically adv 관용적으로

Q: Do you understand the meaning of this idiom?
이 관용구의 의미를 이해하나요?

A: ....

0823 □□□

idle
[ˈaɪdl]

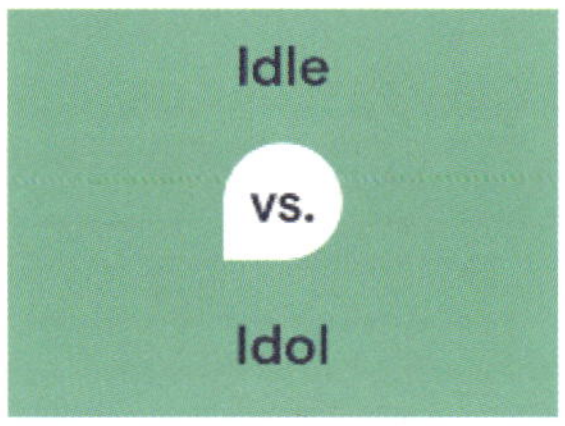

a 한가한, 게으른 v 빈둥거리다

= inactive, lazy, dormant, jobless, unoccupied, waste
+ idleness n 게으름 idly adv 게으르게

Q: Why do some machines stay idle all day?
일부 기계가 왜 하루 종일 작동하지 않나요?

A: ....

0824 □□□

ignore
[ɪgˈnɔːr]

v 무시하다

= disregard, overlook, neglect, dismiss, shun
+ ignorance n 무지 ignorant a 무지한

Q: Did you ignore the warning signs completely?
경고 신호를 완전히 무시한 건가요?

A: ....

0825 □□□

illegal
[ɪˈliːgl]

a 불법적인

= unlawful, illicit, forbidden, prohibited, criminal
+ illegality n 불법성 illegally adv 불법적으로

Q: Is it illegal to park here after hours?
영업시간 후에 여기에 주차하는 것이 불법인가요?

A: ....

0826 □□□

illustrate
[ˈɪləstreɪt]

v 설명하다, 삽화를 넣다

= demonstrate, exemplify, clarify, depict, explain

\+ illustration **n** 삽화, 설명 illustrative **a** 예시가 되는

Q: Can you illustrate your point with an example?
예를 들어 당신의 요점을 설명해 줄 수 있나요?

A: ....

0827 □□□

imaginary
[ɪˈmædʒɪneri]

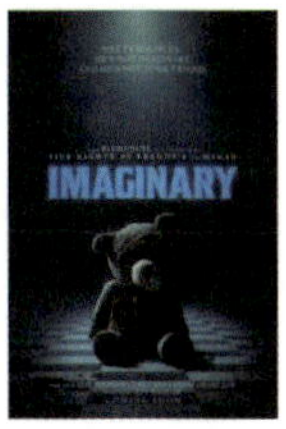

a 상상의

= fictional, unreal, hypothetical, visionary, fantasized

\+ imagination **n** 상상 image **n** 이미지 imagine **v** 상상하다

Q: Did you have any imaginary friends as a child?
어렸을 때 상상 속 친구가 있었나요?

A: ....

0828 □□□

imagination
[ɪˌmædʒɪˈneɪʃn]

n 상상(력)

= creativity, fantasy, vision, inventiveness

\+ imagine **v** 상상하다 imaginative **a** 상상력이 풍부한

Q: How active is your imagination these days?
요즘 당신의 상상력은 얼마나 활발한가요?

A: ....

0829 □□□

imaginative
[ɪˈmædʒɪnətɪv]

a 상상력이 풍부한

= creative, inventive, visionary, resourceful

\+ imagination **n** 상상력 imaginatively **adv** 상상력을 발휘하여

Q: Are you naturally imaginative or more realistic?
당신은 선천적으로 상상력이 풍부한가요 아니면 더 현실적인가요?

A: ....

0830 □□□

imagine
[ɪˈmædʒɪn]

v 상상하다

= envision, conceive, picture, suppose, dream up

\+ imagination **n** 상상 imaginary **a** 상상의

Q: Can you imagine living in another country?
다른 나라에서 사는 것을 상상할 수 있나요?

A: ....

0831 ☐☐☐

imitate
[ˈɪmɪteɪt]

v 모방하다, 흉내 내다

= **mimic, copy, simulate, emulate, impersonate**
\+ **imitation** n 모방 **imitator** n 모방자 **imitative** a 모방적인

Q: Do children often imitate adults around them?
아이들이 주변 어른들을 자주 모방하나요?

A: ....

0832 ☐☐☐

immediate
[ɪˈmiːdiət]

a 즉각적인, 즉시의

= **instant, prompt, direct, closest**
\+ **immediacy** n 즉각성 **immediately** adv 즉시

Q: Is immediate action required for this issue?
이 문제에 즉각적인 조치가 필요한가요?

A: ....

0833 ☐☐☐

immediately
[ɪˈmiːdiətli]

adv 즉시, 곧바로

= **instantly, promptly, at once, directly, right away**
\+ **immediate** a 즉각적인

Q: Did you respond immediately to the message? 메시지에 즉시 답장했나요?

A: ....

0834 ☐☐☐

immigrate
[ˈɪmɪgreɪt]

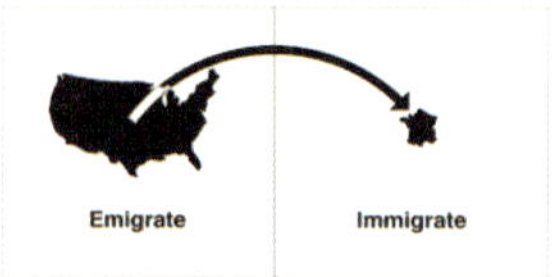

v 이민 오다

= **migrate, settle, relocate, move in**
\+ **immigration** n 이민 **immigrant** n 이민자 **emigration** n 이주, 이민 (떠남)
emigrant n 이주자, 출국 이민자

Q: When did your family immigrate to this country?
당신의 가족은 언제 이 나라로 이민 왔나요?

A: ....

0835 ☐☐☐

immune
[ɪˈmjuːn]

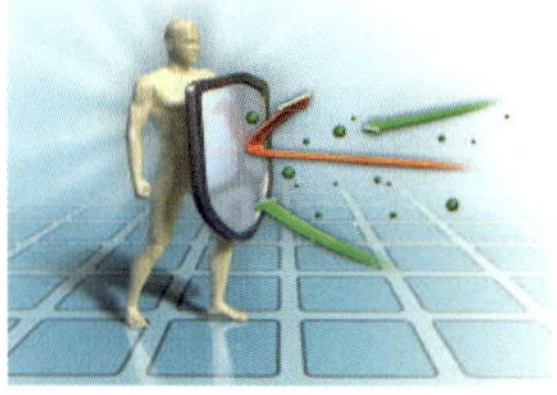

a 면역의, 면역이 있는

= **resistant, protected, unaffected, exempt**
\+ **immunity** n 면역

Q: Are you immune to certain diseases naturally?
특정 질병에 자연적으로 면역이 있나요?

A: ....

0836 □□□

impact
[ˈɪmpækt] n [ɪmˈpækt] v

n 영향, 충격 v 영향을 미치다, 충격을 주다

= effect, influence, collision, force, affect, strike
+ impactful a 영향력 있는

Q: What impact did the new law have locally?
새로운 법이 지역적으로 어떤 영향을 미쳤나요?

A: ....

0837 □□□

impatient
[ɪmˈpeɪʃnt]

a 참을성 없는

= restless, eager, anxious, intolerant, hasty
+ impatience n 조바심, 참을성 없음 impatiently adv 성급하게

Q: Are you impatient when waiting in lines? 줄 서서 기다릴 때 참을성이 없나요?

A: ....

0838 □□□

imply
[ɪmˈplaɪ]

v 암시하다, 의미하다

= suggest, hint, insinuate, signify, indicate
+ implication n 함축, 암시

Q: Did her tone imply something different? 그녀의 말투가 뭔가 다른 것을 암시했나요?

A: ....

0839 □□□

import
[ˈɪmpɔːrt] n [ɪmˈpɔːrt] v

v 수입하다 n 수입(품)

= bring in, introduce, significance, purchase from abroad
+ importer n 수입업자

Q: Does your company import products from overseas?
귀사는 해외에서 제품을 수입하나요?

A: ....

0840 □□□

importance
[ɪmˈpɔːrtns]

n 중요성

= significance, consequence, value, weight, relevance
+ important a 중요한 importantly adv 중요하게도

Q: What's the importance of good communication skills?
훌륭한 의사소통 기술의 중요성은 무엇인가요?

A: ....

DAY 12 | DICTATION TEST

5회 반복 예문 QR

DICTATION TEST 예문 QR을 듣고 다음 빈칸에 올바른 단어를 쓰세요.

821. Can you prove your ______________ at the entrance?
822. Do you understand the meaning of this ______________?
823. Why do some machines stay ______________ all day?
824. Did you ______________ the warning signs completely?
825. Is it ______________ to park here after hours?
826. Can you ______________ your point with an example?
827. Did you have any ______________ friends as a child?
828. How active is your ______________ these days?
829. Are you naturally ______________ or more realistic?
830. Can you ______________ living in another country?
831. Do children often ______________ adults around them?
832. Is ______________ action required for this issue?
833. Did you respond ______________ to the message?
834. When did your family ______________ to this country?
835. Are you ______________ to certain diseases naturally?
836. What ______________ did the new law have locally?
837. Are you ______________ when waiting in lines?
838. Did her tone ______________ something different?
839. Does your company ______________ products from overseas?
840. What's the ______________ of good communication skills?

5회 반복 표제어 QR　5회 반복 예문 QR

DAY 13
30 days

AI 학습자료와 인강 youpass.co.kr

PREVIEW A 다음 단어의 뜻을 한국어로 써보세요.

□ impossible ______	□ increase ______
□ impress ______	□ incredible ______
□ impressed ______	□ indeed ______
□ impression ______	□ independence ______
□ impressive ______	□ independent ______
□ improve ______	□ index ______
□ incident ______	□ indicate ______
□ incline ______	□ indifferent ______
□ include ______	□ individual ______
□ income ______	□ indoor ______

PREVIEW B 사진을 보고 알맞은 영어 단어를 **PREVIEW A**에서 찾아 써보세요.

______

______

______

______

DAY 01 DAY 02 DAY 03 DAY 04 DAY 05 DAY 06 DAY 07 DAY 08 DAY 09 DAY 10 DAY 11 DAY 12 DAY 13 DAY 14 DAY 15 DAY 16 DAY 17 DAY 18 DAY 19 DAY 20 DAY 21 DAY 22 DAY 23 DAY 24 DAY 25 DAY 26 DAY 27 DAY 28 DAY 29 DAY 30

0841 □□□

impossible
[ɪmˈpɑːsəbl]

a 불가능한

= **unachievable, unfeasible, beyond reach, hopeless**

+ **impossibility** n 불가능성

Q: Is it really impossible to finish this on time?
이것을 제시간에 끝내는 것이 정말 불가능한가요?

A: ....

0842 □□□

impress
[ɪmˈpres]

v 깊은 인상을 주다

= **awe, affect, influence, imprint, make an impression**

+ **impression** n 인상 **impressiveness** n 인상적임 **impressive** a 인상적인
impressed a 감명 받은

Q: How can you impress your boss this week?
이번 주에 상사에게 어떻게 깊은 인상을 줄 수 있을까요?

A: ....

0843 □□□

impressed
[ɪmˈprest]

a 감명 받은, 깊은 인상을 받은

= **moved, awed, deeply affected**

+ **impression** n 인상 **impress** v 깊은 인싱을 주다

Q: Were you impressed by the presentation yesterday?
어제 발표에 감명 받았나요?

A: ....

0844 □□□

impression
[ɪmˈpreʃn]

n 인상

= **effect, impact, feeling, notion, imitation**

+ **impress** v 인상을 주다 **impressive** a 인상적인

Q: What's your first impression of the new teacher?
새 선생님에 대한 첫인상은 어떤가요?

A: ....

0845 □□□

impressive
[ɪmˈpresɪv]

a 인상적인

= **striking, remarkable, spectacular, powerful, memorable**

+ **impressiveness** n 인상적임 **impressively** adv 인상적으로

Q: Was the concert performance truly impressive last night?
어젯밤 콘서트 공연이 정말 인상적이었나요?

A: ....

0846 □□□

improve
[ɪmˈpruːv]

v 개선하다, 향상시키다

= **enhance, better, ameliorate, refine, advance**

+ **improvement** **n** 개선, 향상 **improved** **a** 개선된

Q: How can we improve our customer service quickly?
고객 서비스를 어떻게 빠르게 개선할 수 있을까요?

A: ....

0847 □□□

incident
[ˈɪnsɪdənt]

n 사건, 발생한 일

= **event, occurrence, episode, happening, mishap**

+ **incidental** **a** 부수적인 **incidentally** **adv** 우연히, 그런데

Q: Did the incident cause any serious problems afterward?
그 사건이 나중에 심각한 문제를 야기했나요?

A: ....

0848 □□□

incline
[ɪnˈklaɪn] **v** [ˈɪnklaɪn] **n**

v ~하고 싶어 하다, 기울이다 **n** 경사

= **slope, lean, tendency, predispose, prefer**

+ **inclination** **n** 경향, 경사 **inclined** **a** ~하는 경향이 있는

Q: Do you incline to agree with their decision?
그들의 결정에 동의하는 경향이 있나요?

A: ....

0849 □□□

include
[ɪnˈkluːd]

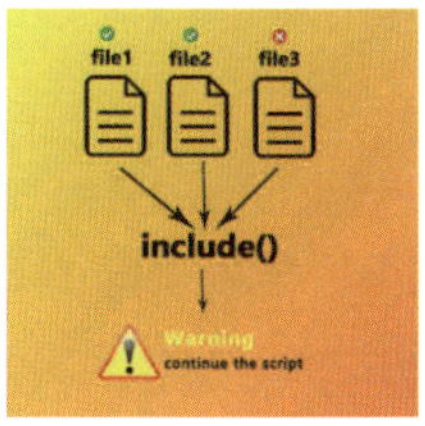

v 포함하다

= **comprise, contain, incorporate, involve, encompass**

+ **inclusion** **n** 포함 **inclusive** **a** 포괄적인

Q: Did they include everyone in the group meeting?
그룹 회의에 모두를 포함시켰나요?

A: ....

0850 □□□

income
[ˈɪnkʌm]

n 수입

= **earnings, revenue, salary, profit**

+ **income tax** 소득세

Q: Is your monthly income enough to cover expenses?
월수입이 지출을 감당하기에 충분한가요?

A: ....

0851 □□□

increase
[ɪnˈkriːs] v [ˈɪnkriːs] n

v 증가하다 n 증가

= grow, expand, rise, multiply, boost, gain
+ increasing a 증가하는 increasingly adv 점점 더

Q: Will the company increase salaries next year?
회사가 내년에 급여를 인상할까요?

A: ....

0852 □□□

incredible
[ɪnˈkredəbl]

a 믿을 수 없는, 엄청난

= unbelievable, amazing, astonishing, extraordinary, fantastic
+ incredibility n 믿을 수 없음 incredibly adv 믿을 수 없을 정도로

Q: Was the view from the mountain incredible?
산에서 본 경치가 믿을 수 없을 정도로 멋졌나요?

A: ....

0853 □□□

indeed
[ɪnˈdiːd]

adv 정말로, 사실

= truly, certainly, in fact, absolutely
+ a friend in need 어려울 때 친구, 이려운 시기에 친해진 친구

Q: Did you indeed finish the work ahead of schedule?
정말로 예정보다 일찍 작업을 마쳤나요?

A: ....

0854 □□□

independence
[ˌɪndɪˈpendəns]

n 독립

= freedom, autonomy, self-reliance, sovereignty
+ independent a 독립적인 independently adv 독립적으로

Q: When did your country gain independence? 당신의 나라는 언제 독립했나요?

A: ....

0855 □□□

independent
[ˌɪndɪˈpendənt]

a 독립적인

= autonomous, self-governing, self-reliant, distinct, uninfluenced
+ independence n 독립 independently adv 독립적으로

Q: Are you financially independent from your parents?
부모님으로부터 재정적으로 독립했나요?

A: ....

0856 □□□

index
[ˈɪndeks]

n 색인, 지수

= guide, list, indicator, measure, register, categorize
+ the cost-of-living index 생활비 지수

Q: Is the index updated regularly on the website?
웹사이트의 색인이 정기적으로 업데이트되나요?

A: ....

0857 □□□

indicate
[ˈɪndɪkeɪt]

v 나타내다, 지시하다

= show, point to, signify, suggest, imply
+ indication n 표시, 징후 indicator n 지표 indicative a 나타내는, 암시하는

Q: Does the data indicate a trend toward growth?
데이터가 성장 추세를 나타내나요?

A: ....

0858 □□□

indifferent
[ɪnˈdɪfrənt]

a 무관심한

= unconcerned, apathetic, detached, neutral, uncaring
+ indifference n 무관심 indifferently adv 무관심하게

Q: Are you indifferent to the new policy changes?
새로운 정책 변화에 무관심한가요?

A: ....

0859 □□□

individual
[ˌɪndɪˈvɪdʒuəl]

n 개인 a 개별적인

= person, single, distinct, personal, unique
+ individuality n 개성 individually adv 개별적으로

Q: Does each individual have equal voting rights?
각 개인이 동등한 투표권을 가지나요?

A: ....

0860 □□□

indoor
[ˌɪnˈdɔːr]

a 실내의

= inside, internal, enclosed, within a building
+ indoors adv 실내에서

Q: Usually, do you prefer indoor or outdoor activities?
보통 실내 활동을 선호하나요, 야외 활동을 선호하나요?

A: ....

DAY 13 | DICTATION TEST

5회 반복 예문 QR

DICTATION TEST 예문 QR을 듣고 다음 빈칸에 올바른 단어를 쓰세요.

841. Is it really ______________ to finish this on time?

842. How can you ______________ your boss this week?

843. Were you ______________ by the presentation yesterday?

844. What's your first ______________ of the new teacher?

845. Was the concert performance truly ______________ last night?

846. How can we ______________ our customer service quickly?

847. Did the ______________ cause any serious problems afterward?

848. Do you ______________ to agree with their decision?

849. Did they ______________ everyone in the group meeting?

850. Is your monthly ______________ enough to cover expenses?

851. Will the company ______________ salaries next year?

852. Was the view from the mountain ______________?

853. Did you ______________ finish the work ahead of schedule?

854. When did your country gain ______________?

855. Are you financially ______________ from your parents?

856. Is the ______________ updated regularly on the website?

857. Does the data ______________ a trend toward growth?

858. Are you ______________ to the new policy changes?

859. Does each ______________ have equal voting rights?

860. Usually, do you prefer ______________ or outdoor activities?

5회 반복 표제어 QR　5회 반복 예문 QR

DAY 14

30 days

AI 학습자료와 인강 youpass.co.kr

PREVIEW A 다음 단어의 뜻을 한국어로 써보세요.

- ☐ industry ____________
- ☐ inevitable ____________
- ☐ infant ____________
- ☐ infect ____________
- ☐ infection ____________
- ☐ inferior ____________
- ☐ influence ____________
- ☐ inform ____________
- ☐ informal ____________
- ☐ information ____________
- ☐ ingredient ____________
- ☐ inhabit ____________
- ☐ inherent ____________
- ☐ inherit ____________
- ☐ initial ____________
- ☐ initiate ____________
- ☐ injure ____________
- ☐ injured ____________
- ☐ injury ____________
- ☐ injustice ____________

PREVIEW B 사진을 보고 알맞은 영어 단어를 PREVIEW A 에서 찾아 써보세요.

____

____

____

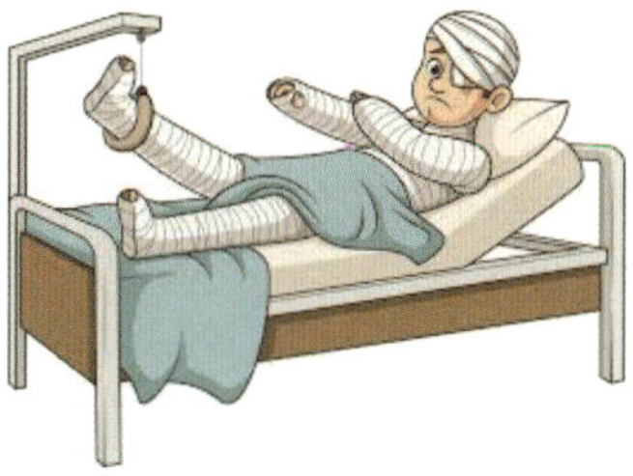
____

0861 □□□

industry
[ˈɪndəstri]

n 산업, 업계

= manufacturing, business, diligence, sector
+ industrial **a** 산업의 **industrious** **a** 근면한 **industrialist** **n** 산업가

Q: Does this new technology have the potential to disrupt the entire industry? 이 새로운 기술이 전체 산업을 뒤흔들 잠재력이 있다고 생각하시나요?

A: ....

0862 □□□

inevitable
[ɪnˈevɪtəbl]

a 피할 수 없는

= unavoidable, inescapable, destined, certain
+ inevitability **n** 불가피함 **inevitably** **adv** 불가피하게

Q: Was the outcome of the game inevitable from start?
경기 결과가 처음부터 피할 수 없는 것이었나요?

A: ....

0863 □□□

infant
[ˈɪnfənt]

n 유아, 아기

= baby, newborn, toddler, very young child
+ infancy **n** 유아기

Q: Is the infant sleeping peacefully through the night?
아기가 밤새도록 평화롭게 자고 있나요?

A: ....

0864 □□□

infect
[ɪnˈfekt]

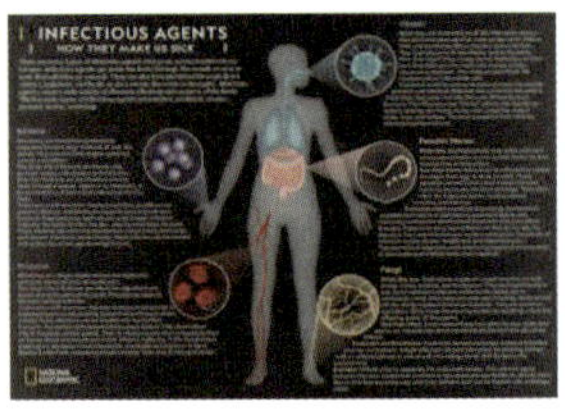

v 감염시키다

= contaminate, pollute, taint, transmit disease
+ infection **n** 감염 **infectious** **a** 전염성의 **infected** **a** 감염된

Q: Can viruses infect people through contact?
바이러스가 접촉을 통해 사람들을 감염시킬 수 있나요?

A: ....

0865 □□□

infection
[ɪnˈfekʃn]

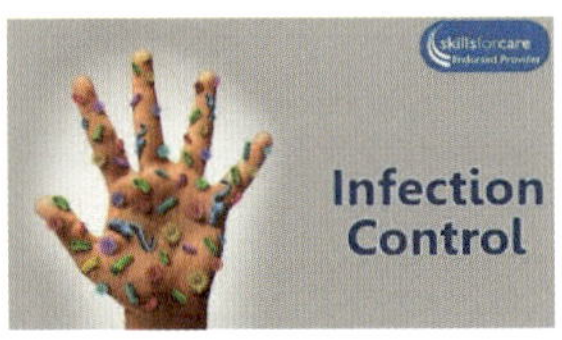

n 감염

= contamination, disease, contagion, inflammation
+ infect **v** 감염시키다 **infectious** **a** 전염성의

Q: Did the infection spread quickly in the hospital?
감염이 병원에서 빠르게 확산되었나요?

A: ....

0866 □□□

inferior
[ɪnˈfɪriər]

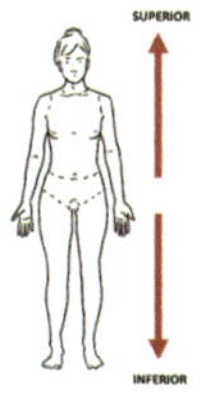

a 열등한, 하위의

= subordinate, lesser, poorer, lower quality
+ inferiority **n** 열등함

Q: Do you feel inferior when compared to others?
다른 사람들과 비교할 때 열등감을 느끼나요?

A: ....

0867 □□□

influence
[ˈɪnfluəns]

n 영향 **v** 영향을 미치다

= impact, sway, effect, power, affect, shape
+ influential **a** 영향력 있는

Q: How does social media influence young people today?
오늘날 소셜 미디어가 젊은 사람들에게 어떻게 영향을 미치나요?

A: ....

0868 □□□

inform
[ɪnˈfɔːrm]

v 알리다, 통지하다

= notify, tell, advise, apprise, communicate
+ information **n** 정보 **informant** **n** 정보원 **informative** **a** 유익한

Q: Did you inform your boss about the delay? 지연에 대해 상사에게 알렸나요?

A: ....

0869 □□□

informal
[ɪnˈfɔːrml]

a 비공식적인

= casual, relaxed, unofficial, conversational
+ informality **n** 비공식성 **informally** **adv** 비공식적으로

Q: Was the meeting more informal than expected?
회의가 예상보다 비공식적이었나요?

A: ....

0870 □□□

information
[ˌɪnfərˈmeɪʃn]

n 정보

= data, facts, knowledge, intelligence, news
+ inform **v** 알리다 **informative** **a** 유익한

Q: Where can I find more information about the event?
행사에 대한 더 많은 정보를 어디서 찾을 수 있나요?

A: ....

0871 □□□

ingredient
[ɪnˈgriːdiənt]

n 재료, 성분

= component, element, part, constituent, factor
+ natural ingredient 천연 소재

Q: Did you forget any important ingredient for cooking?
요리에 중요한 재료를 잊었나요?

A: ....

0872 □□□

inhabit
[ɪnˈhæbɪt]

v 거주하다, 살다

= live in, reside in, occupy, populate
+ inhabitant n 주민 habitation n 거주 inhabited a 사람이 사는

Q: Which animals mostly inhabit this forest area?
어떤 동물들이 이 숲 지역에 주로 서식하나요?

A: ....

0873 □□□

inherent
[ɪnˈhɪrənt]

a 내재하는, 고유한

= intrinsic, innate, built-in, fundamental, essential
+ inherence n 내재성 Inherently adv 선천적으로, 본질적으로

Q: Is risk an inherent part of this business? 위험은 이 사업의 본질적인 부분인가요?

A: ....

0874 □□□

inherit
[ɪnˈherɪt]

v 물려받다, 상속하다

= receive, succeed to, acquire, be bequeathed
+ inheritance n 유산, 상속 inheritor n 상속인

Q: Did you inherit any property from your family?
가족으로부터 재산을 물려받았나요?

A: ....

0875 □□□

initial
[ɪˈnɪʃl]

a 처음의, 초기의 n 첫 글자

= first, original, preliminary, beginning
+ initially adv 처음에

Q: What was your initial reaction to the news?
그 소식에 대한 당신의 첫 반응은 어땠나요?

A: ....

0876 □□□

initiate
[ɪˈnɪʃieɪt]

v 시작하다, 개시하다

= **begin, start, launch, commence, introduce**
+ **initiation** **n** 시작, 개시 **initiative** **n** 솔선, 주도권 **initial** **a** 초기의

Q: Who will initiate the new project next month?
다음 달에 누가 새로운 프로젝트를 시작할 건가요?

A: ....

0877 □□□

injure
[ˈɪndʒər]

v 부상을 입히다

= **harm, hurt, wound, damage, disable**
+ **injury** **n** 부상 **injured** **a** 부상당한 **injurious** **a** 해로운

Q: Did you injure yourself during the sports game? 스포츠 경기 중에 다쳤나요?

A: ....

0878 □□□

injured
[ˈɪndʒərd]

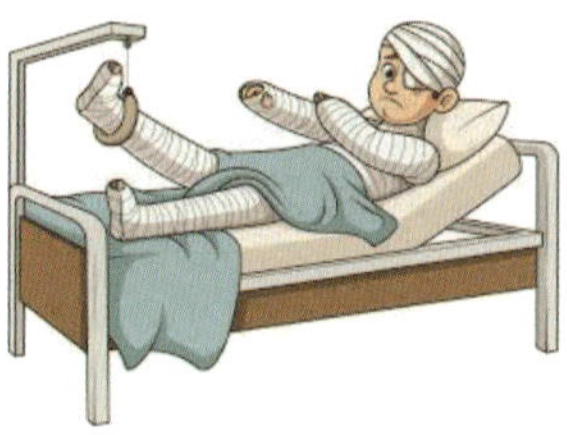

a 부상당한

= **hurt, wounded, damaged, disabled, suffering**
+ **injury** **n** 부상 **injure** **v** 다치게 하다

Q: Are the injured players expected to recover soon?
부상당한 선수들이 곧 회복될 것으로 예상되나요?

A: ....

0879 □□□

injury
[ˈɪndʒəri]

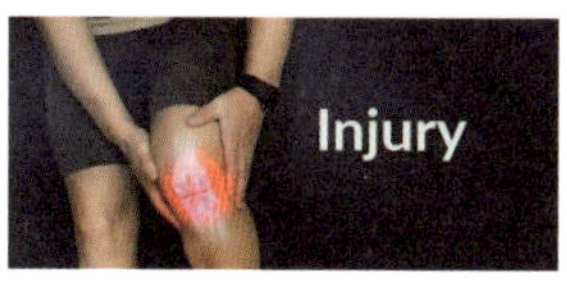

n 부상

= **harm, wound, damage, trauma, impairment**
+ **injure** **v** 다치게 하다 **injurious** **a** 해로운

Q: How serious is the injury from the accident?
사고로 인한 부상이 얼마나 심각한가요?

A: ....

0880 □□□

injustice
[ɪnˈdʒʌstɪs]

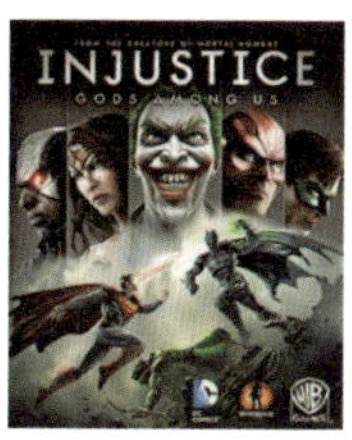

n 불공평, 부당함

= **unfairness, inequity, wrong, grievance**
+ **unjust** **a** 부당한

Q: Have you ever witnessed injustice in your workplace?
직장에서 불의를 목격한 적 있나요?

A: ....

DAY 14 | DICTATION TEST

5회 반복 예문 QR

DICTATION TEST 예문 QR을 듣고 다음 빈칸에 올바른 단어를 쓰세요.

861. Does this new technology have the potential to disrupt the entire ________________?

862. Was the outcome of the game ________________ from start?

863. Is the ________________ sleeping peacefully through the night?

864. Can viruses ________________ people through contact?

865. Did the ________________ spread quickly in the hospital?

866. Do you feel ________________ when compared to others?

867. How does social media ________________ young people today?

868. Did you ________________ your boss about the delay?

869. Was the meeting more ________________ than expected?

870. Where can I find more ________________ about the event?

871. Did you forget any important ________________ for cooking?

872. Which animals mostly ________________ this forest area?

873. Is risk an ________________ part of this business?

874. Did you ________________ any property from your family?

875. What was your ________________ reaction to the news?

876. Who will ________________ the new project next month?

877. Did you ________________ yourself during the sports game?

878. Are the ________________ players expected to recover soon?

879. How serious is the ________________ from the accident?

880. Have you ever witnessed ________________ in your workplace?

5회 반복 표제어 QR 5회 반복 예문 QR

DAY 15

30 days

AI 학습자료와 인강 youpass.co.kr

PREVIEW A 다음 단어의 뜻을 한국어로 써보세요.

□ **inner**	______	□ **inspire**	______
□ **innocent**	______	□ **install**	______
□ **innovation**	______	□ **instance**	______
□ **input**	______	□ **instant**	______
□ **inquire**	______	□ **instead**	______
□ **inquiry**	______	□ **instinct**	______
□ **insert**	______	□ **institute**	______
□ **insight**	______	□ **institution**	______
□ **insist**	______	□ **instruct**	______
□ **inspect**	______	□ **instrument**	______

PREVIEW B 사진을 보고 알맞은 영어 단어를 **PREVIEW A** 에서 찾아 써보세요.

______

______

______

______

0881 □□□

inner
[ˈɪnər]

a 내부의, 내면의

= **internal, interior, central, private, profound**
\+ **inner circle** (조직의 권력을 쥐고 있는) 핵심층[중추 세력]

Q: What's going on in your inner thoughts these days?
요즘 네 마음속엔 무슨 생각이 있나요?

A: ....

0882 □□□

innocent
[ˈɪnəsnt]

a 무고한, 순진한

= **guiltless, blameless, naive, harmless, pure**
\+ **innocence** n 무죄, 순수 **innocently** adv 순수하게, 죄 없이

Q: Do you believe he's innocent of the crime?
그가 그 범죄에 대해 무죄라고 믿나요?

A: ....

0883 □□□

innovation
[ˌɪnəˈveɪʃn]

n 혁신

= **novelty, invention, change, modernization**
\+ **innovate** v 혁신하다 **innovative** a 혁신적인 **innovator** n 혁신가

Q: How does innovation impact business growth overall?
혁신이 전반적인 사업 성장에 어떻게 영향을 미치나요?

A: ....

0884 □□□

input
[ˈɪnpʊt]

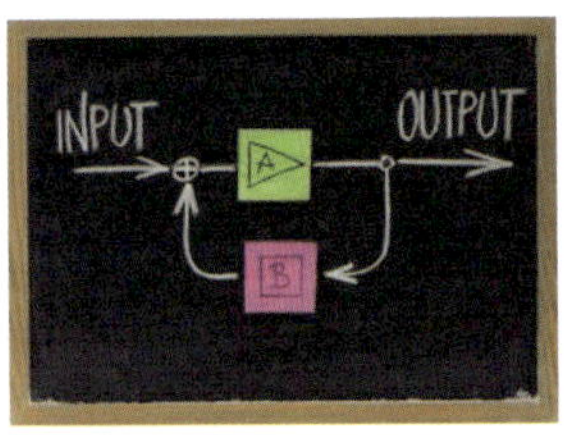

n 투입, 입력 v 입력하다

= **contribution, data, information, ideas, enter, provide**
\+ **input-output table** 투입 산출표(產出表)

Q: Can you provide your input on this matter?
이 문제에 대해 의견을 제시해 줄 수 있나요?

A: ....

0885 □□□

inquire
[ɪnˈkwaɪər]

v 문의하다, 질문하다

= **ask, question, investigate, query, probe**
\+ **inquiry[enquiry]** n 문의, 질문

Q: May I inquire about your availability next week?
다음 주에 시간 괜찮으신지 여쭤 봐도 될까요?

A: ....

0886 □□□

inquiry
[ɪnˈkwaɪəri] [ˈɪnkwəri]

n 문의, 질문, 조사

= **question, investigation, probe, query, examination**
+ **inquire** **v** 묻다, 문의하다

Q: Who should I contact for an inquiry about products?
제품에 대한 문의는 누구에게 해야 하나요?

A: ....

0887 □□□

insert
[ɪnˈsɜːrt]

v 삽입하다, 끼워 넣다

= **put in, place, introduce, embed, inject**
+ **insertion** **n** 삽입

Q: Did you remember to insert the correct password?
올바른 비밀번호를 입력하는 것을 기억했나요?

A: ....

0888 □□□

insight
[ˈɪnsaɪt]

n 통찰력

= **understanding, perception, acumen, discernment, intuition**
+ **insightful** **a** 통찰력 있는

Q: Can you share some insight into the market trends?
시장 동향에 대한 통찰력을 공유해 줄 수 있나요?

A: ....

0889 □□□

insist
[ɪnˈsɪst]

v 주장하다, 고집하다

= **demand, maintain, persist, assert, declare**
+ **insistence** **n** 고집, 주장 **insistent** **a** 끈질긴, 주장하는

Q: Why do you insist on doing it your way? 왜 당신 방식대로 하겠다고 고집하나요?

A: ....

0890 □□□

inspect
[ɪnˈspekt]

v 검사하다, 조사하다

= **examine, check, scrutinize, investigate, review**
+ **inspection** **n** 검사 **inspector** **n** 조사관, 감독관

Q: When will the inspectors come to inspect the site?
언제 검사관들이 현장을 검사하러 올까요?

A: ....

0891 □□□

inspire
[ɪnˈspaɪər]

v 영감을 주다, 고무시키다

= motivate, stimulate, encourage, uplift, animate

+ inspiration **n** 영감 **inspirer** **n** 영감을 주는 사람 **inspiring** **a** 영감을 주는
inspired **a** 영감을 받은

Q: What stories inspire you to keep going forward?
어떤 이야기들이 당신에게 계속 앞으로 나아가도록 영감을 주나요?

A: ……………………………………

0892 □□□

install
[ɪnˈstɔːl]

v 설치하다, 임명하다

= set up, fit, put in place, establish, place

+ installation **n** 설치

Q: Did you install the new software on your computer?
컴퓨터에 새 소프트웨어를 설치했나요?

A: ……………………………………

0893 □□□

instance
[ˈɪnstəns]

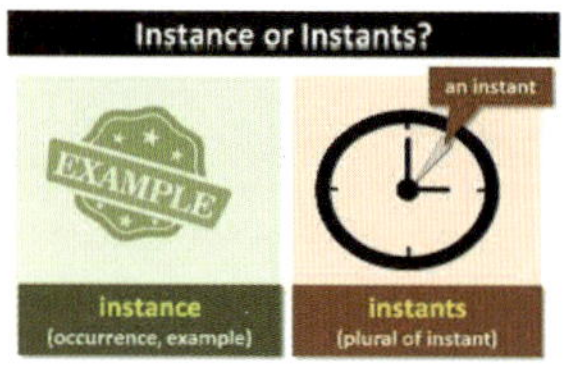

n 사례, 경우

= example, case, occasion, moment

+ for instance 예를 들어 **in the first instance** 우선 먼저

Q: Can you give an instance where this happened?
이런 일이 발생한 사례를 하나 들어줄 수 있나요?

A: ……………………………………

0894 □□□

instant
[ˈɪnstənt]

n 순간, 즉석 **a** 즉각적인

= immediate, momentary, quick, moment, flash

+ instantly **adv** 즉시

Q: Is instant coffee better than fresh brewed coffee?
인스턴트커피가 갓 내린 커피보다 더 낫나요?

A: ……………………………………

0895 □□□

instead
[ɪnˈsted]

adv 대신에

= alternatively, in place of, as a substitute

+ instead of ~ 대신에

Q: Would you choose tea instead of coffee? 커피 대신 차를 선택할 건가요?

A: ……………………………………

0896 □□□

instinct
[ˈɪnstɪŋkt]

n 본능

= intuition, natural tendency, innate behavior, gut feeling
\+ instinctive **a** 본능적인 instinctively **adv** 본능적으로

Q: Do you trust your instinct when making decisions?
결정을 내릴 때 본능을 믿나요?

A: ....

0897 □□□

institute
[ˈɪnstɪtuːt]

n 기관, 협회 **v** 설립하다

= establish, found, initiate, organization, academy
\+ institution **n** 기관, 제도

Q: Is this institute known for its quality education?
이 기관은 양질의 교육으로 유명한가요?

A: ....

0898 □□□

institution
[ˌɪnstɪˈtuːʃn]

n 기관, 제도

= organization, establishment, custom, practice
\+ institute **v** 설립하다 institutional **a** 제도적인

Q: Does this institution offer a wide range of academic programs?
이 기관은 다양한 학술 프로그램을 제공하나요?

A: ....

0899 □□□

instruct
[ɪnˈstrʌkt]

v 지시하다, 가르치다

= teach, educate, direct, order, command
\+ instruction **n** 지시, 교육 instructor **n** 교사, 강사 instructive **a** 유익한, 교육적인

Q: Did the teacher instruct you clearly this morning?
오늘 아침에 선생님이 명확하게 지시했나요?

A: ....

0900 □□□

instrument
[ˈɪnstrəmənt]

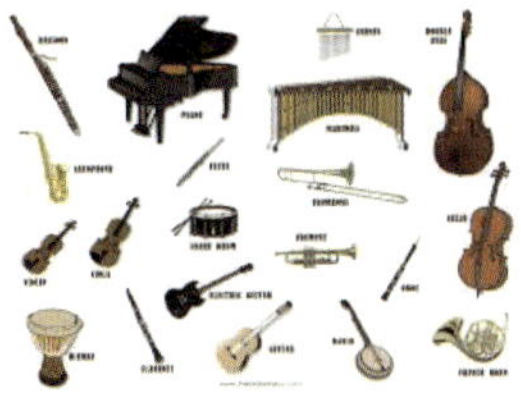

n 도구, 악기

= tool, device, apparatus
\+ instrumental **a** 도움이 되는, 악기의 musical instrument 악기

Q: Can you play any musical instrument well? 어떤 악기를 잘 연주할 수 있나요?

A: ....

DAY 15 | DICTATION TEST

5회 반복 예문 QR

DICTATION TEST 예문 QR을 듣고 다음 빈칸에 올바른 단어를 쓰세요.

881. What's going on in your ________________ thoughts these days?
882. Do you believe he's ________________ of the crime?
883. How does ________________ impact business growth overall?
884. Can you provide your ________________ on this matter?
885. May I ________________ about your availability next week?
886. Who should I contact for an ________________ about products?
887. Did you remember to ________________ the correct password?
888. Can you share some ________________ into the market trends?
889. Why do you ________________ on doing it your way?
890. When will the inspectors come to ________________ the site?
891. What stories ________________ you to keep going forward?
892. Did you ________________ the new software on your computer?
893. Can you give an ________________ where this happened?
894. Is ________________ coffee better than fresh brewed coffee?
895. Would you choose tea ________________ of coffee?
896. Do you trust your ________________ when making decisions?
897. Is this ________________ known for its quality education?
898. Does this ________________ offer a wide range of academic programs?
899. Did the teacher ________________ you clearly this morning?
900. Can you play any musical ________________ well?

5회 반복 표제어 QR　5회 반복 예문 QR

DAY 16
30 days

AI 학습자료와 인강 youpass.co.kr

PREVIEW A 다음 단어의 뜻을 한국어로 써보세요.

□ insult ________	□ interfere ________
□ insurance ________	□ interior ________
□ intake ________	□ internal ________
□ intellectual ________	□ international ________
□ intelligence ________	□ interpret ________
□ intelligent ________	□ interpreter ________
□ intend ________	□ interrupt ________
□ intense ________	□ interval ________
□ interaction ________	□ intonation ________
□ interest ________	□ introduce ________

PREVIEW B 사진을 보고 알맞은 영어 단어를 **PREVIEW A** 에서 찾아 써보세요.

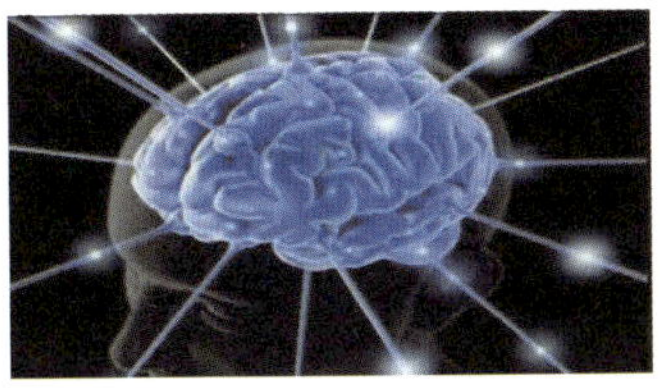
____

____

____

____

0901 □□□

insult
['ɪnsʌlt] n [ɪn'sʌlt] v

n 모욕 v 모욕하다

= offend, disrespect, affront, slight, indignity
+ insulting a 모욕적인 insulted a 모욕당한

Q: Did you feel insulted by what he said earlier?
아까 그가 한 말에 모욕감을 느꼈나요?

A: ....

0902 □□□

insurance
[ɪn'ʃʊrəns]

n 보험

= coverage, protection, assurance, policy
+ insure v 보험에 들다 insurer n 보험회사

Q: Do you have insurance coverage for this accident?
이 사고에 대한 보험 적용을 받나요?

A: ....

0903 □□□

intake
['ɪnteɪk]

n 섭취, 흡입, 유입

= consumption, input, absorption, volume
+ the annual student intake 연간 입학생 수

Q: Is your daily intake of water enough for health?
건강을 위해 하루 물 섭취량이 충분한가요?

A: ....

0904 □□□

intellectual
[ˌɪntə'lektʃuəl]

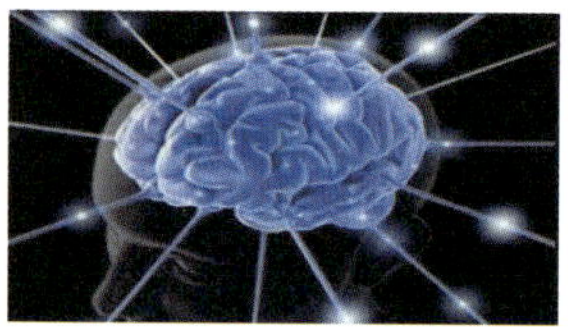

a 지적인 n 지식인

= academic, scholarly, thoughtful, intelligent, thinker
+ intellect n 지성 intelligence n 지능 intellectually adv 지적으로

Q: Are you interested in intellectual discussions? 지적인 토론에 관심이 있나요?

A: ....

0905 □□□

intelligence
[ɪn'telɪdʒəns]

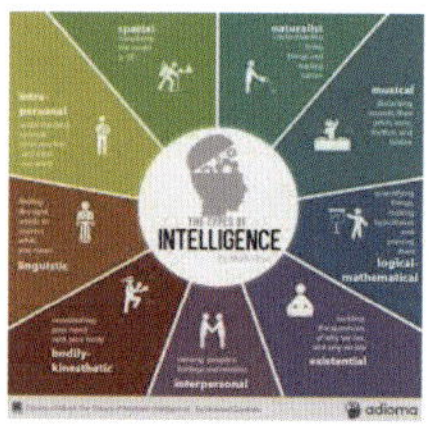

n 지능, 정보

= intellect, mind, brilliance, information, news
+ intelligent a 지능적인

Q: How would you rate your intelligence compared to others?
다른 사람들과 비교해서 당신의 지능을 어떻게 평가하나요?

A: ....

0906 □□□

intelligent
[ɪnˈtelɪdʒənt]

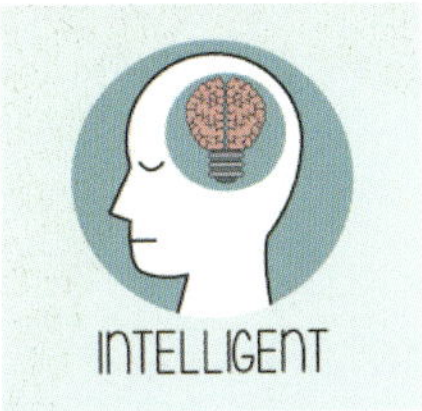

a 지능이 있는, 똑똑한

= smart, clever, bright, rational, discerning
+ intelligence n 지능 intelligently adv 지능적으로

Q: Do you think cats are intelligent animals overall?
고양이가 전반적으로 똑똑한 동물이라고 생각하나요?

A: ....

0907 □□□

intend
[ɪnˈtend]

v ~할 작정이다, 의도하다

= plan, aim, mean, purpose, design
+ intention n 의도 intentional a 고의적인 intentionally adv 고의적으로

Q: Do you intend to finish the project this week?
이번 주에 프로젝트를 마칠 작정인가요?

A: ....

0908 □□□

intense
[ɪnˈtens]

a 강렬한, 격렬한

= strong, powerful, extreme, fierce, passionate
+ intensity n 강도 intensification n 강화 intensify v 강화하다
intensely adv 강렬하게

Q: Was the workout session more intense than usual?
운동 시간이 평소보다 더 강렬했나요?

A: ....

0909 □□□

interaction
[ˌɪntərˈækʃn]

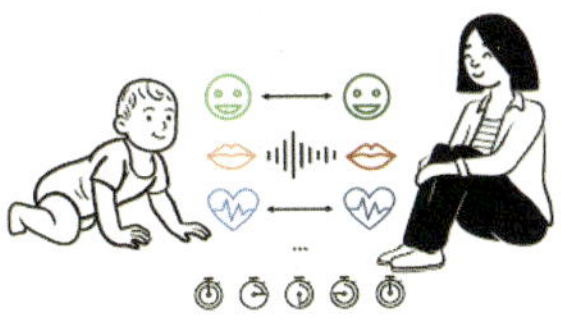

n 상호작용

= communication, interplay, exchange, contact
+ interact v 상호작용하다 interactive a 상호작용하는

Q: How often do you have social interaction at work?
직장에서 사회적 교류를 얼마나 자주 하나요?

A: ....

0910 □□□

interest
[ˈɪntrəst] [ˈɪntərɪst]

n 관심, 흥미, 이자 v 흥미를 끌다

= curiosity, concern, hobby, benefit, involve, attract
+ interesting a 흥미로운 interested a 흥미를 느끼는 interestingly adv 흥미롭게도

Q: What kind of hobbies interest you the most?
어떤 종류의 취미가 당신에게 가장 흥미를 끄나요?

A: ....

0911 □□□

interfere
[ˌɪntərˈfɪr]

v 방해하다, 간섭하다

= **meddle, intervene, obstruct, hinder, intrude**
+ **interference** **n** 방해, 간섭

Q: Does noise interfere with your concentration?
소음이 당신의 집중을 방해하나요?

A: ....

0912 □□□

interior
[ɪnˈtɪriər]

n 내부 **a** 내부의

= **inside, inner, internal, domestic**
+ **interiorly** **adv** 내부에

Q: Is the interior design of your house modern?
당신 집의 인테리어 디자인이 현대적인가요?

A: ....

0913 □□□

internal
[ɪnˈtɜːrnl]

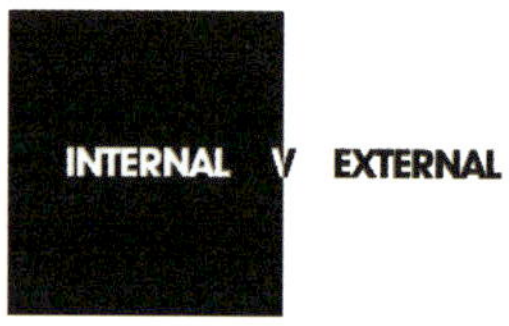

a 내부의, 국내의

= **inner, inside, domestic, inherent, intrinsic**
+ **internalization** **n** 내면화 **internalize** **v** 내면화하다 **internally** **adv** 내부적으로

Q: Have you noticed any internal problems in the system?
시스템 내부에 어떤 문제라도 발견했나요?

A: ....

0914 □□□

international
[ˌɪntərˈnæʃnəl]

a 국제적인

= **global, worldwide, multinational, cross-border**
+ **internationalism** **n** 국제주의 **internationally** **adv** 국제적으로

Q: Are you planning an international trip next summer?
내년 여름에 해외여행을 계획 중인가요?

A: ....

0915 □□□

interpret
[ɪnˈtɜːrprɪt]

v 해석하다, 통역하다

= **explain, translate, clarify, understand, decipher**
+ **interpretation** **n** 해석 **interpreter** **n** 통역사 **interpretive** **a** 해석적인

Q: Can you interpret the meaning of this poem?
이 시의 의미를 해석해 줄 수 있나요?

A: ....

0916 □□□

interpreter
[ɪnˈtɜːrprɪtər]

n 통역사

= **translator, linguist, decipherer**
+ **interpret** **v** 해석하다, 통역하다

Q: Did the interpreter translate everything correctly?
통역사가 모든 것을 정확하게 통역했나요?

A: ....

0917 □□□

interrupt
[ˌɪntəˈrʌpt]

v 방해하다, 중단시키다

= **stop, break in, disturb, cut off, halt**
+ **interruption** **n** 방해, 중단

Q: Do you mind if I interrupt your conversation briefly?
잠시 대화에 끼어들어도 괜찮을까요?

A: ....

0918 □□□

interval
[ˈɪntərvl]

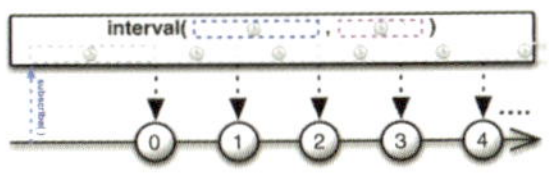

n 간격, 중간 휴식 시간

= **gap, pause, break, period, interim**
+ **after a long interval** 오랜만에

Q: How long is the interval between each session?
각 세션 사이의 간격은 얼마나 되나요?

A: ....

0919 □□□

intonation
[ˌɪntəˈneɪʃn]

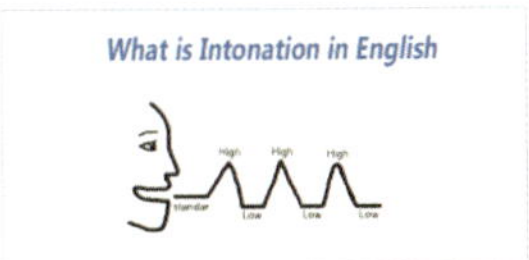

n 억양

= **pitch, tone, accent, modulation**
+ **intone** **v** 억양을 넣다

Q: Is your intonation correct when speaking English?
영어를 말할 때 당신의 억양이 정확한가요?

A: ....

0920 □□□

introduce
[ˌɪntrəˈduːs]

v 소개하다, 도입하다

= **present, initiate, propose, acquaint, insert**
+ **introduction** **n** 소개, 도입 **introductory** **a** 소개하는

Q: Will you introduce yourself to the new members?
새로운 회원들에게 자신을 소개할 건가요?

A: ....

DAY 16 | DICTATION TEST

5회 반복 예문 QR

DICTATION TEST 예문 QR을 듣고 다음 빈칸에 올바른 단어를 쓰세요.

901. Did you feel ________________ by what he said earlier?
902. Do you have ________________ coverage for this accident?
903. Is your daily ________________ of water enough for health?
904. Are you interested in ________________ discussions?
905. How would you rate your ________________ compared to others?
906. Do you think cats are ________________ animals overall?
907. Do you ________________ to finish the project this week?
908. Was the workout session more ________________ than usual?
909. How often do you have social ________________ at work?
910. What kind of hobbies ________________ you the most?
911. Does noise ________________ with your concentration?
912. Is the ________________ design of your house modern?
913. Have you noticed any ________________ problems in the system?
914. Are you planning an ________________ trip next summer?
915. Can you ________________ the meaning of this poem?
916. Did the ________________ translate everything correctly?
917. Do you mind if I ________________ your conversation briefly?
918. How long is the ________________ between each session?
919. Is your ________________ correct when speaking English?
920. Will you ________________ yourself to the new members?

5회 반복 표제어 QR 5회 반복 예문 QR

DAY 17

30 days

AI 학습자료와 인강 youpass.co.kr

PREVIEW A 다음 단어의 뜻을 한국어로 써보세요.

- □ invade ______
- □ invent ______
- □ invest ______
- □ investigate ______
- □ invitation ______
- □ involve ______
- □ iron ______
- □ irritate ______
- □ isolate ______
- □ issue ______
- □ jail ______
- □ jealous ______
- □ joint ______
- □ journey ______
- □ judge ______
- □ justice ______
- □ justify ______
- □ kindness ______
- □ knit ______
- □ knowledge ______

PREVIEW B 사진을 보고 알맞은 영어 단어를 **PREVIEW A**에서 찾아 써보세요.

______

______

______

______

0921 □□□

invade
[ɪnˈveɪd]

v 침략하다, 침범하다

= attack, trespass, occupy, intrude
+ invasion n 침략 invader n 침략자

Q: Did the enemy invade the city without any warning?
적이 아무 경고 없이 도시를 침공했나요?

A: ……………………………………………………

0922 □□□

invent
[ɪnˈvent]

v 발명하다

= create, devise, originate, conceive, discover
+ invention n 발명 inventor n 발명가 inventive a 창의적인

Q: Who will invent the next big technology breakthrough?
다음 큰 기술 혁신은 누가 발명할까요?

A: ……………………………………………………

0923 □□□

invest
[ɪnˈvest]

v 투자하다

= put money into, dedicate, spend, allocate
+ investment n 투자 investor n 투자자

Q: Are you planning to invest money in real estate?
부동산에 돈을 투자할 계획인가요?

A: ……………………………………………………

0924 □□□

investigate
[ɪnˈvestɪgeɪt]

v 조사하다

= probe, examine, research, explore, inquire into
+ investigation n 수사, 조사 investigator n 수사관

Q: Will the police investigate the case thoroughly?
경찰이 사건을 철저히 수사할까요?

A: ……………………………………………………

0925 □□□

invitation
[ˌɪnvɪˈteɪʃn]

n 초대

= request, summons, appeal, welcome
+ invite v 초대하다 invited a 초대받은

Q: Did you receive an invitation to the wedding party?
결혼식 파티 초대장을 받았나요?

A: ……………………………………………………

0926 □□□

involve
[ɪnˈvɑːlv]

v 포함하다, 관련시키다

= include, entail, implicate, engage, absorb
+ involvement **n** 관련, 연루 involved **a** 연루된, 관련된

Q: Does this job involve a lot of traveling abroad?
이 직업은 해외 출장이 많은가요?

A: ....

0927 □□□

iron
[ˈaɪərn]

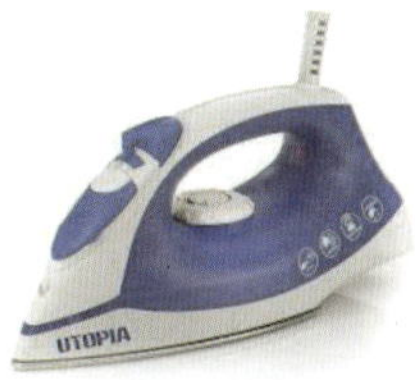

n 철, 철분, 다리미 **v** 다림질하다

= metal, press, smooth, flatten, resolve
+ ironic **a** 아이러니한 ironically **adv** 아이러니하게도

Q: Can you iron the clothes before the meeting tomorrow?
내일 회의 전에 옷을 다림질해 줄 수 있나요?

A: ....

0928 □□□

irritate
[ˈɪrɪteɪt]

v 짜증나게 하다, 자극하다

= annoy, bother, vex, inflame, provoke
+ irritation **n** 짜증, 자극 irritating **a** 짜증나게 하는 irritated **a** 짜증 난

Q: Does loud noise irritate you so much?
큰 소음이 당신을 그렇게 많이 짜증나게 하나요?

A: ....

0929 □□□

isolate
[ˈaɪsəleɪt]

v 고립시키다, 격리하다

= separate, cut off, quarantine, seclude
+ isolation **n** 격리, 고립 isolated **a** 고립된

Q: Did they isolate the patient to prevent infection?
감염을 막기 위해 환자를 격리했나요?

A: ....

0930 □□□

issue
[ˈɪʃuː]

n 문제, 쟁점, 발행 **v** 발행하다

= problem, topic, matter, publication, release, emit
+ issue **n** 문제, 쟁점

Q: What's the main issue causing delays in the project?
프로젝트 지연의 주요 원인은 무엇인가요?

A: ....

0931 □□□

jail
[dʒeɪl]

n 감옥 **v** 투옥하다

= **prison, lockup, detention center, confine, incarcerate**

+ **a ten-year jail sentence 10**년의 실형 선고 **police jail** 경찰서 유치장[보호실] **detention jail** 구치소

Q: How long was he sentenced to jail? 그는 몇 년 형을 받았나요?

A: ....

0932 □□□

jealous
[ˈdʒeləs]

a 질투하는

= **envious, covetous, possessive, suspicious**

+ **jealousy** **n** 질투 **jealously** **adv** 질투심에 불타

Q: Do you feel jealous when your friends succeed?
친구가 성공할 때 질투를 느끼나요?

A: ....

0933 □□□

joint
[dʒɔɪnt]

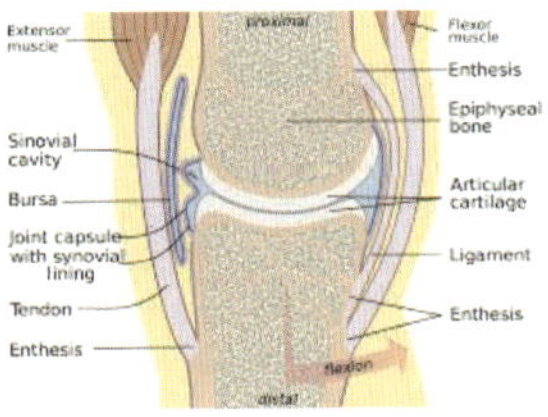

n 관절, 이음매 **a** 공동의

= **shared, common, combined, junction, connection**

+ **jointly** **adv** 공동으로

Q: Is this a joint effort between two companies?
이것은 두 회사 간의 공동 노력인가요?

A: ....

0934 □□□

journey
[ˈdʒɜːrni]

n 여행, 여정

= **trip, voyage, travel, expedition, odyssey**

+ **a journey into the unknown** 미지의 세계로의 여행

Q: How was your journey to the mountains last weekend?
지난 주말 산으로 가는 여행은 어땠나요?

A: ....

0935 □□□

judge
[dʒʌdʒ]

n 판사, 심판 **v** 판단하다

= **evaluate, assess, decide, arbiter, justice, verdict**

+ **judgment[judgement]** **n** 판단 **judgmental[judgemental]** **a** 비판적인

Q: Who will judge the contestants in the competition?
경쟁에서 참가자들을 누가 심사할 건가요?

A: ....

0936 □□□

justice
[ˈdʒʌstɪs]

n 정의, 공정성

= fairness, equity, righteousness, law, legality
\+ just **a** 정당한 unjust **a** 부당한 injustice **n** 불의

Q: Do you believe justice will be served eventually?
결국 정의가 실현될 것이라고 믿나요?

A: ....

0937 □□□

justify
[ˈdʒʌstɪfaɪ]

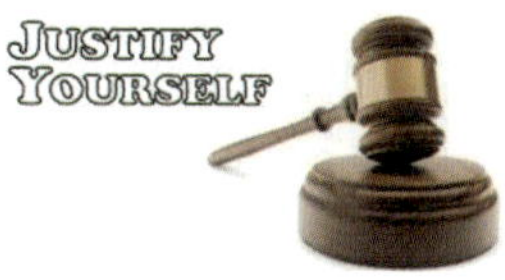

v 정당화하다

= explain, rationalize, legitimize, validate, defend
\+ justification **n** 정당화 justifiable **a** 정당화될 수 있는

Q: Can you justify your decision to quit the job?
직장을 그만둔 결정을 정당화할 수 있나요?

A: ....

0938 □□□

kindness
[ˈkaɪndnəs]

n 친절

= benevolence, compassion, generosity, warmth, goodwill
\+ kind **a** 친절한 kindly **adv** 친절하게

Q: How important is kindness in daily life?
일상생활에서 친절함은 얼마나 중요한가요?

A: ....

0939 □□□

knit
[nɪt]

v 뜨개질하다, 짜다

= weave, interlace, unite, join, fuse
\+ knitting **n** 뜨개질 knitter **n** 뜨개질하는 사람

Q: Did your grandmother teach you how to knit scarves?
할머니가 스카프 뜨개질하는 법을 가르쳐 주셨나요?

A: ....

0940 □□□

knowledge
[ˈnɑːlɪdʒ]

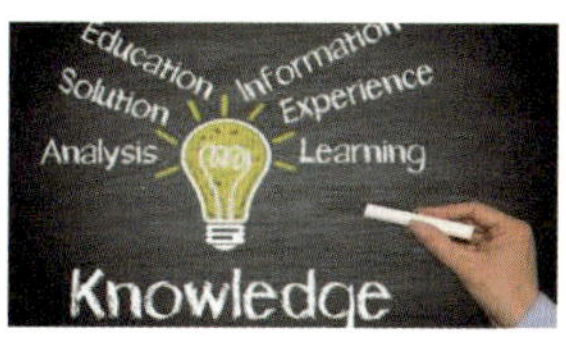

n 지식

= understanding, information, wisdom, expertise, awareness
\+ know **v** 알다 knowledgeable **a** 박식한

Q: Where did you gain all your knowledge about history?
역사에 대한 당신의 모든 지식은 어디서 얻었나요?

A: ....

DAY 17 | DICTATION TEST

5회 반복 예문 QR

DICTATION TEST 예문 QR을 듣고 다음 빈칸에 올바른 단어를 쓰세요.

921. Did the enemy ______________ the city without any warning?
922. Who will ______________ the next big technology breakthrough?
923. Are you planning to ______________ money in real estate?
924. Will the police ______________ the case thoroughly?
925. Did you receive an ______________ to the wedding party?
926. Does this job ______________ a lot of traveling abroad?
927. Can you ______________ the clothes before the meeting tomorrow?
928. Does loud noise ______________ you so much?
929. Did they ______________ the patient to prevent infection?
930. What's the main ______________ causing delays in the project?
931. How long was he sentenced to ______________?
932. Do you feel ______________ when your friends succeed?
933. Is this a ______________ effort between two companies?
934. How was your ______________ to the mountains last weekend?
935. Who will ______________ the contestants in the competition?
936. Do you believe ______________ will be served eventually?
937. Can you ______________ your decision to quit the job?
938. How important is ______________ in daily life?
939. Did your grandmother teach you how to ______________ scarves?
940. Where did you gain all your ______________ about history?

5회 반복 표제어 QR   5회 반복 예문 QR

DAY 18

30 days

AI 학습자료와 인강 youpass.co.kr

PREVIEW A 다음 단어의 뜻을 한국어로 써보세요.

- □ labor ______
- □ laboratory ______
- □ lack ______
- □ ladder ______
- □ landscape ______
- □ lastly ______
- □ latter ______
- □ launch ______
- □ lawyer ______
- □ lay ______
- □ layer ______
- □ league ______
- □ leak ______
- □ lean ______
- □ leap ______
- □ lecture ______
- □ legal ______
- □ legend ______
- □ lend ______
- □ length ______

PREVIEW B 사진을 보고 알맞은 영어 단어를 PREVIEW A 에서 찾아 써보세요.

______

______

______

______

0941 □□□

labor
[ˈleɪbər]

n 노동, 노동력, 출산 **v** 노동하다

= **work, toil, effort, employment, childbirth**

+ **laborer** **n** 노동자 **laborious** **a** 힘든, 고된

Q: Is the labor market improving in your city lately?
최근 당신의 도시 노동 시장이 개선되고 있나요?

A: ....

0942 □□□

laboratory
[ˈlæbrətɔːri] [ləˈbɔːrəˌtɔːri]

n 실험실

= **lab, research facility, workshop**

+ **language laboratory** 어학 실습실 **forensic laboratory** 법의학[과학 수사] 실험실

Q: Have you ever worked in a science laboratory before?
전에 과학 실험실에서 일해본 적 있나요?

A: ....

0943 □□□

lack
[læk]

n 부족, 결핍 **v** 부족하다

= **absence, shortage, deficiency, scarcity, be without**

+ **a lack of charisma** 카리스마 부족

Q: Does this project suffer from a lack of funding?
이 프로젝트는 자금 부족을 겪고 있나요?

A: ....

0944 □□□

ladder
[ˈlædər]

n 사다리

= **steps, stepladder, hierarchy, ascent**

+ **rope ladder** 줄사다리 **extendable ladder** 늘일 수 있는 사다리

Q: Is the ladder safe to use for this repair job?
이 수리 작업에 사다리를 사용해도 안전한가요?

A: ....

0945 □□□

landscape
[ˈlændskeɪp]

n 풍경, 경치

= **scenery, view, terrain, panorama, perspective**

+ **landscape gardener** 정원사 **landscape architect** 조경사

Q: What kind of landscape do you prefer for hiking?
하이킹할 때 어떤 종류의 풍경을 선호하나요?

A: ....

0946 □□□

lastly
['læstli]

adv 마지막으로

= finally, in conclusion, ultimately, eventually

+ last **a** 마지막의

Q: Lastly, do you have any questions before we finish?
마지막으로, 마치기 전에 질문이 있나요?

A: ....

0947 □□□

latter
['lætər]

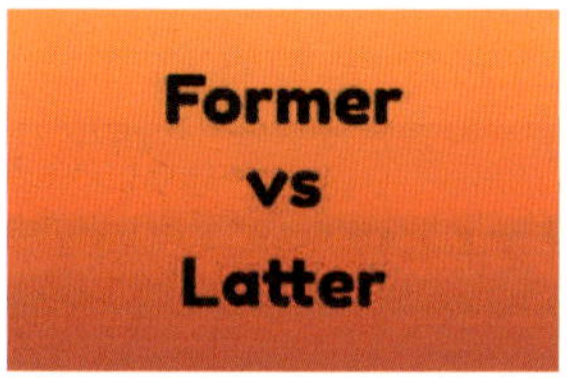

a 후자의

= second, last-mentioned, final

+ a latter-day Robin Hood 현대판 로빈 후드 the latter half of the year 올해[한 해] 후반기에

Q: Do you prefer the latter option in this case? 이 경우 후자의 선택지를 선호하나요?

A: ....

0948 □□□

launch
[lɔːntʃ]

v 시작하다, 발사하다 **n** 시작, 발사

= begin, initiate, propel, release, debut

+ launch pad (우주선 등의) 발사대(launching pad)

Q: When will they launch the new product officially?
언제 새 제품을 공식적으로 출시할 건가요?

A: ....

0949 □□□

lawyer
['lɔɪər]

n 변호사

= attorney, counsel, barrister, legal expert

+ law **n** 법

Q: Did you consult a lawyer about the contract terms?
계약 조건에 대해 변호사와 상담했나요?

A: ....

0950 □□□

lay
[leɪ]

v 놓다, 눕히다, 알을 낳다

= place, put, set down, arrange, present

+ layer **n** 층

Q: Can you lay the table for dinner tonight please?
오늘 밤 저녁 식사 상 좀 차려줄 수 있나요?

A: ....

0951 □□□

layer
[ˈleɪər]

n 층

= **sheet, coating, stratum, level, tier**
+ **ozone layer** 오존층

Q: How many layers does this cake actually have?
이 케이크는 실제로 몇 겹인가요?

A: ....

0952 □□□

league
[liːg]

n 리그, 연맹

= **association, alliance, confederation, division**
+ **big-league** **a** 빅 리그의 **major-league** **a** 메이저 리그의
minor-league **a** 마이너 리그의

Q: Which league does your favorite soccer team play in?
당신이 가장 좋아하는 축구팀은 어느 리그에서 뛰나요?

A: ....

0953 □□□

leak
[liːk]

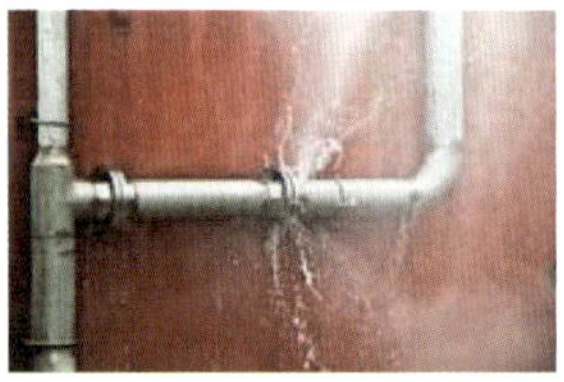

n 누출, 새는 곳 **v** 새다, 누설하다

= **drip, seep, disclose, escape, hole**
+ **leaky** **a** 새는

Q: Is there a water leak somewhere in the basement?
지하실 어딘가에 물이 새나요?

A: ....

0954 □□□

lean
[liːn]

n 기대다, 기울이다 **a** 마른

= **incline, tilt, rest against, slim, thin**
+ **lean on** 기대다, 의지하다

Q: Do you lean more toward traditional or modern style?
전통적인 스타일과 현대적인 스타일 중 어느 쪽에 더 가깝나요?

A: ....

0955 □□□

leap
[liːp]

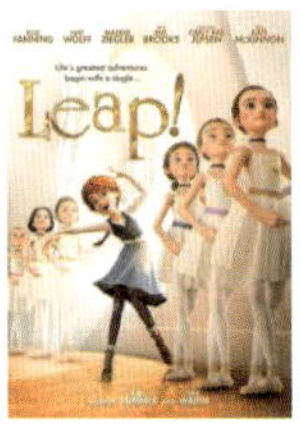

n 도약 **v** 뛰다, 도약하다

= **jump, spring, bound, skip, sudden increase**
+ **leap over a brook** 개울을 뛰어넘다

Q: Did you see the deer leap over the fence?
사슴이 울타리를 뛰어넘는 것을 보셨나요?

A: ....

0956 □□□

lecture
[ˈlektʃər]

n 강의, 강연 **v** 강의하다

= talk, speech, lesson, sermon, reprimand
\+ lecturer **n** 강사

Q: Did you enjoy today's lecture on climate change?
오늘 기후 변화에 대한 강의가 즐거웠나요?

A: ……………………………………………………

0957 □□□

legal
[ˈliːgl]

a 법률의, 합법적인

= lawful, legitimate, valid, permissible, juridical
\+ legality **n** 합법성 legalization **n** 합법화 legally **adv** 법적으로 illegal **a** 불법적인

Q: Is it legal to park here after business hours?
영업시간 후에 여기에 주차하는 것이 합법인가요?

A: ……………………………………………………

0958 □□□

legend
[ˈledʒənd]

n 전설

= myth, fable, story, famous person, folklore
\+ legendary **a** 전설적인

Q: Have you heard the legend about the old castle?
오래된 성에 대한 전설을 들어본 적 있나요?

A: ……………………………………………………

0959 □□□

lend
[lend]

v 빌려주다

= loan, provide, give, impart
\+ lender **n** 대여자

Q: Can you lend me your notes for the exam? 시험 대비 노트 좀 빌려줄 수 있나요?

A: ……………………………………………………

0960 □□□

length
[leŋθ]

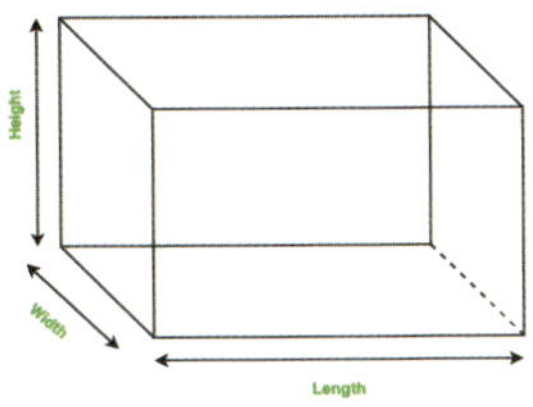

n 길이

= extent, duration, distance, measure
\+ long **a** 긴 lengthen **v** 길게 하다 lengthwise **adv** 길이 방향으로

Q: What's the length of the movie we're watching?
우리가 보고 있는 영화의 길이는 얼마인가요?

A: ……………………………………………………

DAY 18 | DICTATION TEST

5회 반복 예문 QR

DICTATION TEST 예문 QR을 듣고 다음 빈칸에 올바른 단어를 쓰세요.

941. Is the ______________ market improving in your city lately?
942. Have you ever worked in a science ______________ before?
943. Does this project suffer from a ______________ of funding?
944. Is the ______________ safe to use for this repair job?
945. What kind of ______________ do you prefer for hiking?
946. ______________, do you have any questions before we finish?
947. Do you prefer the ______________ option in this case?
948. When will they ______________ the new product officially?
949. Did you consult a ______________ about the contract terms?
950. Can you ______________ the table for dinner tonight please?
951. How many ______________ does this cake actually have?
952. Which ______________ does your favorite soccer team play in?
953. Is there a water ______________ somewhere in the basement?
954. Do you ______________ more toward traditional or modern style?
955. Did you see the deer ______________ over the fence?
956. Did you enjoy today's ______________ on climate change?
957. Is it ______________ to park here after business hours?
958. Have you heard the ______________ about the old castle?
959. Can you ______________ me your notes for the exam?
960. What's the ______________ of the movie we're watching?

5회 반복 표제어 QR　5회 반복 예문 QR

DAY 19

30 days

AI 학습자료와 인강 youpass.co.kr

PREVIEW A 다음 단어의 뜻을 한국어로 써보세요.

□ liberal	________	□ literal	________
□ liberty	________	□ literally	________
□ license	________	□ literate	________
□ lid	________	□ literature	________
□ lightning	________	□ litter	________
□ likely	________	□ load	________
□ limit	________	□ loan	________
□ linguistic	________	□ local	________
□ link	________	□ locate	________
□ liquid	________	□ location	________

PREVIEW B 사진을 보고 알맞은 영어 단어를 **PREVIEW A**에서 찾아 써보세요.

________　________　________　________

0961 □□□

liberal
[ˈlɪbərəl]

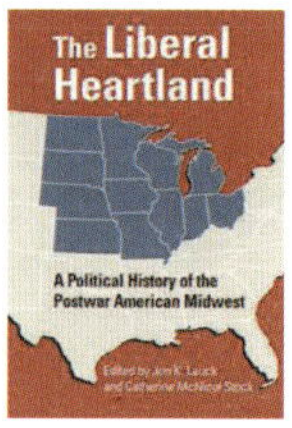

a 자유로운, 진보적인

= generous, open-minded, progressive, tolerant, free
+ liberalism n 자유주의 liberation n 해방 liberty n 자유 liberate v 해방시키다
liberally adv 자유롭게, 관대하게

Q: Are you more liberal or conservative in this issue?
당신은 이 문제에 있어 진보적인가요, 보수적인가요?

A: ……………………………………

0962 □□□

liberty
[ˈlɪbərti]

n 자유

= freedom, independence, autonomy, release
+ liberal a 자유로운

Q: Do you believe in freedom and liberty for everyone?
모든 사람에게 자유와 해방이 있다고 믿나요?

A: ……………………………………

0963 □□□

license
[ˈlaɪsns]

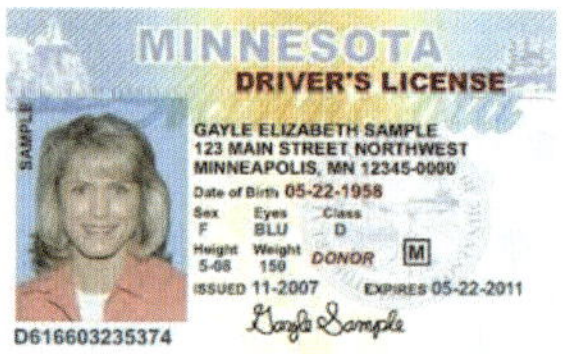

n 면허, 허가 v 허가하다

= permit, authorization, certificate, allow, approve
+ license plate 번호판(number plate)

Q: Did you renew your driver's license? 운전면허를 갱신했나요?

A: ……………………………………

0964 □□□

lid
[lɪd]

n 뚜껑

= cover, top, cap
+ eyelid n (한쪽) 눈꺼풀

Q: Can you put the lid back on the jar properly?
병뚜껑을 제대로 다시 닫아줄 수 있나요?

A: ……………………………………

0965 □□□

lightning
[ˈlaɪtnɪŋ]

n 번개

= flash, bolt, electric discharge
+ lightning rod 피뢰침

Q: Did you see the lightning during last night's storm?
어젯밤 폭풍우 동안 번개를 봤나요?

A: ……………………………………

0966 □□□

likely
[ˈlaɪkli]

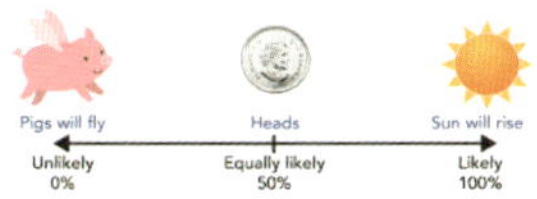

a ~할 것 같은 adv 아마

= probable, apt, plausible, inclined, probably
+ likelihood n 가능성 unlikely a 있을 것 같지 않은

Q: Is it likely that the meeting will be postponed until next week?
회의가 다음 주로 연기될 가능성이 있나요?

A:

0967 □□□

limit
[ˈlɪmɪt]

n 한계, 제한 v 제한하다

= restriction, boundary, ceiling, cap, confine, curb
+ limitation n 제한 limited a 제한된 limitless a 무한한

Q: What's the speed limit on this highway section?
이 고속도로 구간의 제한 속도는 얼마인가요?

A:

0968 □□□

linguistic
[lɪŋˈgwɪstɪk]

a 언어의, 언어학적인

= language, verbal, spoken, semantic
+ linguistics n 언어학 linguist n 언어학자 linguistically adv 언어적으로

Q: Are you interested in linguistic studies or languages?
언어 연구나 언어학에 관심이 있나요?

A:

0969 □□□

link
[lɪŋk]

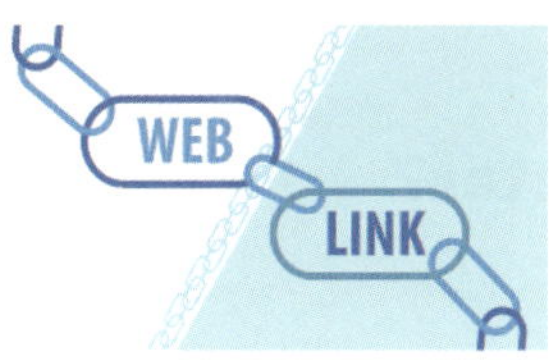

n 연결, 관계 v 연결하다

= connect, associate, relate, bond, connection
+ linkage n 연결

Q: Can you send me the link to that article again?
그 기사 링크 다시 보내줄 수 있나요?

A:

0970 □□□

liquid
[ˈlɪkwɪd]

n 액체 a 액체의

= fluid, solution, flowing, wet
+ liquidity n 유동성

Q: Is this liquid safe to drink without boiling?
이 액체는 끓이지 않고 마셔도 안전한가요?

A:

0971 □□□

literal
[ˈlɪtərəl]

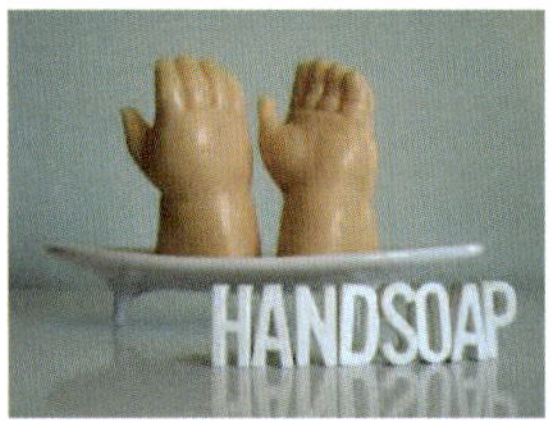

a 문자 그대로의

= exact, precise, factual, word for word
+ literally adv 문자 그대로

Q: Did you take his comment in a literal sense?
그의 말을 문자 그대로 받아들였나요?

A: ....

0972 □□□

literally
[ˈlɪtərəli]

adv 문자 그대로

= actually, precisely, exactly, verbatim
+ literal a 문자 그대로의

Q: Did you literally run five miles this morning?
오늘 아침에 말 그대로 5마일을 달렸나요?

A: ....

0973 □□□

literate
[ˈlɪtərət]

a 읽고 쓸 줄 아는

= educated, able to read and write, knowledgeable
+ literacy n 읽고 쓰는 능력 literature n 문학 illiterate a 문맹의

Q: Is everyone in your community fully literate now?
당신 지역사회의 모든 사람이 이제 완전히 글을 읽을 수 있나요?

A: ....

0974 □□□

literature
[ˈlɪtərətʃər]

n 문학

= writings, books, poetry, prose, scholarly works
+ literate n 글을 읽고 쓸 줄 아는 사람 literary a 문학의

Q: Have you read any classic literature this semester?
이번 학기에 고전 문학을 읽었나요?

A: ....

0975 □□□

litter
[ˈlɪtər]

n 쓰레기 v 쓰레기를 버리다

= rubbish, trash, debris, scatter, mess
+ litter bin (길거리나 공공건물의) 쓰레기통(trash can)

Q: Why do some people still litter in public places?
왜 일부 사람들은 여전히 공공장소에 쓰레기를 버리나요?

A: ....

0976 □□□

load
[loʊd]

n 짐, 부담 v 싣다, 부담을 지우다

= burden, cargo, weight, responsibility, fill, charge
+ loaded a 짐을 실은, 가득 찬

Q: Can you help me load the boxes into the truck?
상자들을 트럭에 싣는 것 좀 도와줄 수 있나요?

A: ....

0977 □□□

loan
[loʊn]

n 대출, 빌려준 돈 v 빌려주다

= credit, advance, borrow, lend, grant
+ loan shark 고리대금업자, 악덕 사채업자

Q: Did you apply for a loan to buy the new house?
새 집을 사기 위해 대출을 신청했나요?

A: ....

0978 □□□

local
[ˈloʊkl]

a 지역의, 현지의 n 지역 주민

= regional, neighborhood, community, nearby, native
+ locality n 지역 localize v 현지화하다 locally adv 현지에서

Q: Do you prefer local food over international cuisine?
국제 요리보다 현지 음식을 선호하나요?

A: ....

0979 □□□

locate
[ˈloʊkeɪt]

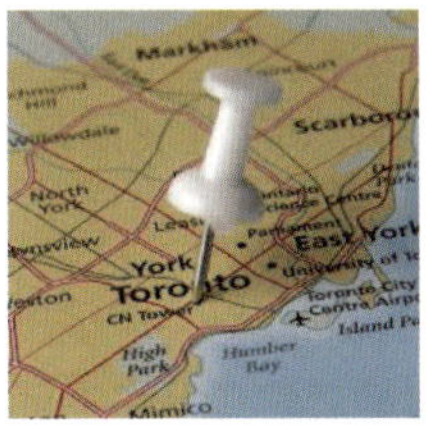

v ~에 위치시키다, 찾아내다

= find, place, situate, position, discover
+ location n 위치 located a 위치한

Q: Can you locate the nearest gas station on your map?
지도에서 가장 가까운 주유소를 찾을 수 있나요?

A: ....

0980 □□□

location
[loʊˈkeɪʃn]

n 위치, 장소

= place, site, position, spot, venue
+ locate v 위치시키다

Q: Is the location of the event easy to find? 행사 장소는 찾기 쉬운가요?

A: ....

DAY 19 | DICTATION TEST

5회 반복 예문 QR

DICTATION TEST 예문 QR을 듣고 다음 빈칸에 올바른 단어를 쓰세요.

961. Are you more ______________ or conservative in this issue?
962. Do you believe in freedom and ______________ for everyone?
963. Did you renew your driver's ______________?
964. Can you put the ______________ back on the jar properly?
965. Did you see the ______________ during last night's storm?
966. Is it ______________ that the meeting will be postponed until next week?
967. What's the speed ______________ on this highway section?
968. Are you interested in ______________ studies or languages?
969. Can you send me the ______________ to that article again?
970. Is this ______________ safe to drink without boiling?
971. Did you take his comment in a ______________ sense?
972. Did you ______________ run five miles this morning?
973. Is everyone in your community fully ______________ now?
974. Have you read any classic ______________ this semester?
975. Why do some people still ______________ in public places?
976. Can you help me ______________ the boxes into the truck?
977. Did you apply for a ______________ to buy the new house?
978. Do you prefer ______________ food over international cuisine?
979. Can you ______________ the nearest gas station on your map?
980. Is the ______________ of the event easy to find?

5회 반복 표제어 QR　5회 반복 예문 QR

DAY 20

30 days

AI 학습자료와 인강 youpass.co.kr

PREVIEW A 다음 단어의 뜻을 한국어로 써보세요.

- ☐ locker ______
- ☐ logic ______
- ☐ logical ______
- ☐ loose ______
- ☐ loosen ______
- ☐ loss ______
- ☐ loyal ______
- ☐ luxury ______
- ☐ lyric ______
- ☐ magnet ______
- ☐ maintain ______
- ☐ major ______
- ☐ majority ______
- ☐ manage ______
- ☐ manipulate ______
- ☐ manner ______
- ☐ manual ______
- ☐ manufacture ______
- ☐ margin ______
- ☐ mass ______

PREVIEW B 사진을 보고 알맞은 영어 단어를 PREVIEW A 에서 찾아 써보세요.

______

______

______

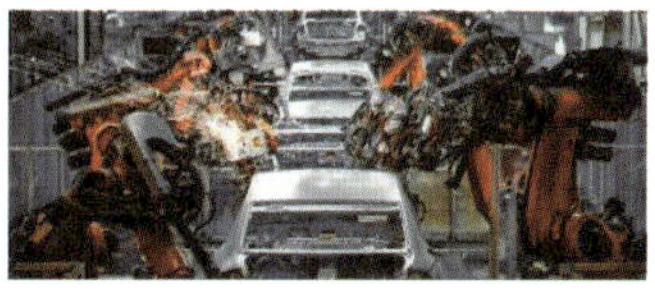
______

0981 □□□

locker
[ˈlɑːkər]

n 사물함

= **compartment, cabinet, storage unit**

+ **locker room** (학교·체육관 등의) 로커룸[탈의실](**changing room**)

Q: Did you remember to lock your locker before class?
수업 전에 사물함 잠그는 것을 기억했나요?

A: ....

0982 □□□

logic
[ˈlɑːdʒɪk]

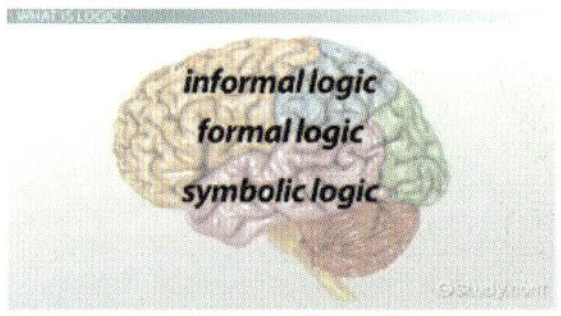

n 논리

= **reason, rationale, common sense, coherence**

+ **logical** **a** 논리적인 **logically** **adv** 논리적으로

Q: Can you explain the logic behind your decision clearly?
당신 결정 뒤에 숨은 논리를 명확하게 설명해 줄 수 있나요?

A: ....

0983 □□□

logical
[ˈlɑːdʒɪkl]

a 논리적인

= **rational, reasonable, sensible, coherent, sound**

+ **logic** **n** 논리 **logically** **adv** 논리적으로

Q: Is it logical to expect results without any effort?
노력 없이 결과를 기대하는 것이 논리적인가요?

A: ....

0984 □□□

loose
[luːs]

a 헐거운, 풀린

= **slack, baggy, detached, unbound, free, release**

+ **looseness** **n** 느슨함 **loosen** **v** 느슨하게 하다 **loosely** **adv** 느슨하게

Q: Are your shoelaces loose or tied tightly right now?
지금 신발 끈이 느슨한가요 아니면 단단히 묶여 있나요?

A: ....

0985 □□□

loosen
[ˈluːsn]

v 늦추다, 풀다

= **relax, slacken, release, untie**

+ **loose** **a** 느슨한

Q: Can you loosen the screws with this screwdriver?
이 드라이버로 나사를 풀 수 있나요?

A: ....

0986 □□□

loss
[lɔːs]

n 손실, 손해

= **defeat, setback, disadvantage, deficit, bereavement**

+ **loss-leader** **n** (상점에서 손님을 끌기 위한) 특가품 **at a loss** (무엇·무슨 말을 해야 할지) 모르는[어쩔 줄을 모르는]

Q: How did you cope with the loss of your pet?
반려동물을 잃은 슬픔을 어떻게 극복했나요?

A: ....

0987 □□□

loyal
[ˈlɔɪəl]

a 충성스러운, 충실한

= **faithful, devoted, allegiance, steadfast, true**

+ **loyalty** **n** 충성 **loyally** **adv** 충성스럽게

Q: Are you always loyal to your favorite sports team?
당신이 가장 좋아하는 스포츠 팀에 항상 충성하나요?

A: ....

0988 □□□

luxury
[ˈlʌkʃəri]

n 사치(품), 호화로움 **a** 호화로운

= **extravagance, indulgence, opulence, comfort, lavish**

+ **luxurious** **a** 고급스러운 **luxuriously** **adv** 호화롭게

Q: What kind of luxury items do you like to buy?
어떤 종류의 명품을 사는 것을 좋아하나요?

A: ....

0989 □□□

lyric
[ˈlɪrɪk]

n 가사 **a** 서정적인

= **poetic, musical, words to a song**

+ **lyrics** **n** 가사 **lyrical** **a** 서정적인

Q: Can you remember the lyrics to that popular song?
그 인기 있는 노래의 가사를 기억할 수 있나요?

A: ....

0990 □□□

magnet
[ˈmægnət]

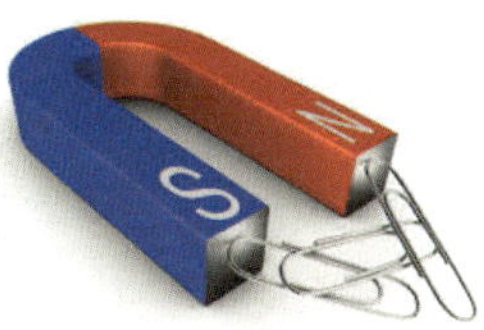

n 자석

= **attractor, lure, pull, charm**

+ **magnetism** **n** 자기 **magnetization** **n** 자화 **magnetize** **v** 자화시키다 **magnetic** **a** 자성의, 매력적인

Q: Is this magnet strong enough to hold the papers?
이 자석이 종이들을 고정할 만큼 충분히 강한가요?

A: ....

0991 □□□

maintain
[meɪnˈteɪn]

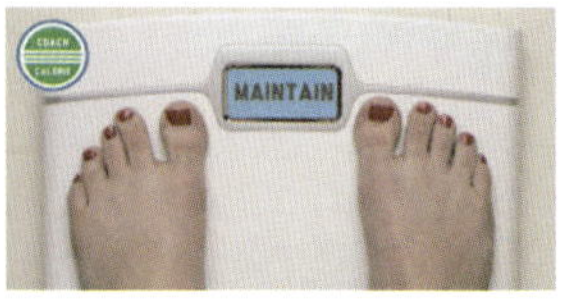

v 유지하다, 주장하다

= **preserve, keep, support, assert, uphold, continue**
+ **maintenance** **n** 유지, 보수

Q: How do you maintain your car in good condition?
차를 좋은 상태로 유지하기 위해 어떻게 하나요?

A: ....

0992 □□□

major
[ˈmeɪdʒər]

a 주요한, 전공의 **n** 전공, 소령

= **principal, main, significant, important, primary, specialty**
+ **majority** **n** 대부분, 다수 **majorly** **adv** 주로, 크게

Q: What was your major when you studied at university?
대학에서 공부할 때 전공이 무엇이었나요?

A: ....

0993 □□□

majority
[məˈdʒɔːrəti]

n 대다수

= **most, bulk, larger part, greater number**
+ **major** **a** 주요한

Q: Does the majority agree with the proposed plan?
대부분이 제안된 계획에 동의하나요?

A: ....

0994 □□□

manage
[ˈmænɪdʒ]

v 관리하다, 경영하다, (간신히) 해내다, (공들여) 하다

= **control, supervise, handle, cope, succeed, direct**
+ **management** **n** 관리 **manager** **n** 관리자 **manageable** **a** 관리할 수 있는

Q: Can you manage your time effectively during exams?
시험 기간 동안 시간을 효과적으로 관리할 수 있나요?

A: ....

0995 □□□

manipulate
[məˈnɪpjuleɪt]

v 조작하다, 능숙하게 다루다

= **control, influence, exploit, operate, handle**
+ **manipulation** **n** 조작 **manipulator** **n** 조작자 **manipulative** **a** 조작적인

Q: Is it easy to manipulate the controls on this device?
이 장치의 조작부는 다루기 쉽나요?

A: ....

0996 □□□

manner
[ˈmænər]

n 방식, 태도

= way, style, conduct, behavior, custom
+ a fussy manner 신경질적인 태도 a casual manner 태평스러운 태도

Q: Do you think manners are important in daily life?
일상생활에서 예절이 중요하다고 생각하나요?

A:

0997 □□□

manual
[ˈmænjuəl]

n 설명서 a 수동의

= handbook, guide, physical, by hand, instructional
+ manually adv 손으로, 수동으로

Q: Did you read the manual before assembling the furniture?
가구를 조립하기 전에 설명서를 읽었나요?

A:

0998 □□□

manufacture
[ˌmænjuˈfæktʃər]

v 제조하다 n 제조

= produce, make, fabricate, create, production
+ manufacturer n 제조업자 manufacturing n 제조업

Q: Where do they manufacture most of their products?
그들은 대부분의 제품을 어디서 제조하나요?

A:

0999 □□□

margin
[ˈmɑːrdʒɪn]

n 여백, 가장자리, 차이

= edge, border, leeway, profit, difference
+ marginal a 미미한, 변두리의 marginally adv 약간, 미미하게

Q: Does the company have enough profit margin to invest in new research? 그 회사는 새로운 연구에 투자할 만큼 충분한 이윤폭을 가지고 있나요?

A:

1000 □□□

mass
[mæs]

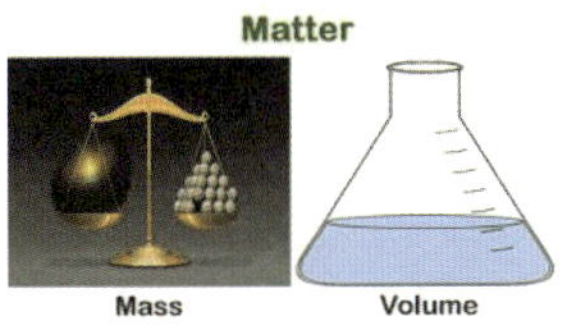

n 덩어리, 대중, 질량 a 대규모의

= bulk, quantity, crowd, large amount, aggregate
+ massive a 거대한 mess n 엉망진창

Q: How do you measure the mass of this heavy object?
이 무거운 물체의 질량은 어떻게 측정하나요?

A:

DAY 20 | DICTATION TEST

5회 반복 예문 QR

DICTATION TEST 예문 QR을 듣고 다음 빈칸에 올바른 단어를 쓰세요.

981. Did you remember to ____________ your locker before class?
982. Can you explain the ____________ behind your decision clearly?
983. Is it ____________ to expect results without any effort?
984. Are your shoelaces ____________ or tied tightly right now?
985. Can you ____________ the screws with this screwdriver?
986. How did you cope with the ____________ of your pet?
987. Are you always ____________ to your favorite sports team?
988. What kind of ____________ items do you like to buy?
989. Can you remember the ____________ to that popular song?
990. Is this ____________ strong enough to hold the papers?
991. How do you ____________ your car in good condition?
992. What was your ____________ when you studied at university?
993. Does the ____________ agree with the proposed plan?
994. Can you ____________ your time effectively during exams?
995. Is it easy to ____________ the controls on this device?
996. Do you think ____________ are important in daily life?
997. Did you read the ____________ before assembling the furniture?
998. Where do they ____________ most of their products?
999. Does the company have enough profit ____________ to invest in new research?
1000. How do you measure the ____________ of this heavy object?

5회 반복 표제어 QR　5회 반복 예문 QR

DAY 21

30 days

AI 학습자료와 인강 youpass.co.kr

PREVIEW A 다음 단어의 뜻을 한국어로 써보세요.

□ massive	______	□ mechanic	______
□ master	______	□ mechanical	______
□ masterpiece	______	□ medical	______
□ material	______	□ meditate	______
□ mature	______	□ medium	______
□ maximum	______	□ melt	______
□ mayor	______	□ memorable	______
□ meaning	______	□ memorial	______
□ meanwhile	______	□ memory	______
□ measure	______	□ mend	______

PREVIEW B 사진을 보고 알맞은 영어 단어를 **PREVIEW A** 에서 찾아 써보세요.

______

______

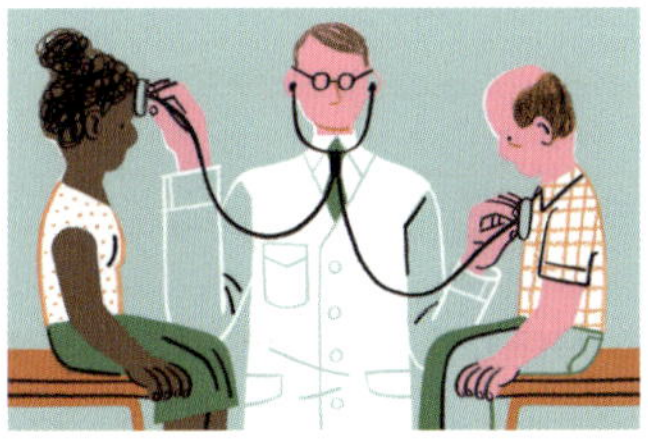
______

______

1001 □□□

massive
[ˈmæsɪv]

a 거대한, 육중한

= huge, enormous, colossal, immense, bulky
+ mass **n** 덩어리, 질량 **massiveness** **n** 거대함 **massively** **adv** 대규모로, 엄청나게

Q: Did the recent earthquake cause massive damage to the city?
최근 지진이 도시에 엄청난 피해를 입혔나요?

A: ....

1002 □□□

master
[ˈmæstər]

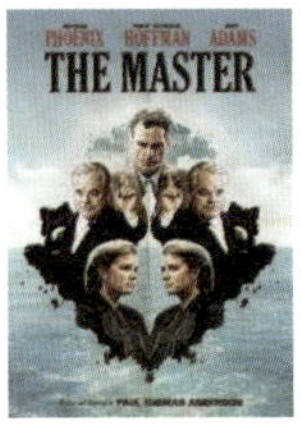

n 달인, 주인 **v** 통달하다

= expert, maestro, chief, commander, acquire, dominate
+ mastery **n** 숙달, 통달 **masterful** **a** 명인 솜씨의

Q: Do you think it's possible to master a new language in just one year? 한 해 만에 새로운 언어를 숙달하는 것이 가능하다고 생각하시나요?

A: ....

1003 □□□

masterpiece
[ˈmæstərpiːs]

n 걸작, 명작

= magnum opus, classic, finest work
+ appreciate Picasso's masterpiece 피카소의 명작을 감상하다

Q: Have you ever seen a masterpiece in a famous museum?
유명한 박물관에서 명작을 본 적 있나요?

A: ....

1004 □□□

material
[məˈtɪriəl]

n 재료, 물질 **a** 물질적인

= substance, fabric, content, physical, relevant
+ materialism **n** 유물론 **materialist** **n** 유물론자 **materialize** **v** 구체화하다, 실현되다 **materially** **adv** 실질적으로

Q: What kind of material is used for this jacket?
이 재킷은 어떤 종류의 재료로 만들어졌나요?

A: ....

1005 □□□

mature
[məˈtʃʊr] [məˈtʃʊər]

a 성숙한 **v** 성숙해지다

= grown-up, adult, ripe, developed, mellow, age
+ maturity **n** 성숙 **maturely** **adv** 성숙하게

Q: Do you think he's mature enough for this responsibility?
그가 이 책임을 맡을 만큼 충분히 성숙하다고 생각하나요?

A: ....

1006 □□□

maximum
[ˈmæksɪməm]

n 최대치 a 최대의

= most, highest, top, utmost, greatest amount

+ maximal a 최대의 maximize v 극대화하다

Q: What is the maximum speed allowed on this road?
이 도로 구간의 최고 허용 속도는 얼마인가요?

A: ....

1007 □□□

mayor
[ˈmeɪər]

n (한 도시의 장) 시장

= city head, civic leader, chief magistrate

+ mayoral n 시장의

Q: Has the mayor announced new plans for the city?
시장이 도시에 대한 새로운 계획을 발표했나요?

A: ....

1008 □□□

meaning
[ˈmiːnɪŋ]

n 의미, 뜻

= sense, significance, implication, definition, purpose

+ mean v 의미하다 meaningful a 의미 있는 meaningless a 무의미한
meaningfully adv 의미 있게

Q: Can you explain the meaning of this difficult word?
이 어려운 단어의 의미를 설명해 줄 수 있나요?

A: ....

1009 □□□

meanwhile
[ˈmiːnwaɪl]

adv 그러는 동안에, 한편

= in the meantime, simultaneously, at the same time

+ in the meanwhile (두 가지 시점·사건들) 그 동안[사이]에, (다음 일이 있을) 그때까지
for the meanwhile 당분간

Q: I was busy working. What did you do meanwhile?
나는 일하느라 바빴어요. 그동안 당신은 무엇을 했나요?

A: ....

1010 □□□

measure
[ˈmeʒər]

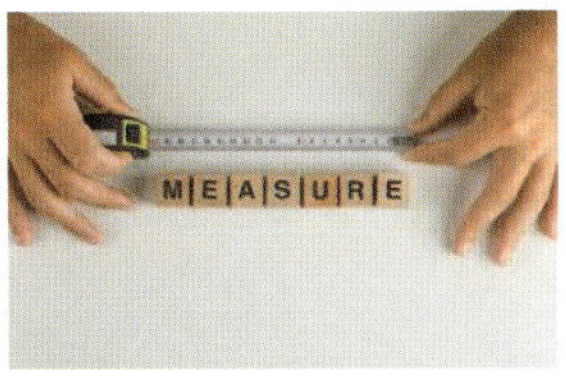

v 측정하다 n 측정, 조치

= quantify, assess, determine, size, amount, extent

+ measurement n 측정 measurable a 측정 가능한 measurably adv 측정할 수 있게

Q: How do you measure the success of your projects?
프로젝트의 성공을 어떻게 측정하나요?

A: ....

1011 □□□

mechanic
[məˈkænɪk]

n 정비사, 역학

= technician, engineer, repairman
+ mechanics n 역학, 기계학 mechanical a 기계적인

Q: Did the mechanic fix your car quickly this time?
이번에 정비사가 차를 빨리 고쳐줬나요?

A: ....

1012 □□□

mechanical
[məˈkænɪkl]

a 기계적인

= automated, automatic, machine-like, robotic
+ mechanic n 정비사 mechanism n 메커니즘 mechanically adv 기계적으로

Q: Are you interested in mechanical engineering or design?
기계 공학이나 디자인에 관심이 있나요?

A: ....

1013 □□□

medical
[ˈmedɪkl]

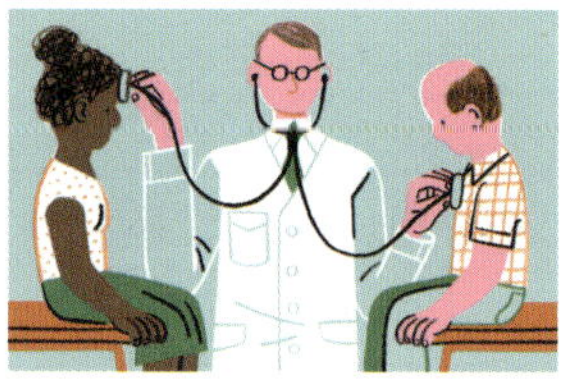

a 의학의, 의료의

= health, clinical, therapeutic, curative
+ medicine n 의학, 약 medically adv 의학적으로

Q: Do you have any medical conditions I should know about?
제가 알아야 할 의학적 상태가 있나요?

A: ....

1014 □□□

meditate
[ˈmedɪteɪt]

v 명상하다

= contemplate, reflect, ponder, muse, ruminate
+ meditation n 명상 meditative a 명상적인

Q: How often do you meditate to relieve your stress?
스트레스 해소를 위해 얼마나 자주 명상하나요?

A: ....

1015 □□□

medium
[ˈmiːdiəm]

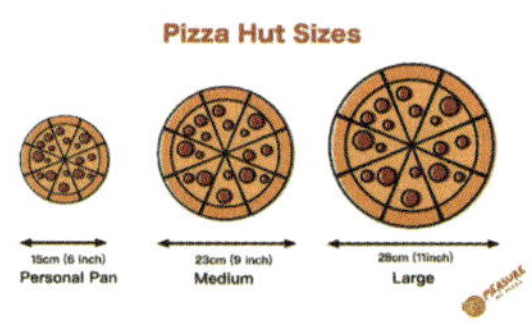

n 매개체, 중간 a 중간의

= average, intermediate, means, channel, environment
+ medium-sized a 중간 크기[치수]의

Q: Is the medium size shirt available in green color?
녹색 색상으로 중간 사이즈 셔츠가 있나요?

A: ....

1016 □□□

melt
[melt]

v 녹다, 녹이다

= **thaw, liquefy, dissolve, soften, fade**

+ **melt away** 차츰 사라지다[사라지게 하다] **melt something down** (특히 물건을 만드는 데 쓰기 위해 금속 · 왁스를) 녹이다

Q: How long does it take for ice to melt indoors?
실내에서 얼음이 녹는 데 얼마나 걸리나요?

A: ....

1017 □□□

memorable
[ˈmemərəbl]

a 기억할 만한

= **unforgettable, distinctive, remarkable, impressive**

+ **memory** **n** 기억 **memorability** **n** 기억에 남을 만함 **memorize** **v** 기억하다 **memorably** **adv** 기억에 남을 만큼

Q: What was the most memorable moment of your trip?
여행 중 가장 기억에 남는 순간은 무엇이었나요?

A: ....

1018 □□□

memorial
[məˈmɔːriəl]

n 기념물 **a** 기념의

= **monument, tribute, remembrance, commemorative**

+ **memorialize** **v** 기념하다

Q: Did you visit the memorial for the fallen soldiers?
전사자들을 위한 기념비를 방문했나요?

A: ....

1019 □□□

memory
[ˈeməri]

n 기억, 추억

= **recollection, recall, remembrance, reminiscence, storage**

+ **memorize** **v** 기억하다 **memorable** **a** 기억할 만한

Q: Can you recall the memory of your first day at school?
학교 첫날의 기억을 떠올릴 수 있나요?

A: ....

1020 □□□

mend
[mend]

v 고치다, 수선하다

= **repair, fix, patch, heal, restore**

+ **mend your ways** 행실을 고치다 **mend your fences** 불화[관계]를 개선하다

Q: Do you know how to mend torn clothes by yourself?
찢어진 옷을 혼자서 수선할 줄 아나요?

A: ....

DAY 21 | DICTATION TEST

5회 반복 예문 QR

DICTATION TEST 예문 QR을 듣고 다음 빈칸에 올바른 단어를 쓰세요.

1001. Did the recent earthquake cause ______________ damage to the city?
1002. Do you think it's possible to ______________ a new language in just one year?
1003. Have you ever seen a ______________ in a famous museum?
1004. What kind of ______________ is used for this jacket?
1005. Do you think he's ____________ enough for this responsibility?
1006. What is the ______________ speed allowed on this road?
1007. Has the ______________ announced new plans for the city?
1008. Can you explain the ______________ of this difficult word?
1009. I was busy working. What did you do ______________?
1010. How do you ______________ the success of your projects?
1011. Did the ______________ fix your car quickly this time?
1012. Are you interested in ______________ engineering or design?
1013. Do you have any __________ conditions I should know about?
1014. How often do you ______________ to relieve your stress?
1015. Is the ______________ size shirt available in green color?
1016. How long does it take for ice to ______________ indoors?
1017. What was the most ______________ moment of your trip?
1018. Did you visit the ______________ for the fallen soldiers?
1019. Can you recall the ______________ of your first day at school?
1020. Do you know how to ______________ torn clothes by yourself?

5회 반복 표제어 QR　5회 반복 예문 QR

DAY 22

30 days

AI 학습자료와 인강 youpass.co.kr

PREVIEW A 다음 단어의 뜻을 한국어로 써보세요.

□ **mental**	______	□ **metal**	______
□ **mention**	______	□ **metaphor**	______
□ **mentor**	______	□ **method**	______
□ **merchant**	______	□ **migrate**	______
□ **mercy**	______	□ **military**	______
□ **merely**	______	□ **minimize**	______
□ **merit**	______	□ **minimum**	______
□ **merry**	______	□ **minor**	______
□ **mess**	______	□ **miserable**	______
□ **messy**	______	□ **mission**	______

PREVIEW B 사진을 보고 알맞은 영어 단어를 **PREVIEW A** 에서 찾아 써보세요.

______　______　______　______

1021 □□□

mental
[ˈmentl]

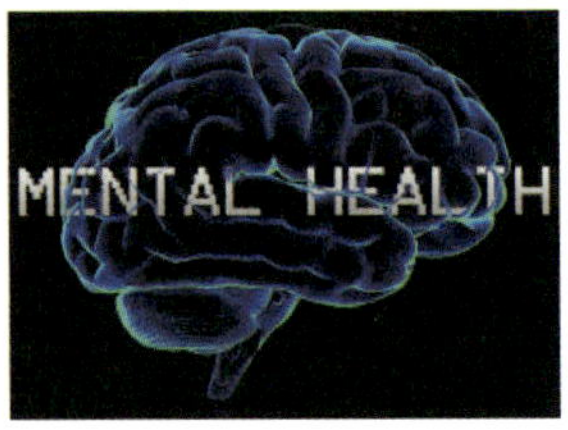

a 정신의, 마음의

= intellectual, cognitive, psychological, inner
+ mentality n 사고방식 mentally adv 정신적으로

Q: Do you take care of your mental health regularly enough?
정신 건강을 충분히 꾸준히 관리하나요?

A: ....

1022 □□□

mention
[ˈmenʃn]

v 언급하다 n 언급

= state, refer to, remark, note, allusion
+ not to mention ~은 말할 것도 없고[물론이고] don't mention it (고맙다는 말에 대한 정중한 인사로) 별 말씀을요

Q: Did you mention the meeting time to your team yesterday?
어제 팀에게 회의 시간을 언급했나요?

A: ....

1023 □□□

mentor
[ˈmentɔːr]

n 멘토, 조언자

= guide, coach, advisor, tutor
+ mentorship n 멘토링

Q: Have you ever had a mentor to guide your career path?
경력 경로를 안내해 줄 멘토가 있었나요?

A: ....

1024 □□□

merchant
[ˈmɜːrtʃənt]

n 상인

= trader, dealer, vendor, shopkeeper
+ merchandise n 상품

Q: Is the merchant selling fresh vegetables at the market today?
상인이 오늘 시장에서 신선한 채소를 팔고 있나요?

A: ....

1025 □□□

mercy
[ˈmɜːrsi]

n 자비, 연민

= compassion, leniency, pity, clemency
+ merciful a 자비로운 merciless a 무자비한 mercifully adv 자비롭게

Q: Will you show mercy to someone who made a mistake?
실수한 사람에게 자비를 베풀 건가요?

A: ....

1026 □□□

merely
[ˈmɪrli]

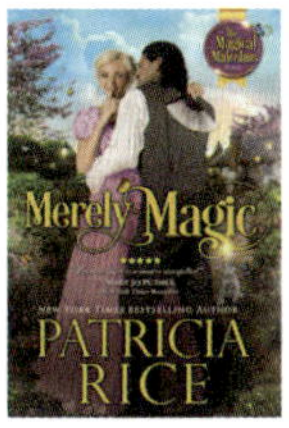

adv 단지, 그저

= **simply, just, only, solely**
+ **mere** **a** 겨우, 단지

Q: Is it merely a coincidence or something more important?
단지 우연인가요, 아니면 더 중요한 무엇인가요?

A: ....

1027 □□□

merit
[ˈmerɪt]

n 장점, 공로 **v** ~할 가치가 있다

= **worth, value, virtue, deserve, earn**
+ **meritorious** **a** 칭찬할 만한

Q: Does this job candidate have enough merit for the position?
이 지원자는 그 자리에 충분한 자격이 있나요?

A: ....

1028 □□□

merry
[ˈmeri]

a 즐거운, 명랑한

= **cheerful, joyful, festive, cheerful**
+ **merriment** **n** 흥겨움 **merrily** **adv** 즐겁게

Q: Did you have a merry Christmas with your family?
가족과 함께 즐거운 크리스마스를 보냈나요?

A: ....

1029 □□□

mess
[mes]

n 엉망진창, 혼란 **v** 엉망으로 만들다

= **disorder, clutter, confusion, muddle, dirty, tangle**
+ **messy** **a** 지저분한

Q: How do you clean up a mess after cooking dinner?
저녁 식사 후에 어지러운 것을 어떻게 치우나요?

A: ....

1030 □□□

messy
[ˈmesi]

a 지저분한, 엉망인

= **untidy, disarranged, chaotic, dirty, disorganized**
+ **mess** **n** 혼란 **messily** **adv** 지저분하게

Q: Is your room messy or well organized most of the time?
방이 대부분 어지럽나요 아니면 잘 정리되어 있나요?

A: ....

1031 □□□

metal
[ˈmetl]

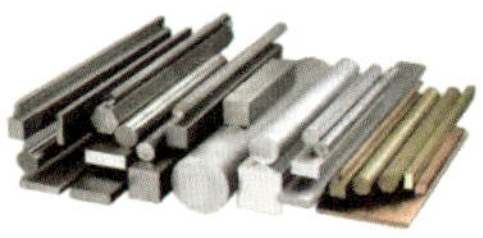

n 금속

= alloy, element, ore
\+ metallic **a** 금속성의

Q: What type of metal is used to make this jewelry piece?
이 장신구는 어떤 종류의 금속으로 만들어졌나요?

A: ....

1032 □□□

metaphor
[ˈmetəfɔːr]

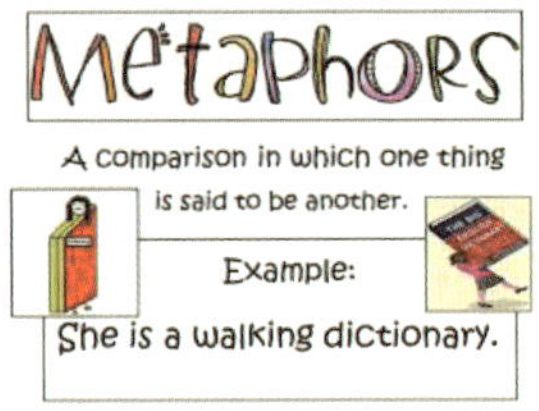

n 은유, 비유

= analogy, symbol, figure of speech, simile
\+ metaphorical **a** 은유적인 metaphorically **adv** 은유적으로

Q: Can you explain the metaphor in this poem clearly?
이 시의 은유를 명확하게 설명해 줄 수 있나요?

A: ....

1033 □□□

method
[ˈmeθəd]

n 방법, 방식

= approach, technique, procedure, system, way
\+ methodical **a** 체계적인 methodically **adv** 체계적으로

Q: Which method do you prefer to study for exams?
시험 공부할 때 어떤 방법을 선호하나요?

A: ....

1034 □□□

migrate
[ˈmaɪgreɪt]

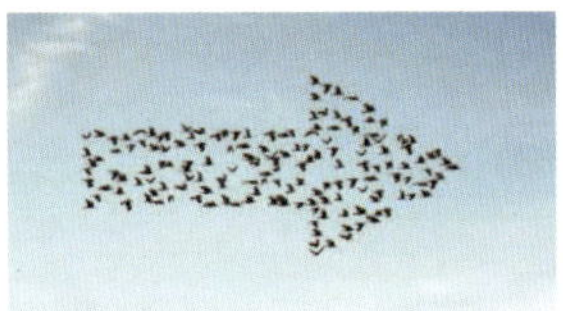

v 이주하다

= relocate, move, resettle, journey
\+ migration **n** 이주 migrant **n** 이주자

Q: Do birds migrate south during the winter season?
겨울 동안 새들이 남쪽으로 이동하나요?

A: ....

1035 □□□

military
[ˈmɪlɪteri]

n 군대 **a** 군사의

= armed forces, army, martial, warlike
\+ military service 군 복무 military band 군악대 military police 헌병대

Q: Have you ever considered joining the military service?
군 복무를 고려해 본 적 있나요?

A: ....

1036 □□□

minimize
[ˈmɪnɪmaɪz]

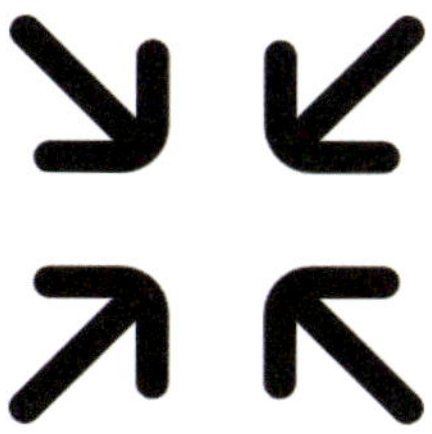

v 최소화하다

= **reduce, diminish, lessen, decrease, mitigate**
\+ **minimization** **n** 최소화 **minimal** **a** 최소의

Q: How can we minimize errors in our daily work routines?
일상 업무 루틴에서 오류를 어떻게 최소화할 수 있을까요?

A:

1037 □□□

minimum
[ˈmɪnɪməm]

n 최소한도 **a** 최소의

= **least, lowest, smallest, absolute least**
\+ **minimal** **a** 최소의 **minimize** **v** 최소화하다

Q: What is the minimum age required to vote in your country?
당신의 나라에서 투표할 수 있는 최소 연령은 몇 살인가요?

A:

1038 □□□

minor
[ˈmaɪnər]

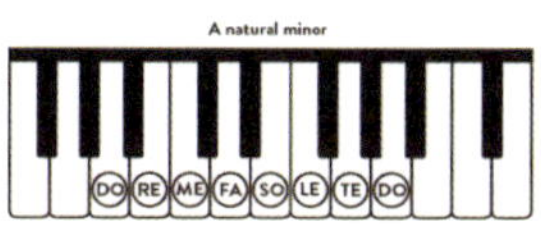

a 사소한, 미성년의 **n** 미성년자, (음악) 단조

= **secondary, lesser, trivial, unimportant, slight**
\+ **minority** **n** 소수

Q: Is this problem minor or does it need urgent attention?
이 문제는 사소한가요 아니면 긴급한 주의가 필요한가요?

A:

1039 □□□

miserable
[ˈmɪzərəbl]

a 비참한, 불쌍한

= **unhappy, wretched, sad, dreadful, pathetic**
\+ **misery** **n** 비참함 **miserably** **adv** 비참하게

Q: Did the team feel miserable after losing the championship game? 팀은 챔피언 결정전에서 진 후에 비참함을 느꼈나요?

A:

1040 □□□

mission
[ˈmɪʃn]

n 임무, 사명

= **task, objective, assignment, purpose, quest**
\+ **missionary** **a** 선교의

Q: What was the mission of your volunteer group last weekend?
지난 주말 당신의 자원봉사 그룹의 임무는 무엇이었나요?

A:

DAY 22 | DICTATION TEST

5회 반복 예문 QR

DICTATION TEST 예문 QR을 듣고 다음 빈칸에 올바른 단어를 쓰세요.

1021. Do you take care of your ______________ health regularly enough?

1022. Did you ______________ the meeting time to your team yesterday?

1023. Have you ever had a ______________ to guide your career path?

1024. Is the ______________ selling fresh vegetables at the market today?

1025. Will you show ______________ to someone who made a mistake?

1026. Is it ______________ a coincidence or something more important?

1027. Does this job candidate have enough ______________ for the position?

1028. Did you have a ______________ Christmas with your family?

1029. How do you clean up a ______________ after cooking dinner?

1030. Is your room ______________ or well organized most of the time?

1031. What type of ______________ is used to make this jewelry piece?

1032. Can you explain the ______________ in this poem clearly?

1033. Which ______________ do you prefer to study for exams?

1034. Do birds ______________ south during the winter season?

1035. Have you ever considered joining the ______________ service?

1036. How can we ______________ errors in our daily work routines?

1037. What is the ______________ age required to vote in your country?

1038. Is this problem ______________ or does it need urgent attention?

1039. Did the team feel ______________ after losing the championship game?

1040. What was the ______________ of your volunteer group last weekend?

5회 반복 표제어 QR 5회 반복 예문 QR

DAY 23

30 days

AI 학습자료와 인강 youpass.co.kr

PREVIEW A 다음 단어의 뜻을 한국어로 써보세요.

□ mixture ________	□ moreover ________
□ moderate ________	□ mostly ________
□ modern ________	□ motion ________
□ modest ________	□ motivate ________
□ modify ________	□ motto ________
□ monitor ________	□ mount ________
□ monster ________	□ movement ________
□ mood ________	□ mud ________
□ moonlight ________	□ multiple ________
□ moral ________	□ multiply ________

PREVIEW B 사진을 보고 알맞은 영어 단어를 PREVIEW A 에서 찾아 써보세요.

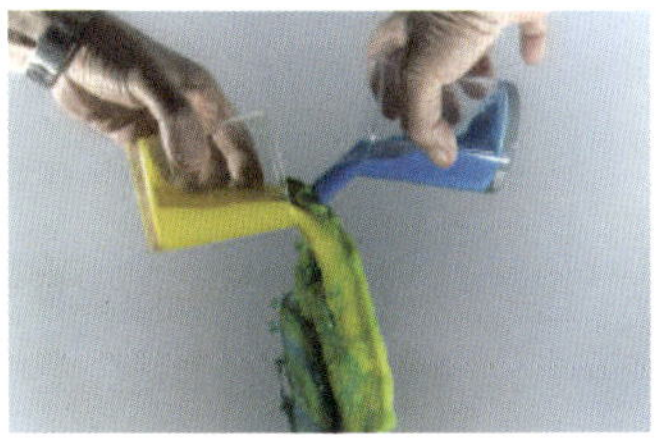
____

____

____

____

1041 □□□

mixture
[ˈmɪkstʃər]

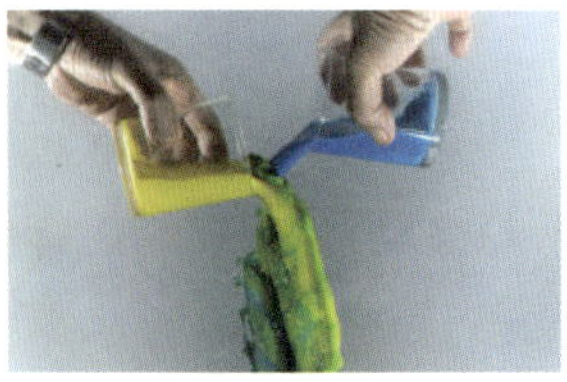

n 혼합물

= **blend, compound, mix, concoction, combination**
+ **mix** **v** 섞다

Q: What's the best mixture of ingredients for this recipe?
이 요리법에 가장 좋은 재료 혼합은 무엇인가요?

A: ....

1042 □□□

moderate
[ˈmɑːdərət] **a** [ˈmɑːdəreɪt] **v**

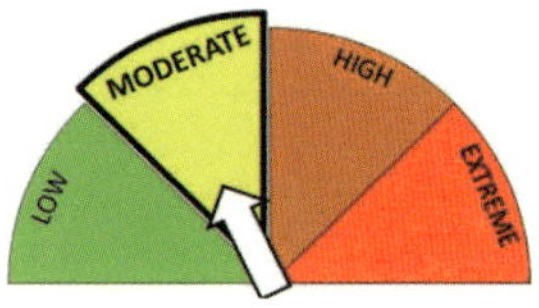

a 보통의, 적당한 **v** 완화하다

= **temperate, reasonable, average, mild, adjust, lessen**
+ **moderation** **n** 절제, 완화 **moderately** **adv** 적당히

Q: Do you prefer moderate exercise or intense workouts?
적당한 운동을 선호하나요 아니면 강도 높은 운동을 선호하나요?

A: ....

1043 □□□

modern
[ˈmɑːdərn]

a 현대의

= **contemporary, current, new, recent, advanced**
+ **modernity** **n** 현대성 **modernization** **n** 현대화 **modernize** **v** 현대화하다

Q: Is your house decorated in a modern or traditional style?
당신의 집은 현대적인 스타일로 꾸며져 있나요 아니면 전통적인 스타일로 꾸며져 있나요?

A: ....

1044 □□□

modest
[ˈmɑːdɪst]

a 겸손한, 보통의

= **humble, unpretentious, discreet, reserved, small**
+ **modesty** **n** 겸손 **modestly** **adv** 겸손하게

Q: Do you think children should be taught to be modest from an early age? 어린이들은 어릴 때부터 겸손함을 배워야 한다고 생각하나요?

A: ....

1045 □□□

modify
[ˈmɑːdɪfaɪ]

v 수정하다, 변경하다

= **change, alter, adjust, adapt, revise**
+ **modification** **n** 수정, 변경 **modified** **a** 수정된

Q: Can you modify the design to make it more user-friendly?
디자인을 수정해서 더 사용자 친화적으로 만들 수 있나요?

A: ....

1046 □□□

monitor
[ˈmɑːnɪtər]

n 모니터 v 감시하다

= **observe, watch, track, supervise, screen**

+ **name a person for monitor** ~을 반장으로 임명하다

Q: How often do you monitor your progress during training?
훈련 중에 진행 상황을 얼마나 자주 모니터링하나요?

A: ....

1047 □□□

monster
[ˈmɑːnstər]

n 괴물

= **creature, beast, fiend, giant**

+ **monstrous** a 괴물 같은, 엄청난

Q: Have you watched the movie about the sea monster?
바다 괴물에 대한 영화를 봤나요?

A: ....

1048 □□□

mood
[muːd]

n 기분, 분위기

= **atmosphere, disposition, temper, feeling, humor**

+ **moody** a 변덕스러운, 기분 변화가 심한

Q: What usually puts you in a good mood during work?
보통 일할 때 무엇이 당신의 기분을 좋게 만드나요?

A: ....

1049 □□□

moonlight
[ˈmuːnlaɪt]

n 달빛

= **lunar glow, moonbeams, lunar light**

+ **the Moonlight Sonata** 월광곡

Q: Did you see the moonlight shining over the calm lake?
고요한 호수 위로 비치는 달빛을 봤나요?

A: ....

1050 □□□

moral
[ˈmɔːrəl]

a 도덕적인 n 도덕

= **ethical, virtuous, righteous, lesson, principle**

+ **morality** n 도덕성 **morals** n 도덕률 **morally** adv 도덕적으로 **immoral** a 부도덕한

Q: What moral lesson did you learn from that story?
그 이야기에서 어떤 도덕적인 교훈을 얻었나요?

A: ....

1051 □□□

moreover
[mɔːrˈoʊvər]

adv 더욱이, 게다가

= furthermore, in addition, besides, additionally
+ and moreover 그리고 게다가

Q: Moreover, do you think this plan will succeed eventually?
게다가, 이 계획이 결국 성공할 것이라고 생각하나요?

A: ....

1052 □□□

mostly
[ˈmoʊstli]

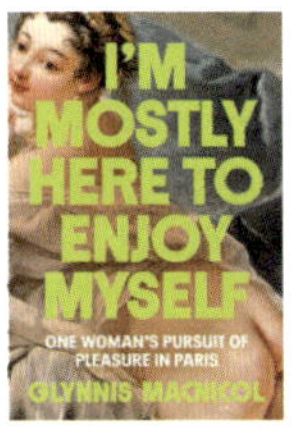

adv 주로, 대개

= mainly, chiefly, primarily, generally, usually
+ most **a** 대부분의

Q: Do you mostly work from home or go to the office?
주로 재택근무를 하나요 아니면 사무실에 가나요?

A: ....

1053 □□□

motion
[ˈmoʊʃn]

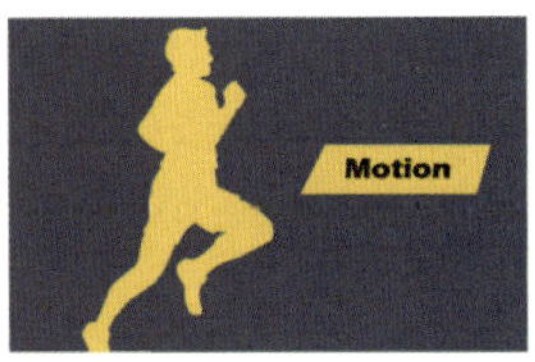

n 움직임, 동작 **v** 동작으로 지시하다

= movement, gesture, proposal, move, signal
+ motionless **a** 움직이지 않는

Q: Can you explain the motion of planets around the sun?
태양 주위 행성의 움직임을 설명해 줄 수 있나요?

A: ....

1054 □□□

motivate
[ˈmoʊtɪveɪt]

v 동기를 부여하다

= inspire, stimulate, encourage, impel, prompt
+ motivation **n** 동기 부여 motive **n** 동기 motivated **a** 동기 부여된
motivating **a** 동기 부여하는

Q: What motivates you to keep going when things get tough?
어려울 때 계속 나아가도록 무엇이 당신을 동기 부여하나요?

A: ....

1055 □□□

motto
[ˈmɑːtoʊ]

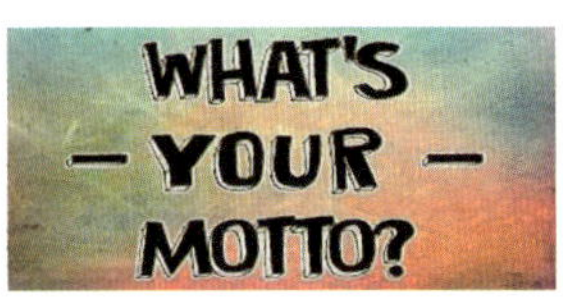

n 좌우명, 표어

= slogan, maxim, adage, saying
+ school motto 교훈 National Motto (미국의) 국시(國是) (In God we trust (우리는 하나님을 믿습니다))

Q: Do you have a personal motto that guides your life?
삶을 이끄는 개인적인 좌우명이 있나요?

A: ....

1056 □□□

mount
[maʊnt]

v 오르다, 설치하다 **n** 산, 탑재물

= ascend, climb, get on, install, prepare, peak

+ mountain **n** 산

Q: How long will it take to mount the television?
텔레비전을 설치하는 데 얼마나 걸릴까요?

A: ....

1057 □□□

movement
[ˈmuːvmənt]

n 움직임, (사회적) 운동

= motion, action, trend, campaign, gesture

+ move **v** 움직이다

Q: Are you involved in any social or political movement now?
지금 어떤 사회적 또는 정치적 운동에 참여하고 있나요?

A: ....

1058 □□□

mud
[mʌd]

n 진흙

= dirt, mire, muck, sludge

+ muddy **a** 진흙투성이의

Q: Did your boots get covered in mud after walking through the field? 밭을 가로질러 걷고 나서 부츠에 진흙이 잔뜩 묻은 건가요?

A: ....

1059 □□□

multiple
[ˈmʌltɪpl]

a 다수의, 복합의 **n** 배수

= numerous, various, many, diverse, manifold

+ multiply **v** 곱하다, 증식하다

Q: Have you visited multiple countries during your vacation?
휴가 동안 여러 나라를 방문했나요?

A: ....

1060 □□□

multiply
[ˈmʌltɪplaɪ]

v 곱하다, 증가시키다

= increase, procreate, reproduce, calculate

+ multiplication **n** 곱셈 multiple **a** 다수의

Q: Can you multiply these numbers quickly without a calculator?
계산기 없이 이 숫자들을 빠르게 곱할 수 있나요?

A: ....

DAY 23 | DICTATION TEST

5회 반복 예문 QR

DICTATION TEST 예문 QR을 듣고 다음 빈칸에 올바른 단어를 쓰세요.

1041. What's the best ______________ of ingredients for this recipe?

1042. Do you prefer ______________ exercise or intense workouts?

1043. Is your house decorated in a ______________ or traditional style?

1044. Do you think children should be taught to be ______________ from an early age?

1045. Can you ______________ the design to make it more user-friendly?

1046. How often do you ______________ your progress during training?

1047. Have you watched the movie about the sea ______________?

1048. What usually puts you in a good ______________ during work?

1049. Did you see the ______________ shining over the calm lake?

1050. What ______________ lesson did you learn from that story?

1051. ______________, do you think this plan will succeed eventually?

1052. Do you ______________ work from home or go to the office?

1053. Can you explain the ______________ of planets around the sun?

1054. What ______________ you to keep going when things get tough?

1055. Do you have a personal ______________ that guides your life?

1056. How long will it take to ______________ the television?

1057. Are you involved in any social or political ______________ now?

1058. Did your boots get covered in ______________ after walking through the field?

1059. Have you visited ______________ countries during your vacation?

1060. Can you ______________ these numbers quickly without a calculator?

5회 반복 표제어 QR　5회 반복 예문 QR

DAY 24

30 days

AI 학습자료와 인강 youpass.co.kr

PREVIEW A 다음 단어의 뜻을 한국어로 써보세요.

- ☐ murder ______
- ☐ muscle ______
- ☐ mutual ______
- ☐ mysterious ______
- ☐ myth ______
- ☐ narrator ______
- ☐ narrow ______
- ☐ native ______
- ☐ natural ______
- ☐ navigate ______
- ☐ navy ______
- ☐ nearby ______
- ☐ necessary ______
- ☐ necessity ______
- ☐ negative ______
- ☐ neglect ______
- ☐ negotiate ______
- ☐ neighborhood ______
- ☐ nerve ______
- ☐ nervous ______

PREVIEW B 사진을 보고 알맞은 영어 단어를 **PREVIEW A**에서 찾아 써보세요.

______

______

______

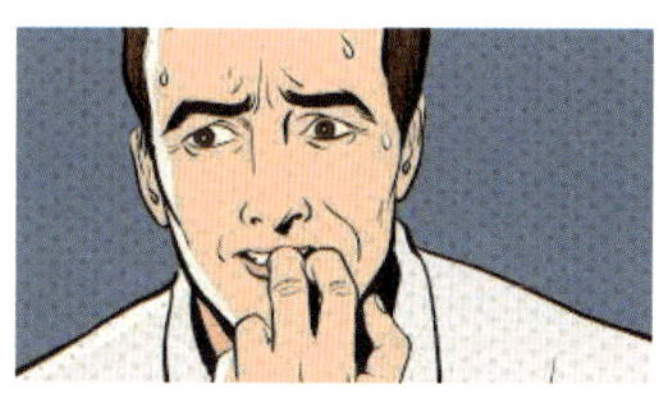
______

1061 □□□

murder
[ˈmɜːrdər]

n 살인 v 살인하다

= kill, assassinate, slay, homicide
+ murderer n 살인자 murderous a 살인적인

Q: Did the detective solve the murder case that happened a month ago? 그 형사가 한 달 전에 발생된 그 살인 사건을 해결했나요?

A: ....

1062 □□□

muscle
[ˈmʌsl]

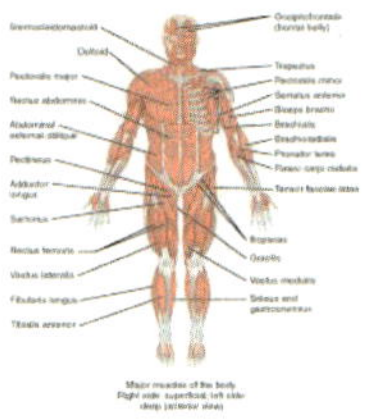

n 근육

= sinew, strength, power, brawn
+ muscular a 근육의

Q: How often do you exercise to build muscle strength?
근력을 키우기 위해 얼마나 자주 운동하나요?

A: ....

1063 □□□

mutual
[ˈmjuːtʃuəl]

a 상호간의, 공통의

= reciprocal, shared, joint, common, collaborative
+ mutually adv 상호간에

Q: Is there mutual respect between the team members?
팀원들 사이에 상호 존중이 있나요?

A: ....

1064 □□□

mysterious
[mɪˈstɪriəs]

a 신비로운, 불가사의한

= puzzling, enigmatic, secretive, obscure, strange
+ mystery n 미스터리 mysteriously adv 신비롭게

Q: What do you think caused that mysterious noise last night?
어젯밤 그 신비로운 소음은 무엇 때문이라고 생각하나요?

A: ....

1065 □□□

myth
[mɪθ]

n 신화, 근거 없는 믿음

= legend, fable, falsehood, folklore, fiction
+ mythical a 신화적인

Q: Have you heard the myth about the lost city underwater?
수중의 잃어버린 도시에 대한 신화를 들어본 적 있나요?

A: ....

1066 □□□

narrator
[nəˈreɪtər]

n 해설자, 내레이터

= storyteller, speaker, commentator, chronicler
\+ narrate **v** 이야기하다, 묘사하다 narration **n** 서술

Q: Did the narrator explain the story clearly in the documentary?
다큐멘터리에서 내레이터가 이야기를 명확하게 설명했나요?

A: ....

1067 □□□

narrow
[ˈnæroʊ]

a 좁은 **v** 좁아지다

= confined, tight, restricted, limited, constrict
\+ narrowness **n** 좁음 narrowly **adv** 간신히, 좁게

Q: Is the road to your house too narrow for big cars?
당신 집으로 가는 길이 큰 차가 다니기에는 너무 좁나요?

A: ....

1068 □□□

native
[ˈneɪtɪv]

a 토착의, 타고난 **n** 원주민

= indigenous, local, original, innate, natural
\+ native speaker (특정 언어를) 모국어로 하는 사람[모국어 사용자]

Q: Are you a native speaker of English or another language?
영어 원어민인가요 아니면 다른 언어 원어민인가요?

A: ....

1069 □□□

natural
[ˈnætʃərəl]

a 자연의, 타고난

= inherent, normal, organic, unadulterated, spontaneous
\+ nature **n** 자연 naturally **adv** 자연스럽게 unnatural **a** 부자연스러운

Q: Do you prefer natural remedies or pharmaceutical medicine?
천연 치료법과 의약품 중 어느 것을 선호하나요?

A: ....

1070 □□□

navigate
[ˈnævɪgeɪt]

v 항해하다, 길을 찾다

= steer, guide, direct, cruise, traverse
\+ navigation **n** 항해, 길 찾기 navigator **n** 항해사

Q: Can you navigate the city without using a GPS device?
GPS 장치 없이 도시를 돌아다닐 수 있나요?

A: ....

1071 □□□

navy
[ˈneɪvi]

n 해군

= fleet, marine, naval force

+ naval **a** 해군의

Q: Have you ever thought about joining the navy after school?
학교 졸업 후 해군에 입대하는 것을 생각해 본 적 있나요?

A: ……………………………………

1072 □□□

nearby
[ˈnɪrbaɪ]

a 근처의 **adv** 근처에

= close, adjacent, neighboring, proximity

+ nearby towns 가까운 도시

Q: Is there a good restaurant nearby that you would recommend?
근처에 추천해 줄 만한 좋은 식당이 있나요?

A: ……………………………………

1073 □□□

necessary
[ˈnesəseri]

a 필요한

= essential, vital, required, compulsory, inevitable

+ necessity **n** 필요성 **necessarily** **adv** 필연적으로

Q: Is it necessary to bring identification for the event?
행사에 신분증을 가져가는 것이 필요한가요?

A: ……………………………………

1074 □□□

necessity
[nəˈsesəti]

n 필요성, 필수품

= essential, requirement, need, prerequisite, imperative

+ necessary **a** 필요한

Q: How do you handle the necessity of waking up early every day? 매일 일찍 일어나야 하는 필요성을 어떻게 다루나요?

A: ……………………………………

1075 □□□

negative
[ˈnegətɪv]

a 부정적인, 음수의 **n** 부정적인 것

= adverse, unfavorable, pessimistic, harmful, minus

+ negativity **n** 부정성 **negatively** **adv** 부정적으로

Q: Did you receive any negative feedback from your boss today?
오늘 상사에게 부정적인 피드백을 받았나요?

A: ……………………………………

1076 □□□

neglect
[nɪˈglekt]

v 무시하다, 소홀히 하다 n 방치

= disregard, ignore, overlook, abandon, fail to care for
+ negligence n 태만, 부주의 negligent a 태만한

Q: Why do some people neglect their responsibilities so often?
왜 일부 사람들은 그렇게 자주 책임을 소홀히 하는 걸까요?

A: ....

1077 □□□

negotiate
[nɪˈgoʊʃieɪt]

v 협상하다

= bargain, mediate, discuss, arrange, settle
+ negotiation n 협상 negotiator n 협상가

Q: Are you willing to negotiate the price for this car?
이 차 가격을 협상할 의향이 있나요?

A: ....

1078 □□□

neighborhood
[ˈneɪbərˌhʊd]

n 이웃, 근처

= district, area, community, vicinity, locality
+ a neighborhood store 근처의 가게

Q: How safe is your neighborhood during late night hours?
늦은 밤 시간에 당신의 동네는 얼마나 안전한가요?

A: ....

1079 □□□

nerve
[nɜːrv]

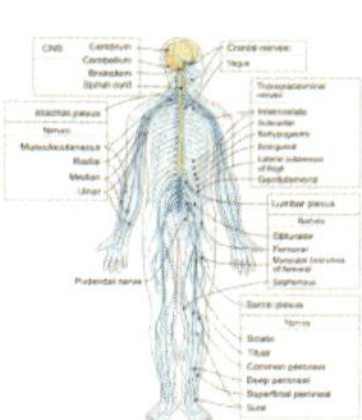

n 신경, 용기

= courage, bravery, boldness, apprehension, fiber
+ nervous a 초조한 nervy a 뻔뻔스러운

Q: Do you lose your nerve before giving the big presentation?
큰 발표를 하기 전에 용기를 잃나요?

A: ....

1080 □□□

nervous
[ˈnɜːrvəs]

a 초조한, 긴장한

= anxious, uneasy, tense, agitated, apprehensive
+ nerve n 신경 nervousness n 초조함 nervously adv 초조하게

Q: Do you get nervous before speaking in front of crowds?
군중 앞에서 말하기 전에 긴장하게 되나요?

A: ....

DAY 24 | DICTATION TEST

5회 반복 예문 QR

DICTATION TEST 예문 QR을 듣고 다음 빈칸에 올바른 단어를 쓰세요.

1061. Did the detective solve the ______________ case that happened a month ago?
1062. How often do you exercise to build ______________ strength?
1063. Is there ______________ respect between the team members?
1064. What do you think caused that ______________ noise last night?
1065. Have you heard the ______________ about the lost city underwater?
1066. Did the ______________ explain the story clearly in the documentary?
1067. Is the road to your house too ______________ for big cars?
1068. Are you a ______________ speaker of English or another language?
1069. Do you prefer ______________ remedies or pharmaceutical medicine?
1070. Can you ______________ the city without using a GPS device?
1071. Have you ever thought about joining the ______________ after school?
1072. Is there a good restaurant ______________ that you would recommend?
1073. Is it ______________ to bring identification for the event?
1074. How do you handle the ______________ of waking up early every day?
1075. Did you receive any ______________ feedback from your boss today?
1076. Why do some people ______________ their responsibilities so often?
1077. Are you willing to ______________ the price for this car?
1078. How safe is your ______________ during late night hours?
1079. Do you lose your ______________ before giving the big presentation?
1080. Do you get ______________ before speaking in front of crowds?

5회 반복 표제어 QR 5회 반복 예문 QR

DAY 25

30 days

AI 학습자료와 인강 youpass.co.kr

PREVIEW A 다음 단어의 뜻을 한국어로 써보세요.

□ **nest** ______	□ **northern** ______
□ **net** ______	□ **notice** ______
□ **neuron** ______	□ **novel** ______
□ **neutral** ______	□ **nowadays** ______
□ **nevertheless** ______	□ **nuclear** ______
□ **newborn** ______	□ **numerous** ______
□ **noble** ______	□ **nutrient** ______
□ **norm** ______	□ **obey** ______
□ **normal** ______	□ **object** ______
□ **normally** ______	□ **objective** ______

PREVIEW B 사진을 보고 알맞은 영어 단어를 PREVIEW A에서 찾아 써보세요.

______

______

______

______

1081 □□□

nest
[nest]

n 둥지, 보금자리 v 둥지를 틀다

= den, lair, abode, build a nest, settle
+ a nest of thieves 도둑들의 소굴

Q: Did you see the bird building its nest in the tree?
나무에 새가 둥지를 짓는 것을 보았나요?

A:

1082 □□□

net
[net]

n 그물, 망, 순이익 a 순수한

= mesh, web, trap, final, actual, capture
+ fishnet n 어망, 그물 모양 직물

Q: How much net profit did the company make last year?
작년에 그 회사는 얼마의 순이익을 냈나요?

A:

1083 □□□

neuron
[ˈnʊrɑːn] [ˈnjʊrɑːn]

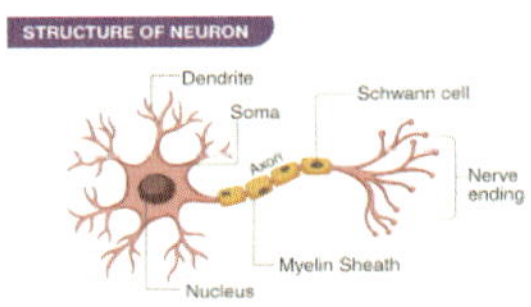

n 뉴런, 신경세포

= nerve cell, brain cell
+ neural a 신경의

Q: Can you explain how a neuron sends signals in the brain?
뉴런이 뇌에서 어떻게 신호를 보내는지 설명해 줄 수 있나요?

A:

1084 □□□

neutral
[ˈnuːtrəl] [ˈnjuːtrəl]

a 중립적인

= impartial, unbiased, objective, unaligned, indifferent
+ neutrality n 중립성 neutralize v 중화하다, 무효화하다 neutrally adv 중립적으로

Q: Are you remaining neutral in the argument between friends?
친구들 간의 논쟁에서 중립을 지키고 있는 건가요?

A:

1085 □□□

nevertheless
[ˌnevərðəˈles]

adv 그럼에도 불구하고

= however, nonetheless, still, even so
+ a small but nevertheless important change 사소하지만 그럼에도 불구하고 중요한 변화

Q: Nevertheless, do you think the plan will work eventually?
그럼에도 불구하고, 그 계획이 결국 성공할 것이라고 생각하나요?

A:

1086 □□□

newborn
[ˈnuːbɔːrn] [ˈnjuːbɔːrn]

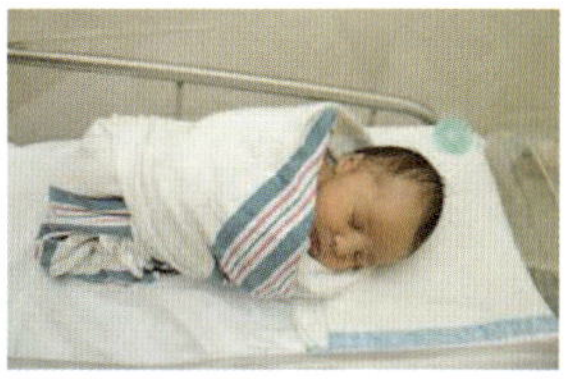

a 갓 태어난 n 신생아

= infant, baby, recently born
+ a newborn baby 갓난아기

Q: Have you visited your friend's newborn baby at the hospital?
병원에 있는 친구의 갓 태어난 아기를 방문해 본적 있나요?

A: ....

1087 □□□

noble
[ˈnoʊbl]

a 고귀한, 숭고한 n 귀족

= honorable, aristocratic, dignified, grand, high-minded
+ nobility n 고귀함, 귀족 nobly adv 고귀하게

Q: Do you think helping others is a noble act nowadays?
요즘에도 다른 사람들을 돕는 것이 고귀한 행동이라고 생각하나요?

A: ....

1088 □□□

norm
[nɔːrm]

n 규범, 기준

= standard, rule, average, typical, benchmark
+ normality n 정상 normal a 정상적인

Q: Is working from home becoming the new norm everywhere now? 재택근무가 이제 어디서나 새로운 표준이 되고 있나요?

A: ....

1089 □□□

normal
[ˈnɔːrml]

a 정상적인, 보통의

= regular, ordinary, common, standard, typical
+ normality n 정상 normally adv 정상적으로, 보통 abnormal a 비정상적인

Q: Is it normal to feel nervous before a big interview?
큰 면접 전에 긴장하는 것이 정상인가요?

A: ....

1090 □□□

normally
[ˈnɔːrməli]

adv 보통, 일반적으로

= usually, typically, ordinarily, generally
+ normal a 정상적인

Q: Do you normally have breakfast before leaving the house?
보통 집을 나서기 전에 아침 식사를 하나요?

A: ....

1091 □□□

northern
[ˈnɔːrðərn]

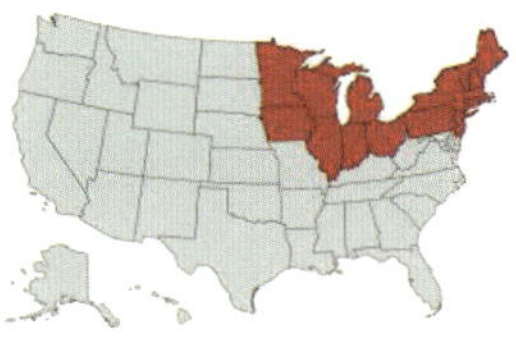

a 북쪽의

= northerly, boreal, arctic
+ north **n** 북쪽

Q: Have you ever traveled to the northern part of the country?
그 나라의 북부 지역으로 여행해 본 적 있나요?

A: ....

1092 □□□

notice
[ˈnoʊtɪs]

n 통지, 주목 **v** 알아차리다

= observe, see, perceive, announcement, attention
+ noticeable **a** 눈에 띄는 noticeably **adv** 눈에 띄게

Q: Did you notice the changes in the schedule this morning?
오늘 아침 일정 변경을 알아차렸나요?

A: ....

1093 □□□

novel
[ˈnɑːvl]

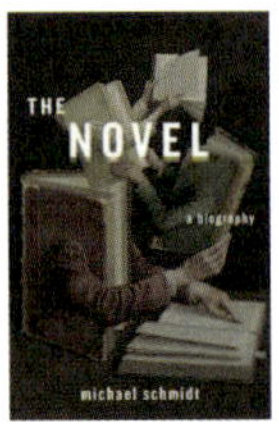

n 소설 **a** 새로운

= new, unique, original, fresh, book, fiction
+ novelty **n** 참신함, 신기함

Q: Are you reading a novel for your English class this semester?
이번 학기에 영어 수업을 위해 소설을 읽고 있나요?

A: ....

1094 □□□

nowadays
[ˈnaʊədeɪz]

adv 요즘에는

= currently, today, presently, in these times
+ the youth of nowadays 요즘의 청년들

Q: Do you think people communicate less nowadays than before?
요즘 사람들이 예전보다 덜 소통한다고 생각하나요?

A: ....

1095 □□□

nuclear
[ˈnuːkliər] [ˈnjuːkliər]

a 핵의, 원자력의

= atomic, core, central, relating to nucleus
+ nucleus **n** 핵

Q: In your opinion, are nuclear power plants safe to operate?
당신의 의견으로는 원자력 발전소가 운영하기에 안전한가요?

A: ....

1096 □□□

numerous
[ˈnuːmərəs] [ˈnjuːmərəs]

a 수많은

= many, abundant, plentiful, countless
+ number n 숫자 numeration n 계산

Q: Have you faced numerous challenges in your recent project?
최근 프로젝트에서 수많은 어려움에 직면하고 있나요?

A: ....

1097 □□□

nutrient
[ˈnuːtriənt] [ˈnjuːtriənt]

n 영양소

= nourishment, sustenance, food element
+ nutrition n 영양 nutritious a 영양가 있는

Q: Which nutrient is most important for a balanced diet?
균형 잡힌 식단에서 가장 중요한 영양소는 무엇인가요?

A: ....

1098 □□□

obey
[oʊˈbeɪ]

v 복종하다, 따르다

= comply, conform, follow, adhere to
+ obedience n 복종 obedient a 복종하는

Q: Do children always obey their parents without question?
아이들이 항상 부모님께 무조건 복종하나요?

A: ....

1099 □□□

object
[ˈɑːbdʒekt] n [əbˈdʒekt] v

n 물체, 목적, 대상 v 반대하다

= item, thing, purpose, aim, protest, disagree
+ objection n 반대 objective a 객관적인

Q: Did you find the object you lost in the living room?
거실에서 잃어버린 물건을 찾았나요?

A: ....

1100 □□□

objective
[əbˈdʒektɪv]

n 목표 a 객관적인

= goal, aim, purpose, impartial, unbiased, factual
+ objectivity n 객관성 objectively adv 객관적으로

Q: What is the main objective of your marketing strategy?
당신의 마케팅 전략의 주요 목표는 무엇인가요?

A: ....

DAY 25 | DICTATION TEST

5회 반복 예문 QR

DICTATION TEST 예문 QR을 듣고 다음 빈칸에 올바른 단어를 쓰세요.

1081. Did you see the bird building its ______________ in the tree?

1082. How much ______________ profit did the company make last year?

1083. Can you explain how a ______________ sends signals in the brain?

1084. Are you remaining ______________ in the argument between friends?

1085. ______________, do you think the plan will work eventually?

1086. Have you visited your friend's ______________ baby at the hospital?

1087. Do you think helping others is a ______________ act nowadays?

1088. Is working from home becoming the new ______________ everywhere now?

1089. Is it ______________ to feel nervous before a big interview?

1090. Do you ______________ have breakfast before leaving the house?

1091. Have you ever traveled to the ______________ part of the country?

1092. Did you ______________ the changes in the schedule this morning?

1093. Are you reading a ______________ for your English class this semester?

1094. Do you think people communicate less ______________ than before?

1095. In your opinion, are ______________ power plants safe to operate?

1096. Have you faced ______________ challenges in your recent project?

1097. Which ______________ is most important for a balanced diet?

1098. Do children always ______________ their parents without question?

1099. Did you find the ______________ you lost in the living room?

1100. What is the main ______________ of your marketing strategy?

5회 반복 표제어 QR　5회 반복 예문 QR

DAY 26
30 days

AI 학습자료와 인강 youpass.co.kr

PREVIEW A 다음 단어의 뜻을 한국어로 써보세요.

□ observe ________	□ offer ________
□ obstacle ________	□ official ________
□ obtain ________	□ omit ________
□ obvious ________	□ operate ________
□ occasion ________	□ operation ________
□ occupation ________	□ operator ________
□ occupy ________	□ opinion ________
□ occur ________	□ opponent ________
□ odd ________	□ opportunity ________
□ offend ________	□ oppose ________

PREVIEW B 사진을 보고 알맞은 영어 단어를 **PREVIEW A** 에서 찾아 써보세요.

____

____

____

____

1101 □□□

observe
[əbˈzɜːrv]

v 관찰하다, 준수하다

= **watch, notice, perceive, monitor, follow, remark**

+ **observation** **n** 관찰 **observer** **n** 관찰자 **observant** **a** 관찰력 있는

Q: Did you observe any changes during the experiment?

실험하는 동안 어떤 변화라도 관찰했나요?

A: ....

1102 □□□

obstacle
[ˈɑːbstəkl]

n 장애물

= **barrier, hindrance, impediment, hurdle, obstruction**

+ **obstacle course** (경기·훈련용) 장애물 코스

Q: What was the biggest obstacle you faced during the project?

프로젝트를 진행하면서 직면했던 가장 큰 장애물은 무엇이었나요?

A: ....

1103 □□□

obtain
[əbˈteɪn]

v 얻다, 획득하다

= **get, acquire, procure, gain, achieve**

+ **obtainable** **a** 얻을 수 있는

Q: How quickly can I obtain a copy of the official report?

공식 보고서 사본을 어떻게 빨리 구할 수 있나요?

A: ....

1104 □□□

obvious
[ˈɑːbviəs]

a 명백한, 분명한

= **clear, evident, apparent, plain, manifest**

+ **obviousness** **n** 명백함 **obviously** **adv** 분명히

Q: In this situation, is it obvious who made the mistake?

이 상황에서 누가 실수를 했는지 명백한가요?

A: ....

1105 □□□

occasion
[əˈkeɪʒn]

n 경우, 때, 특별한 행사

= **event, instance, opportunity, moment, reason**

+ **occasional** **a** 가끔의 **occasionally** **adv** 가끔

Q: What occasion are you planning to celebrate next month?

다음 달에 어떤 행사를 기념할 계획인가요?

A: ....

1106 ☐☐☐

occupation
[ˌɑːkjuˈpeɪʃn]

n 직업, 점령

= **profession, job, vocation, taking control, possession**

+ **occupy** **v** 점령하다, 차지하다 **occupant** **n** 점유자 **occupational** **a** 직업의

Q: What occupation do you think suits your skills best?
어떤 직업이 당신의 기술과 가장 잘 맞을 것 같다고 생각하나요?

A: ....

1107 ☐☐☐

occupy
[ˈɑːkjupaɪ]

v 차지하다, 점령하다

= **inhabit, possess, take up, engage, absorb**

+ **occupation** **n** 점유, 직업 **occupant** **n** 점유자

Q: Does this new project require us to occupy the entire third floor of the building? 이 새로운 프로젝트 때문에 우리가 건물 3층 전체를 차지해야 하나요?

A: ....

1108 ☐☐☐

occur
[əˈkɜːr]

v 발생하다, 일어나다

= **happen, take place, arise, transpire, come to mind**

+ **occurrence** **n** 발생, 사건

Q: Did the problem occur before or after the software update?
문제가 소프트웨어 업데이트 전 또는 후에 발생했나요?

A: ....

1109 ☐☐☐

odd
[ɑːd]

a 이상한, 홀수의

= **strange, unusual, peculiar, eccentric, uneven**

+ **oddity** **n** 특이함, 기묘함 **oddly** **adv** 이상하게

Q: Isn't it odd that he didn't show up for the meeting today?
오늘 그가 회의에 나타나지 않은 것이 이상하지 않나요?

A: ....

1110 ☐☐☐

offend
[əˈfend]

v 기분을 상하게 하다, 범죄를 저지르다

= **insult, upset, affront, annoy, violate**

+ **offense[offence]** **n** 위반, 범죄 **offender** **n** 범죄자 **offensive** **a** 모욕적인, 공격적인

Q: Did you offend anyone with your comment unintentionally?
의도치 않게 당신의 발언으로 누군가를 불쾌하게 했었나요?

A: ....

1111 □□□

offer
[ˈɔːfər]

v 제안하다, 제공하다 **n** 제안

= **propose, present, provide, tender, suggestion**
+ **special offer** 특가품, 특가 판매

Q: Can you offer any advice for improving my presentation?
제 발표를 개선하는 데 도움이 될 만한 조언을 해줄 수 있나요?

A: ....

1112 □□□

official
[əˈfɪʃl]

a 공식적인 **n** 공무원, 임원

= **authorized, formal, legitimate, public servant, executive**
+ **officially** **adv** 공식적으로

Q: When will the official results of the election be announced?
선거의 공식 결과는 언제 발표될 예정인가요?

A: ....

1113 □□□

omit
[oʊˈmɪt]

v 생략하다, 빠뜨리다

= **exclude, leave out, neglect, forget, miss**
+ **omission** **n** 생략, 누락

Q: Did you omit any important details from your report yesterday?
어제 보고서에서 중요한 세부 사항을 누락했었나요?

A: ....

1114 □□□

operate
[ˈɑːpəreɪt]

v 작동하다, 수술하다

= **function, work, manage, perform surgery, control**
+ **operation** **n** 작동, 수술 **operator** **n** 조작자, 운전자 **operational** **a** 작동 가능한

Q: Can you operate this machine without any prior training?
사전 교육 없이 이 기계를 작동할 수 있나요?

A: ....

1115 □□□

operation
[ˌɑːpəˈreɪʃn]

n 작전, 수술, 운영

= **process, procedure, surgery, mission, action**
+ **operate** **v** 작동하다, 수술하다 **operator** **n** 조작자

Q: How long will the operation to fix the system take?
시스템을 고치는 데 드는 작업은 얼마나 걸릴까요?

A: ....

1116 □□□

operator
[ˈɑːpəreɪtər]

n 운영자, (기계) 조작원

= **driver, manager, technician, controller**
+ **operate** **v** 조작하다

Q: Is the operator available to answer questions about the device? 장치에 대한 질문에 답변해 줄 운영 담당자가 있나요?

A: ....

1117 □□□

opinion
[əˈpɪnjən]

n 의견

= **view, belief, judgment, sentiment, stance**
+ **public opinion** 여론

Q: What is your honest opinion about the new policy changes?
새로운 정책 변경에 대한 당신의 솔직한 의견은 무엇인가요?

A: ....

1118 □□□

opponent
[əˈpoʊnənt]

n 반대자, 상대방

= **rival, adversary, competitor, foe**
+ **oppose** **v** 반대하다

Q: Did your opponent prepare well for the upcoming match?
상대방이 다가오는 경기에 잘 준비했었나요?

A: ....

1119 □□□

opportunity
[ˌɑːpərˈtuːnəti]

n 기회

= **chance, possibility, opening, occasion**
+ **equality of opportunity** 기회 균등

Q: Are you planning to take this opportunity to study abroad?
이 기회를 잡고 유학을 갈 계획인가요?

A: ....

1120 □□□

oppose
[əˈpoʊz]

v 반대하다

= **resist, object to, combat, defy, contradict**
+ **opposition** **n** 반대 **opposing** **a** 반대하는 **opposite** **a** 반대의

Q: Do you oppose the new regulations proposed by the government?
정부가 제안한 새 규제에 반대하나요?

A: ....

DAY 26 | DICTATION TEST

5회 반복 예문 QR

DICTATION TEST 예문 QR을 듣고 다음 빈칸에 올바른 단어를 쓰세요.

1101. Did you ______________ any changes during the experiment?

1102. What was the biggest ______________ you faced during the project?

1103. How quickly can I ______________ a copy of the official report?

1104. In this situation, is it ______________ who made the mistake?

1105. What ______________ are you planning to celebrate next month?

1106. What ______________ do you think suits your skills best?

1107. Does this new project require us to ______________ the entire third floor of the building?

1108. Did the problem ______________ before or after the software update?

1109. Isn't it ______________ that he didn't show up for the meeting today?

1110. Did you ______________ anyone with your comment unintentionally?

1111. Can you ______________ any advice for improving my presentation?

1112. When will the ______________ results of the election be announced?

1113. Did you ______________ any important details from your report yesterday?

1114. Can you ______________ this machine without any prior training?

1115. How long will the ______________ to fix the system take?

1116. Is the ______________ available to answer questions about the device?

1117. What is your honest ______________ about the new policy changes?

1118. Did your ______________ prepare well for the upcoming match?

1119. Are you planning to take this ______________ to study abroad?

1120. Do you ______________ the new regulations proposed by the government?

5회 반복 표제어 QR   5회 반복 예문 QR

DAY 27
30 days

AI 학습자료와 인강 youpass.co.kr

PREVIEW A 다음 단어의 뜻을 한국어로 써보세요.

□ opposite ______	□ origin ______
□ optimist ______	□ original ______
□ option ______	□ originate ______
□ order ______	□ otherwise ______
□ ordinary ______	□ outcome ______
□ organ ______	□ outline ______
□ organic ______	□ output ______
□ organization ______	□ outstanding ______
□ organize ______	□ overall ______
□ orient ______	□ overcome ______

PREVIEW B 사진을 보고 알맞은 영어 단어를 **PREVIEW A** 에서 찾아 써보세요.

______

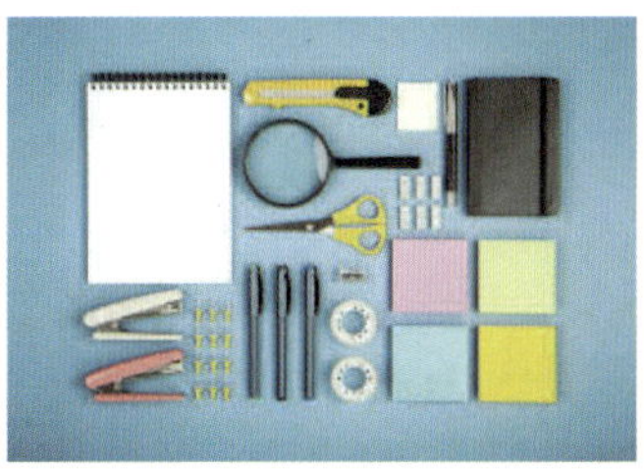
______

______

______

1121 □□□

opposite
[ˈɑːpəzɪt]

a 반대의 n 반대편

= contrary, contrasting, reverse, facing, antagonist
+ opposition n 반대

Q: Do you think our political views are completely opposite, or is there some common ground? 우리의 정치적 견해가 완전히 반대라고 생각하시나요, 아니면 공통점을 찾을 수 있을까요?

A:

1122 □□□

optimist
[ˈɑːptɪmɪst]

n 낙천주의자

= positive thinker, idealist, hopeful person
+ optimism n 낙관주의 optimistic a 낙관적인 optimistically adv 낙관적으로

Q: Are you naturally an optimist when facing tough challenges? 힘든 난관에 직면했을 때에도 천성적으로 낙천적인가요?

A:

1123 □□□

option
[ˈɑːpʃn]

n 선택(권)

= choice, alternative, selection, possibility
+ optional a 선택적인 optionally adv 선택적으로

Q: Do you have any other option besides taking this job offer? 이 직업 제안을 받아들이는 것 외에 다른 선택지가 있나요?

A:

1124 □□□

order
[ˈɔːrdər]

n 순서, 주문, 명령 v 주문하다, 명령하다

= command, sequence, arrangement, stability, request, arrange
+ orderly a 정돈된

Q: Did you place the order for the new equipment last week? 지난주에 새 장비 주문했나요?

A:

1125 □□□

ordinary
[ˈɔːrdəneri]

a 평범한, 보통의

= common, usual, normal, regular, average
+ ordinariness n 평범함 ordinarily adv 보통, 일반적으로 extraordinary a 비범한

Q: Is today just an ordinary day or something special for you? 오늘은 당신에게 그저 평범한 날인가요 아니면 특별한 날인가요?

A:

1126 □□□

organ
[ˈɔːrgən]

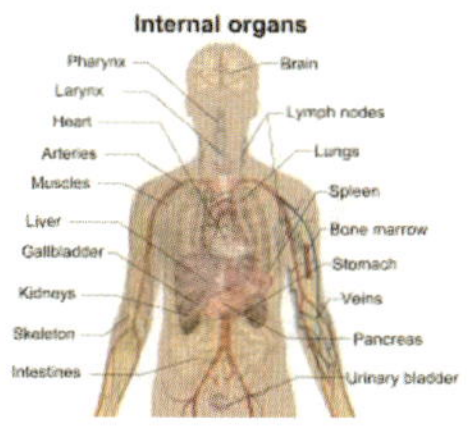

n 기관, 장기, 오르간

= part, instrument, body part, apparatus
+ organic **a** 유기적인

Q: Can you name the organ responsible for pumping blood?
혈액 펌프질을 담당하는 기관 이름을 말할 수 있나요?

A: ……………………………………

1127 □□□

organic
[ɔːrˈgænɪk]

a 유기농의, 유기체의

= natural, biological, chemical-free, fundamental
+ organism **n** 유기체 **organically** **adv** 유기적으로

Q: Do you usually prefer buying organic fruits over regular ones?
보통 유기농 과일을 일반 과일보다 선호하나요?

A: ……………………………………

1128 □□□

organization
[ˌɔːrgənɪˈzeɪʃn]

n 조직, 단체

= structure, institution, group, arrangement
+ organize **v** 조직하다 **organizer** **n** 조직자 **organized** **a** 조직된

Q: Is your organization planning any events for this coming month? 당신의 조직은 이번 달에 어떤 행사를 계획하고 있나요?

A: ……………………………………

1129 □□□

organize
[ˈɔːrgənaɪz]

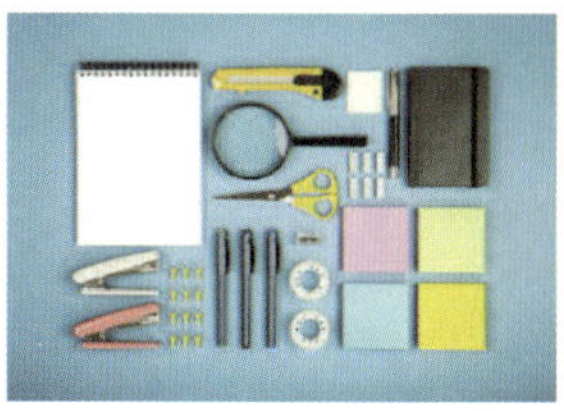

v 조직하다, 정리하다

= arrange, categorize, systematize, plan, coordinate
+ organization **n** 조직 **organized** **a** 조직된

Q: How do you organize your work schedule during busy periods?
바쁜 시기에 업무 일정을 어떻게 정리하나요?

A: ……………………………………

1130 □□□

orient
[ˈɔːriənt]

v ~의 방향을 정하다, 적응시키다

= direct, align, guide, adapt, familiarize
+ orientation **n** 방향, 지향 **oriented** **a** ~을 지향하는

Q: Does this map orient us toward the nearest hiking trail?
이 지도가 우리를 가장 가까운 등산로 방향으로 안내해 줄까요?

A: ……………………………………

1131 □□□

origin
[ˈɔːrɪdʒɪn]

n 기원, 근원

= source, beginning, root, genesis, derivation
+ originate **v** 시작되다, 유래하다 original **a** 원래의, 독창적인

Q: Do you know the origin of this traditional dish from your country? 당신 나라의 이 전통 요리 기원을 아나요?

A: ....

1132 □□□

original
[əˈrɪdʒənl]

a 원래의, 독창적인 **n** 원본

= initial, authentic, creative, novel, unique
+ origin **n** 기원 originality **n** 독창성 originally **adv** 원래는

Q: Is this the original version of the software you purchased?
이것이 당신이 구입한 소프트웨어의 원본 버전인가요?

A: ....

1133 □□□

originate
[əˈrɪdʒɪneɪt]

v 비롯되다, 시작하다

= begin, start, stem from, create, devise
+ origin **n** 기원

Q: Where does jazz music originate from historically speaking?
역사적으로 말하자면 재즈 음악은 어디에서 유래했나요?

A: ....

1134 □□□

otherwise
[ˈʌðərwaɪz]

adv 그렇지 않으면, 다른 방법으로

= else, differently, in other respects, if not
+ unless otherwise noted[mentioned] 달리 언급이 없으면

Q: Study hard for the exam. Otherwise, you might really regret it. Got it? 시험공부 열심히 해. 그렇지 않으면 정말 후회할 거야. 알겠지?

A: ....

1135 □□□

outcome
[ˈaʊtkʌm]

n 결과

= result, consequence, effect, aftermath, conclusion
+ achieve the desired outcome 소기의 성과를 거두다

Q: What was the final outcome of your business negotiation?
사업 협상의 최종 결과는 무엇이었나요?

A: ....

1136 □□□

outline
[ˈaʊtlaɪn]

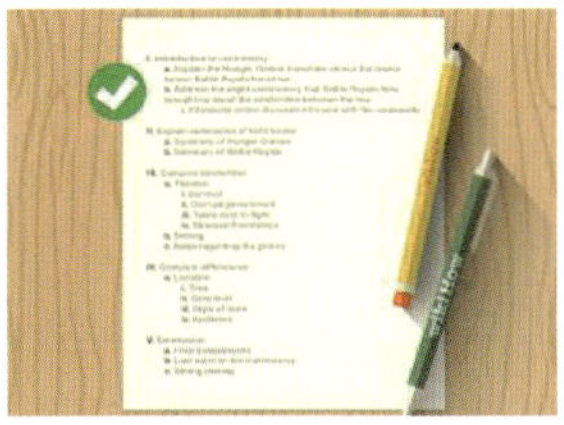

n 개요, 윤곽 **v** 개요를 설명하다

= summary, sketch, framework, draft, delineate

+ a sharp outline 선명한[뚜렷한] 윤곽 **the broad outline of a proposal** 제안 내용의 전반적인 개요

Q: Can you provide an outline of the main points for the meeting?
회의 주요 요점에 대한 개요를 제공해 줄 수 있나요?

A: ....

1137 □□□

output
[ˈaʊtpʊt]

n 생산량, 출력

= production, yield, result, product, data

+ data output 데이터 출력 **an output device** 출력 장치

Q: Is the output from this machine meeting your quality standards?
이 기계의 생산물이 당신의 품질 기준을 충족하나요?

A: ....

1138 □□□

outstanding
[aʊtˈstændɪŋ]

a 뛰어난, 미결제의

= excellent, superb, remarkable, unpaid, prominent

+ outstandingness n 뛰어남 **outstandingly adv** 뛰어나게

Q: Do you have any outstanding tasks to complete before Friday?
금요일 전에 완료해야 할 미완료 작업이 있나요?

A: ....

1139 □□□

overall
[ˌoʊvərˈɔːl]

a 전반적인 **adv** 전반적으로 **n** 멜빵바지

= general, comprehensive, total, encompassing, entirely

+ overall responsibility 전반적인 책임

Q: What is your overall impression of the new restaurant?
새 레스토랑에 대한 당신의 전반적인 인상은 어떤가요?

A: ....

1140 □□□

overcome
[ˌoʊvərˈkʌm]

v 극복하다

= conquer, defeat, surmount, get over, prevail

+ overcomer n 극복하는 사람

Q: How did you overcome the difficulties in your last project?
지난 프로젝트에서 어려움을 어떻게 극복했나요?

A: ....

DAY 27 | DICTATION TEST

5회 반복 예문 QR

DICTATION TEST 예문 QR을 듣고 다음 빈칸에 올바른 단어를 쓰세요.

1121. Do you think our political views are completely ________________, or is there some common ground?
1122. Are you naturally an ________________ when facing tough challenges?
1123. Do you have any other ________________ besides taking this job offer?
1124. Did you place the ________________ for the new equipment last week?
1125. Is today just an ________________ day or something special for you?
1126. Can you name the ________________ responsible for pumping blood?
1127. Do you usually prefer buying ________________ fruits over regular ones?
1128. Is your ________________ planning any events for this coming month?
1129. How do you ________________ your work schedule during busy periods?
1130. Does this map ________________ us toward the nearest hiking trail?
1131. Do you know the ________________ of this traditional dish from your country?
1132. Is this the ________________ version of the software you purchased?
1133. Where does jazz music ________________ from historically speaking?
1134. Study hard for the exam. ________________, you might really regret it. Got it?
1135. What was the final ________________ of your business negotiation?
1136. Can you provide an ________________ of the main points for the meeting?
1137. Is the ________________ from this machine meeting your quality standards?
1138. Do you have any ________________ tasks to complete before Friday?
1139. What is your ________________ impression of the new restaurant?
1140. How did you ________________ the difficulties in your last project?

5회 반복 표제어 QR 5회 반복 예문 QR

DAY 28

30 days

AI 학습자료와 인강 youpass.co.kr

PREVIEW A 다음 단어의 뜻을 한국어로 써보세요.

- □ overlap ____________
- □ overlook ____________
- □ overseas ____________
- □ overwhelm ____________
- □ owe ____________
- □ oxygen ____________
- □ pale ____________
- □ panic ____________
- □ parade ____________
- □ paragraph ____________
- □ parallel ____________
- □ paralyze ____________
- □ pardon ____________
- □ participate ____________
- □ particle ____________
- □ particular ____________
- □ partner ____________
- □ passage ____________
- □ passenger ____________
- □ passion ____________

PREVIEW B 사진을 보고 알맞은 영어 단어를 PREVIEW A 에서 찾아 써보세요.

____

____

____

____

1141 □□□

overlap
[ˌoʊvər'læp]

v 겹치다, 중복되다 **n** 중복

= extend over, coincide, superimpose, intersection

+ overlap area 겹친 면적 **overlap test** 중첩 시험

Q: Do your work hours often overlap with your colleagues' schedules? 당신의 근무 시간이 동료들의 일정과 자주 겹치나요?

A: ......

1142 □□□

overlook
[ˌoʊvər'lʊk]

v 간과하다, 내려다보다

= miss, ignore, disregard, supervise, pardon

+ overlook a person's mistake 남의 실수를 눈감아 주다

Q: Did you overlook any important details in the project proposal?
프로젝트 제안서에서 중요한 세부 사항을 놓쳤나요?

A: ......

1143 □□□

overseas
[ˌoʊvər'siːz]

adv 해외로 **a** 해외의

= abroad, foreign, international, across the sea

+ overseas development[markets/trade] 해외 개발[시장/무역]

Q: Have you ever worked overseas or studied in a foreign country? 해외에서 일하거나 외국에서 공부해 본 적 있나요?

A: ......

1144 □□□

overwhelm
[ˌoʊvər'welm]

v 압도하다

= overpower, inundate, engulf, devastate, dismay

+ overwhelming a 압도적인 **overwhelmed a** 압도된

Q: Do you ever feel overwhelmed when too many tasks pile up?
너무 많은 업무가 쌓일 때 압도당한다고 느끼나요?

A: ......

1145 □□□

owe
[oʊ]

v 빚지다, ~의 덕분이다

= be indebted, be obligated, be due

= owing a 빚지고 있는 **owing to ~** 때문에

Q: Do you owe anyone money from your recent business deals?
최근 사업 거래에서 누구에게 빚진 돈이 있나요?

A: ......

1146 □□□

oxygen
[ˈɑːksɪdʒən]

n 산소

= air, life gas, essential element
+ oxygen mask 산소마스크

Q: How much oxygen do we normally need to survive each day?
우리가 정상적으로 매일 생존하는 데 얼마나 많은 산소가 필요한가요?

A: ....

1147 □□□

pale
[peɪl]

a 창백한, 옅은

= light, faint, dim, pallid, colorless, blanch
+ paleness **n** 창백함

Q: Did his face turn pale when he heard the bad news?
그가 나쁜 소식을 들었을 때 얼굴이 창백해졌나요?

A: ....

1148 □□□

panic
[ˈpænɪk]

n 공황 **v** 공황 상태에 빠지다

= alarm, fright, terror, anxiety, sudden fear
+ panicky **a** 공황 상태의

Q: Did you panic when you missed your flight this morning?
오늘 아침 비행기를 놓쳤을 때 당황했나요?

A: ....

1149 □□□

parade
[pəˈreɪd]

n 행진, 퍼레이드 **v** 행진하다

= procession, march, display, show off
+ parade ground 연병장

Q: Are you planning to watch the parade downtown this weekend?
이번 주말에 시내에서 퍼레이드를 볼 계획인가요?

A: ....

1150 □□□

paragraph
[ˈpærəgræf]

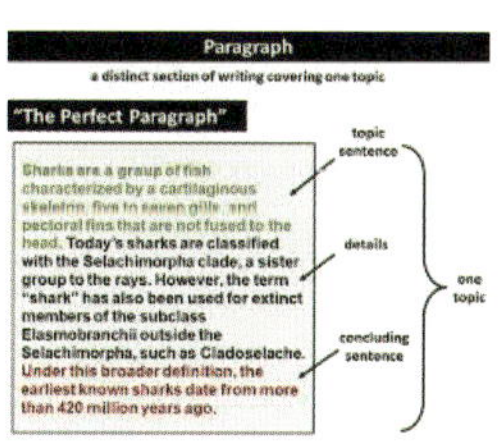

n 단락

= section, passage, clause, segment of text
+ an editorial paragraph 짧은 사설(社說)

Q: Can you write a paragraph explaining your opinion clearly?
당신의 의견을 명확하게 설명하는 한 단락을 쓸 수 있나요?

A: ....

1151 □□□

parallel
[ˈpærəlel]

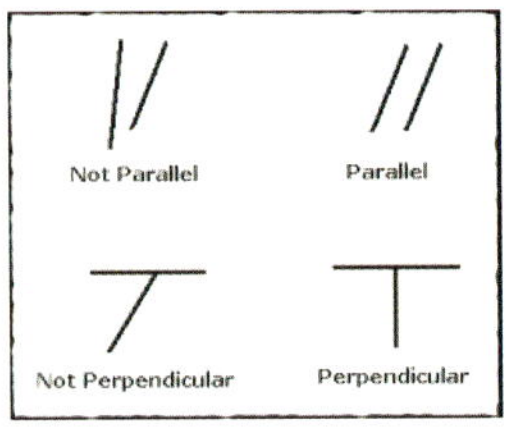

a 평행한, 유사한 n 평행선, 유사점

= analogous, equivalent, corresponding, concurrent, line
+ **parallelly** adv 평행하게, ~와 동시에

Q: Are the two roads running parallel to each other?
두 도로가 서로 평행하게 나 있나요?

A:

1152 □□□

paralyze
[ˈpærəlaɪz]

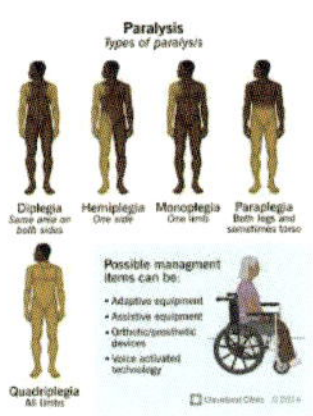

v 마비시키다

= disable, immobilize, cripple, freeze, stun
+ **paralysis** n 마비 **paralyzed** a 마비된

Q: Can a fear of failure paralyze your ability to try new things?
실패에 대한 두려움이 새로운 것을 시도하는 당신의 능력을 마비시키기도 하나요?

A:

1153 □□□

pardon
[ˈpɑːrdn]

n 용서 v 용서하다

= forgive, excuse, condone, absolution, forgiveness
+ **pardonable** a 용서할 수 있는

Q: Could you pardon me for interrupting your important conversation? 중요한 대화에 방해해서 용서해 주시겠어요?

A:

1154 □□□

participate
[pɑːrˈtɪsɪpeɪt]

v 참여하다

= join, take part, engage, involve
+ **participation** n 참여 **participant** n 참가자 **participating** a 참여하는

Q: Will you participate in the company's charity event next week?
다음 주에 회사 자선 행사에 참여할 건가요?

A:

1155 □□□

particle
[ˈpɑːrtɪkl]

n 입자, 미립자

= fragment, speck, molecule, atom, bit
+ **particulate** a 입자의

Q: Did the scientist detect any particle movement during the test? 과학자가 테스트 중에 어떤 입자 움직임이라도 감지했나요?

A:

1156 □□□

particular
[pər'tɪkjələr]

a 특정한, 까다로운

= **specific, distinct, precise, individual, detailed**
+ **particularity** **n** 특이성 **particularly** **adv** 특히

Q: Is there a particular reason you chose that restaurant tonight?
오늘 밤 그 레스토랑을 선택한 특별한 이유가 있나요?

A: ....

1157 □□□

partner
['pɑːrtnər]

n 파트너, 동반자

= **associate, collaborator, colleague, spouse, join**
+ **partnership** **n** 협력, 동반자 관계

Q: Have you introduced your partner to your family?
가족에게 당신의 파트너를 소개했나요?

A: ....

1158 □□□

passage
['pæsɪdʒ]

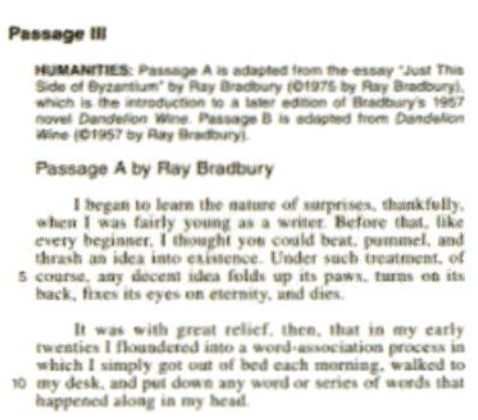
Passage III

HUMANITIES: Passage A is adapted from the essay "Just This Side of Byzantium" by Ray Bradbury (©1975 by Ray Bradbury), which is the introduction to a later edition of Bradbury's 1957 novel *Dandelion Wine*. Passage B is adapted from *Dandelion Wine* (©1957 by Ray Bradbury).

Passage A by Ray Bradbury

I began to learn the nature of surprises, thankfully, when I was fairly young as a writer. Before that, like every beginner, I thought you could beat, pummel, and thrash an idea into existence. Under such treatment, of course, any decent idea folds up its paws, turns on its back, fixes its eyes on eternity, and dies.

It was with great relief, then, that in my early twenties I floundered into a word-association process in which I simply got out of bed each morning, walked to my desk, and put down any word or series of words that happened along in my head.

n 통로, 구절, 통과

= **corridor, path, extract, journey, transition**
+ **pass** **v** 지나가다

Q: Can you find the passage in the book about ancient history?
고대 역사에 대한 책에서 그 구절을 찾을 수 있나요?

A: ....

1159 □□□

passenger
['pæsɪndʒər]

n 승객

= **traveler, commuter, rider, fare payer**
+ **passenger seat** (자동차의) 조수석 **front-seat passenger** 앞좌석 승객

Q: Did the passengers complain about the flight delay?
승객들이 비행 지연에 대해 불평했나요?

A: ....

1160 □□□

passion
['pæʃn]

n 열정

= **strong emotion, fervor, zeal, enthusiasm, obsession**
+ **passionate** **a** 열정적인 **passionately** **adv** 열정적으로

Q: What is your biggest passion outside of your regular work?
정규 업무 외에 당신의 가장 큰 열정은 무엇인가요?

A: ....

DAY 28 | DICTATION TEST

5회 반복 예문 QR

DICTATION TEST 예문 QR을 듣고 다음 빈칸에 올바른 단어를 쓰세요.

1141. Do your work hours often ______________ with your colleagues' schedules?

1142. Did you ______________ any important details in the project proposal?

1143. Have you ever worked ______________ or studied in a foreign country?

1144. Do you ever feel ______________ when too many tasks pile up?

1145. Do you ______________ anyone money from your recent business deals?

1146. How much ______________ do we normally need to survive each day?

1147. Did his face turn ______________ when he heard the bad news?

1148. Did you ______________ when you missed your flight this morning?

1149. Are you planning to watch the ______________ downtown this weekend?

1150. Can you write a ______________ explaining your opinion clearly?

1151. Are the two roads running ______________ to each other?

1152. Can a fear of failure ______________ your ability to try new things?

1153. Could you ______________ me for interrupting your important conversation?

1154. Will you ______________ in the company's charity event next week?

1155. Did the scientist detect any ______________ movement during the test?

1156. Is there a ______________ reason you chose that restaurant tonight?

1157. Have you introduced your ______________ to your family?

1158. Can you find the ______________ in the book about ancient history?

1159. Did the ______________ complain about the flight delay?

1160. What is your biggest ______________ outside of your regular work?

5회 반복 표제어 QR　5회 반복 예문 QR

DAY 29

30 days

AI 학습자료와 인강 youpass.co.kr

PREVIEW A 다음 단어의 뜻을 한국어로 써보세요.

□ passive ______	□ penalty ______
□ paste ______	□ per ______
□ path ______	□ perceive ______
□ patient ______	□ perform ______
□ pattern ______	□ performance ______
□ pause ______	□ perhaps ______
□ pave ______	□ period ______
□ peaceful ______	□ permanent ______
□ pedestrian ______	□ permit ______
□ peer ______	□ persist ______

PREVIEW B 사진을 보고 알맞은 영어 단어를 **PREVIEW A**에서 찾아 써보세요.

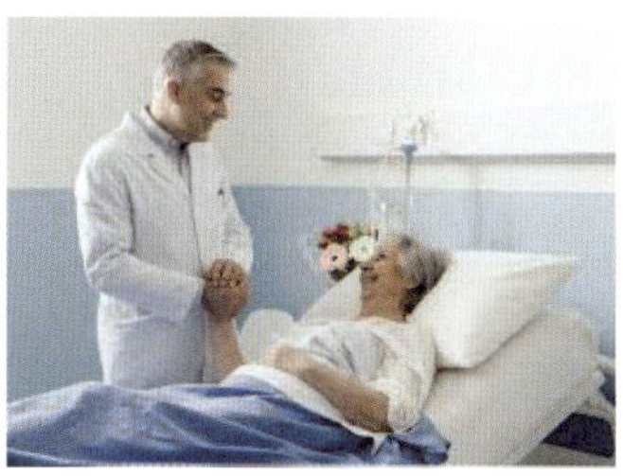
______

______

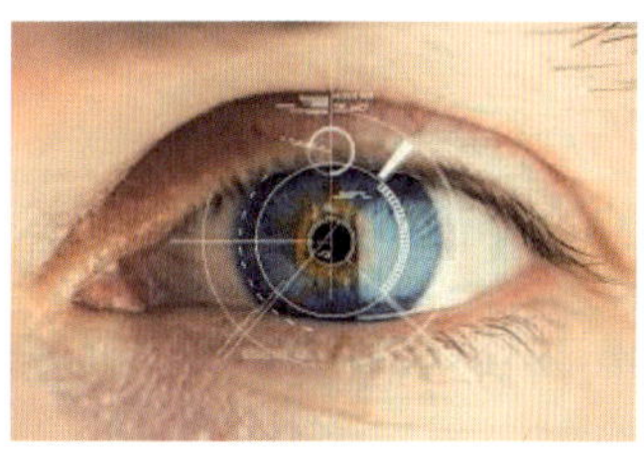
______

______

1161 □□□

passive
[ˈpæsɪv]

a 수동적인

= inactive, submissive, receptive, unresisting

+ passivity **n** 수동성 **passively** **adv** 수동적으로

Q: Are you usually passive or active during group discussions at work? 직장에서 그룹 토론 중에 보통 수동적인가요 아니면 적극적인가요?

A: ....

1162 □□□

paste
[peɪst]

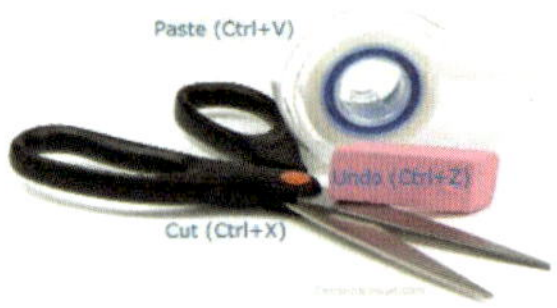

n 풀, 반죽 **v** 붙이다

= glue, adhesive, dough, spread, stick

+ cut-and-paste **a** 풀과 가위로 만든, 잘라 붙여 만든 **scissors-and-paste** **a** 가위와 풀로 편집한, 남의 책을 오려내어 편집하는, 독창성이 없는

Q: Can you paste the link into the email before sending it?
이메일 보내기 전에 링크를 이메일에 붙여 넣을 수 있나요?

A: ....

1163 □□□

path
[pæθ]

n 길, 경로

= way, route, trail, course, track

+ a concrete path 콘크리트 길 **a career path** 진로 계획

Q: Does this forest path lead directly to the old lighthouse?
이 숲길이 오래된 등대로 곧장 이어지나요?

A: ....

1164 □□□

patient
[ˈpeɪʃnt]

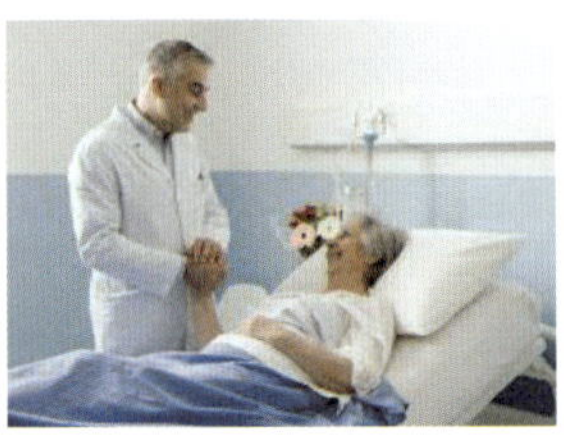

n 환자 **a** 참을성 있는

= tolerant, enduring, persistent, calm, sick person

+ patience **n** 인내심 **patiently** **adv** 인내심 있게 **impatient** **a** 성급한

Q: Do you think doctors always need to be incredibly patient with their patients? 의사들은 환자들에게 항상 엄청나게 인내심을 가져야 한다고 생각하시나요?

A: ....

1165 □□□

pattern
[ˈpætərn]

n 양식, 패턴, 무늬

= design, model, motif, example, arrangement

+ changing patterns of behaviour 행동 양식의 변화

Q: Do you see a pattern in your spending habits each month?
매달 당신의 소비 습관에서 패턴이 발견되나요?

A: ....

1166 □□□

pause
[pɔːz]

n 잠시 멈춤 v 잠시 멈추다

= halt, break, stop, interruption, hesitate
+ pause for breath 숨을 돌리기 위해 잠깐 멈추다

Q: Should we pause the meeting for a short break?
회의를 잠시 쉬었다가 갈까요?

A: ....

1167 □□□

pave
[peɪv]

v (도로를) 포장하다

= surface, cover, lay, prepare the way
+ pavement n 포장 도로

Q: Will they pave the road outside your house this summer?
올여름에 당신 집 밖의 도로를 포장할 건가요?

A: ....

1168 □□□

peaceful
[ˈpiːsfl]

a 평화로운

= calm, tranquil, serene, harmonious, quiet
+ peace n 평화 peacefully adv 평화롭게

Q: Is your neighborhood peaceful during the late evening hours?
늦은 저녁 시간에 당신의 동네는 평화로운가요?

A: ....

1169 □□□

pedestrian
[pəˈdestriən]

n 보행자

= walker, foot traveler, ordinary, common
+ pedestrian crossing 횡단보도(crosswalk, zebra crossing)

Q: Do pedestrians have the right-of-way at this crosswalk?
이 횡단보도에서는 보행자가 우선인가요?

A: ....

1170 □□□

peer
[pɪr]

n 또래, 동료 v 자세히 들여다보다

= look closely, gaze, associate, equal, noble
+ peerage n 귀족의 신분

Q: Do you often ask your peers for feedback on your projects?
자주 동료들에게 프로젝트에 대한 피드백을 요청하나요?

A: ....

1171 □□□

penalty
[ˈpenəlti]

n 벌금, 처벌

= **punishment, fine, sanction, disadvantage**
+ **penalize** **v** 벌칙을 가하다

Q: What penalty will the team face if they break the rules again?
팀이 다시 규칙을 어기면 어떤 벌칙을 받게 될까요?

A: ....

1172 □□□

per
[pɜːr]

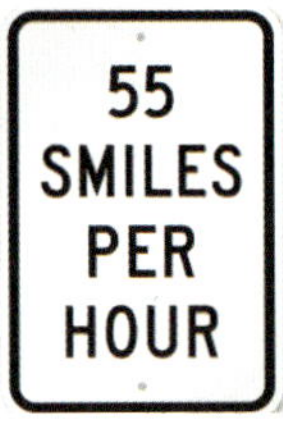

prep ~당, ~마다

= **each, every, by means of, through**
+ **per person** 1인당 **per night** 1박에

Q: How much do you get paid per hour at your current job?
현재 직장에서 시간당 얼마를 받나요?

A: ....

1173 □□□

perceive
[pərˈsiːv]

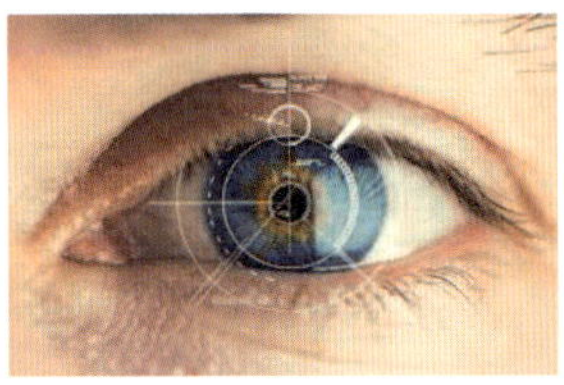

v 감지하다, 인식하다

= **discern, recognize, notice, comprehend, sense**
+ **perception** **n** 인식 **perceptive** **a** 지각력 있는 **perceivable** **a** 인지할 수 있는

Q: Do you perceive any immediate threats to our project's timeline? 우리 프로젝트 일정에 대한 즉각적인 위협을 인지하고 계신가요?

A: ....

1174 □□□

perform
[pərˈfɔːrm]

v 수행하다, 공연하다

= **execute, accomplish, stage, enact, function**
+ **performance** **n** 공연, 성과 **performer** **n** 연기자, 연주자

Q: Can you perform the task without any assistance from others?
다른 사람의 도움 없이 작업을 수행할 수 있나요?

A: ....

1175 □□□

performance
[pərˈfɔːrməns]

n 성능, 공연, 실행

= **show, execution, act, accomplishment, function**
+ **perform** **v** 공연하다, 수행하다

Q: Did your performance improve after the new training sessions?
새로운 훈련 세션 후에 당신의 실적이 향상되었나요?

A: ....

1176 □□□

perhaps
[pər'hæps]

adv 아마도

= maybe, possibly, conceivably, perchance

+ Perhaps that's true. 어쩌면 그것은 사실일 거야.

Q: Perhaps we should reconsider our strategy for the upcoming negotiations? 아마도 우리가 다가오는 협상을 위한 전략을 재고해야 할까요?

A: ....

1177 □□□

period
['pɪriəd]

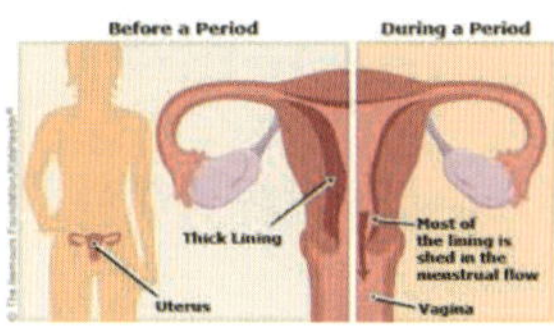

n 기간, 시대, 마침표, 생리[월경]기간

= duration, interval, era, menstruation, point

+ periodic **a** 주기적인 **periodically** **adv** 주기적으로

Q: How long is the trial period for the new software system?
새 소프트웨어 시스템의 시험 기간은 얼마나 되나요?

A: ....

1178 □□□

permanent
['pɜːrmənənt]

a 영구적인, 영원한

= lasting, fixed, constant, perpetual, enduring

+ permanence **n** 영구성 **permanently** **adv** 영구적으로

Q: Are you looking for a permanent position or just temporary work? 영구적인 직책을 찾고 있나요 아니면 임시직을 찾고 있나요?

A: ....

1179 □□□

permit
['pɜːrmɪt] **n** [pər'mɪt] **v**

v 허락하다, 허용하다 **n** 허가증

= allow, authorize, grant, license, pass, leave

+ permission **n** 허가

Q: Do I need a permit to park my car in this area overnight?
이 지역에 밤새 주차하려면 허가가 필요한가요?

A: ....

1180 □□□

persist
[pər'sɪst]

v 고집하다, 지속하다

= continue, persevere, endure, carry on, insist

+ persistence **n** 고집, 끈기 **persistent** **a** 끈기 있는 **persistently** **adv** 끈질기게

Q: Will you persist in trying despite the difficulties you're facing?
당신이 직면한 어려움에도 불구하고 계속 시도할 건가요?

A: ....

DAY 01 DAY 02 DAY 03 DAY 04 DAY 05 DAY 06 DAY 07 DAY 08 DAY 09 DAY 10 DAY 11 DAY 12 DAY 13 DAY 14 DAY 15 DAY 16 DAY 17 DAY 18 DAY 19 DAY 20 DAY 21 DAY 22 DAY 23 DAY 24 DAY 25 DAY 26 DAY 27 DAY 28 DAY 29 DAY 30

DAY 29 | DICTATION TEST

5회 반복 예문 QR

DICTATION TEST 예문 QR을 듣고 다음 빈칸에 올바른 단어를 쓰세요.

1161. Are you usually ________________ or active during group discussions at work?

1162. Can you ________________ the link into the email before sending it?

1163. Does this forest ________________ lead directly to the old lighthouse?

1164. Do you think doctors always need to be incredibly patient with their ________________?

1165. Do you see a ________________ in your spending habits each month?

1166. Should we ________________ the meeting for a short break?

1167. Will they ________________ the road outside your house this summer?

1168. Is your neighborhood ________________ during the late evening hours?

1169. Do ________________ have the right-of-way at this crosswalk?

1170. Do you often ask your ________________ for feedback on your projects?

1171. What ________________ will the team face if they break the rules again?

1172. How much do you get paid ________________ hour at your current job?

1173. Do you ________________ any immediate threats to our project's timeline?

1174. Can you ________________ the task without any assistance from others?

1175. Did your ________________ improve after the new training sessions?

1176. ________________ we should reconsider our strategy for the upcoming negotiations?

1177. How long is the trial ________________ for the new software system?

1178. Are you looking for a ________________ position or just temporary work?

1179. Do I need a ________________ to park my car in this area overnight?

1180. Will you ________________ in trying despite the difficulties you're facing?

5회 반복 표제어 QR　5회 반복 예문 QR

DAY 30

30 days

PREVIEW A 다음 단어의 뜻을 한국어로 써보세요.

- □ personal ____________
- □ personality ____________
- □ personnel ____________
- □ perspective ____________
- □ persuade ____________
- □ pesticide ____________
- □ phase ____________
- □ phenomenon ____________
- □ philosophy ____________
- □ photographer ____________
- □ phrase ____________
- □ physical ____________
- □ physician ____________
- □ physics ____________
- □ pile ____________
- □ pillow ____________
- □ pioneer ____________
- □ pipe ____________
- □ pity ____________
- □ plain ____________

PREVIEW B 사진을 보고 알맞은 영어 단어를 PREVIEW A 에서 찾아 써보세요.

____

____

____

____

1181 □□□

personal
['pɜːrsənl]

a 개인적인

= **private, individual, intimate, subjective, own**

+ **person** **n** 사람 **personality** **n** 성격 **personalization** **n** 개인화
personalize **v** 개인화하다 **personally** **adv** 개인적으로

Q: Is this a personal decision or one by the whole team?
이것이 개인적인 결정인가요, 아니면 팀 전체의 결정인가요?

A: ....

1182 □□□

personality
[ˌpɜːrsə'næləti]

n 성격, 개성

= **character, disposition, temperament, nature**

+ **personal** **a** 개인의

Q: How would you describe your friend's personality?
친구의 성격을 어떻게 묘사할 건가요?

A: ....

1183 □□□

personnel
[ˌpɜːrsə'nel]

n 직원, 인원

= **staff, employees, workforce, human resources**

+ **anti-personnel** **a** 인명 살상용인, 대인 (무기인) **skilled personnel** 숙련된 직원들

Q: Does the company have enough personnel now?
회사가 지금 충분한 인력을 가지고 있나요?

A: ....

1184 □□□

perspective
[pər'spektɪv]

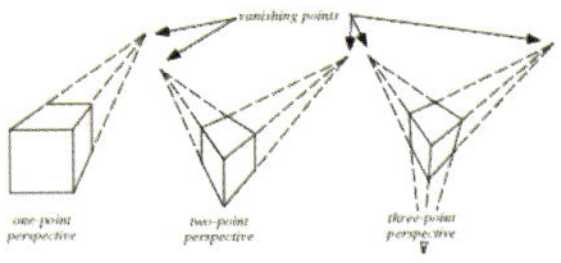

n 관점, 시각

= **viewpoint, outlook, angle, standpoint, vision**

+ **a global perspective** 범세계적인 관점[시각]

Q: Can you share your perspective on the changes?
변화에 대한 당신의 관점을 공유해 줄 수 있나요?

A: ....

1185 □□□

persuade
[pər'sweɪd]

v 설득하다

= **convince, induce, influence, urge, sway**

+ **persuasion** **n** 설득 **persuasive** **a** 설득력 있는

Q: How do you persuade someone to agree with you?
누군가를 당신에게 동의하도록 어떻게 설득하나요?

A: ....

1186 □□□

pesticide
[ˈpestɪsaɪd]

n 살충제

= insecticide, herbicide, chemical spray

\+ pesticide-free produce 무농약 농산물

Q: Do organic farms use any type of pesticide, or are they completely chemical-free? 유기농 농장에서도 어떤 종류의 살충제를 사용하나요, 아니면 완전히 화학 물질이 없나요?

A:

1187 □□□

phase
[feɪz]

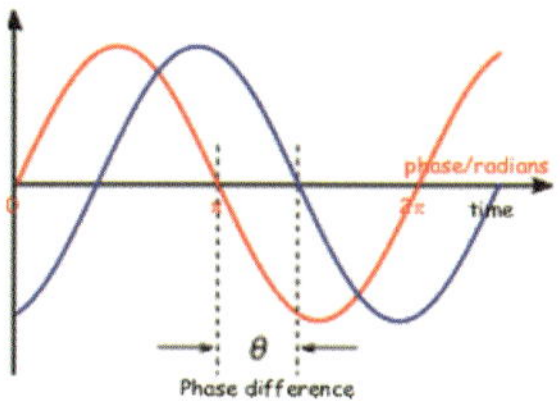

n 단계, 국면

= stage, period, aspect, develop gradually

\+ the design phase 계획 단계

Q: Which phase of the moon is it tonight? 오늘 밤은 어떤 달의 위상인가요?

A:

1188 □□□

phenomenon
[fəˈnɑːmɪnɑːn]

n 현상

= occurrence, event, marvel, rarity, fact

\+ phenomenal **a** 경이적인 phenomenally **adv** 경이롭게

Q: Have you seen a phenomenon like a solar eclipse? 일식과 같은 현상을 본 적 있나요?

A:

1189 □□□

philosophy
[fəˈlɑːsəfi]

n 철학

= wisdom, beliefs, principles, theory, outlook

\+ philosopher **n** 철학자 philosophical **a** 철학적인 philosophically **adv** 철학적으로

Q: What philosophy do you follow in life? 인생에서 어떤 철학을 따르나요?

A:

1190 □□□

photographer
[fəˈtɑːgrəfər]

n 사진작가

= cameraman, photojournalist, artist

\+ photography **n** 사진술 photograph **v** 사진을 찍다 photographic **a** 사진의

Q: Did the photographer capture the event well? 사진작가가 그 행사를 잘 포착했나요?

A:

1191 □□□

phrase
[freɪz]

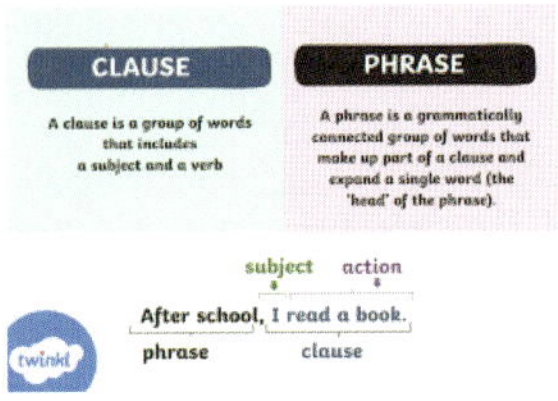

n 구, 문구 **v** 표현하다

= expression, idiom, saying, segment, articulate
+ noun phrase 명사구(문장 속에서 명사처럼 주어•목적어•보어•전치사의 목적어로 쓰이는 구)

Q: Can you explain that phrase simply? 그 구절을 간단하게 설명해 줄 수 있나요?

A: ....

1192 □□□

physical
[ˈfɪzɪkl]

a 신체의, 물리적인

= bodily, corporeal, tangible, material, athletic
+ physics **n** 물리학 physician **n** 의사 physicist **n** 물리학자
physically **adv** 신체적으로, 물리적으로

Q: Do you prefer physical books or digital ones?
실물 책과 디지털 책 중 어느 것을 선호하나요?

A: ....

1193 □□□

physician
[fɪˈzɪʃn]

n (내과) 의사

= doctor, medical practitioner, medic
+ physical **a** 신체의

Q: Have you visited a physician this year? 올해 의사에게 진찰을 받았나요?

A: ....

1194 □□□

physics
[ˈfɪzɪks]

n 물리학

= natural science, mechanics, properties of matter
+ physicist **n** 물리학자 physical **a** 물리적인

Q: Did you enjoy physics in school? 학교에서 물리학을 재미있게 배웠나요?

A: ....

1195 □□□

pile
[paɪl]

n 더미, 쌓아 올린 것 **v** 쌓다

= heap, stack, mound, accumulation, accumulate
+ pile up (양이) 많아지다[쌓이다]

Q: Is there a pile of work on your desk? 당신 책상에 일이 쌓여 있나요?

A: ....

1196 □□□

pillow
[ˈpɪloʊ]

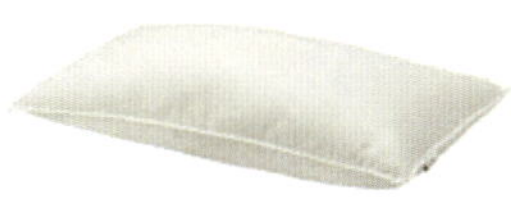

n 베개

= cushion, headrest, bolster

\+ **pillow one's head on one's arm** 팔베개를 하다

Q: Which do you sleep better with: a soft pillow or a firm one?
부드러운 베개와 단단한 베개 중 어느 것으로 잠을 더 잘 자나요?

A: ....

1197 □□□

pioneer
[ˌpaɪəˈnɪr]

n 개척자, 선구자 **v** 개척하다

= trailblazer, innovator, explorer, initiate, lead

\+ **the pioneer spirit** 개척자 정신

Q: Who is the pioneer of modern computers? 현대 컴퓨터의 선구자는 누구인가요?

A: ....

1198 □□□

pipe
[paɪp]

n 파이프, 관

= tube, conduit, duct, smoke, whistle

\+ **pipeline** **n** 파이프라인

Q: Did the plumber fix the broken pipe? 배관공이 망가진 파이프를 고쳤나요?

A: ....

1199 □□□

pity
[ˈpɪti]

n 연민, 동정 **v** 불쌍히 여기다

= compassion, sympathy, sorrow, lament, commiserate

\+ **pitiful** **a** 불쌍한 **pitiless** **a** 무자비한

Q: Is it a pity the concert got canceled? 콘서트가 취소된 것이 안타깝나요?

A: ....

1200 □□□

plain
[pleɪn]

a 평범한, 명백한 **n** 평원

= simple, clear, obvious, flat, unadorned, prairie

\+ **plainly** **adv** 분명히, 수수하게

Q: Do you like plain coffee or coffee with cream?
블랙커피를 좋아하나요, 아니면 크림 넣은 커피를 좋아하나요?

A: ....

DAY 30 | DICTATION TEST

5회 반복 예문 QR

DICTATION TEST 예문 QR을 듣고 다음 빈칸에 올바른 단어를 쓰세요.

1181. Is this a ______________ decision or one by the whole team?
1182. How would you describe your friend's ______________?
1183. Does the company have enough ______________ now?
1184. Can you share your ______________ on the changes?
1185. How do you ______________ someone to agree with you?
1186. Do organic farms use any type of ______________, or are they completely chemical-free?
1187. Which ______________ of the moon is it tonight?
1188. Have you seen a ______________ like a solar eclipse?
1189. What ______________ do you follow in life?
1190. Did the ______________ capture the event well?
1191. Can you explain that ______________ simply?
1192. Do you prefer ______________ books or digital ones?
1193. Have you visited a ______________ this year?
1194. Did you enjoy ______________ in school?
1195. Is there a ______________ of work on your desk?
1196. Which do you sleep better with: a soft ______________ or a firm one?
1197. Who is the ______________ of modern computers?
1198. Did the plumber fix the broken ______________?
1199. Is it a ______________ the concert got canceled?
1200. Do you like ______________ coffee or coffee with cream?

대기중 영단어 1800 리스트

1. abandon
2. ability
3. aboard
4. abroad
5. absence
6. absolute
7. absorb
8. abstract
9. academic
10. accent
11. accept
12. access
13. accident
14. accompany
15. accomplish
16. account
17. accurate
18. accuse
19. achieve
20. acid
21. acquire
22. activate
23. active
24. adapt
25. addicted
26. addition
27. address
28. adequate
29. adjust
30. admire
31. admission
32. admit
33. adolescent
34. adopt
35. advance
36. advantage
37. advertise
38. advise
39. advocate
40. affect
41. afford
42. afterward
43. agent
44. aggressive
45. agriculture
46. aid
47. aim
48. aircraft
49. alike
50. aloud
51. alter
52. alternative
53. although
54. altitude
55. amaze
56. ambiguous
57. amount
58. amuse
59. amusement
60. analyze
61. ancestor
62. ancient
63. angle
64. anniversary
65. announce
66. announcer
67. annoy
68. annual
69. anonymous
70. anticipate
71. antique
72. anxiety
73. anxious
74. anytime
75. anyway
76. apart
77. apologize
78. apology
79. apparent
80. appeal
81. appear
82. appearance
83. applaud
84. apply
85. appoint
86. appreciate
87. approach
88. appropriate
89. approve
90. approximately
91. aptitude
92. architecture
93. argue
94. argument
95. arise
96. army
97. arouse
98. arrange
99. arrangement
100. arrest
101. arrogant
102. article
103. artificial
104. ashamed
105. asleep
106. aspect
107. aspire
108. assemble
109. assess
110. asset
111. assign
112. assist
113. associate
114. association
115. assume
116. astronaut
117. astronomer
118. athlete
119. atmosphere
120. atom
121. attach
122. attain
123. attempt
124. attend
125. attention
126. attitude
127. attract
128. attraction
129. attractive
130. attribute
131. audience
132. author
133. authority
134. automatic
135. automobile
136. available
137. avenue
138. average
139. avoid
140. await
141. awake
142. award
143. aware
144. awesome
145. awful
146. awkward
147. background
148. bacteria
149. badly
150. balance
151. bald
152. ban
153. bandage
154. banner
155. bar
156. barely
157. barrier
158. basis
159. bear
160. beat
161. beg
162. behave
163. behavior
164. belief
165. belong
166. bend
167. benefit
168. beside
169. besides
170. bet
171. bias
172. bill
173. billion
174. bind
175. biology
176. birth
177. bit
178. bitter
179. blame
180. blend
181. bless
182. block
183. bold
184. bond
185. boost
186. booth
187. border
188. bother
189. bow
190. brain
191. branch
192. breathe
193. breed
194. brief
195. brilliant
196. broad
197. broadcast
198. budget
199. bullet
200. bunch
201. burden
202. burst
203. bury
204. bush
205. business
206. cable
207. cage
208. calculate
209. campaign
210. canal
211. cancer
212. candidate
213. candle
214. capable
215. capital
216. capture
217. carbon
218. cardboard
219. career
220. carnival
221. carve
222. cast
223. castle
224. casual
225. caution
226. cautious
227. cease
228. ceiling
229. celebrate
230. cell
231. ceremony
232. certain
233. certainly
234. certificate
235. chain
236. challenge
237. champion
238. character
239. characteristic
240. charge
241. charity
242. charm
243. chart
244. chase
245. cheat
246. chef
247. chemical
248. chemistry
249. cherish
250. chest
251. chief
252. childhood
253. chop
254. chore
255. chronic
256. circuit
257. circulate
258. circumstance
259. circus
260. cite
261. citizen
262. civil
263. claim
264. clarify
265. classic
266. classical
267. classify
268. clerk
269. clever
270. cliff
271. climate
272. climbing
273. closet
274. clue
275. coal
276. coast
277. coincide
278. collaborate
279. collapse
280. colleague
281. collection
282. collective
283. college
284. combat
285. combine
286. comfort
287. comfortable
288. command
289. comment
290. commerce
291. commercial
292. commit
293. committee
294. common
295. commonly
296. communicate
297. communication
298. community
299. commute
300. companion
301. company

302. compare
303. comparison
304. compass
305. compete
306. competition
307. competitive
308. complain
309. complaint
310. complement
311. complete
312. completely
313. complex
314. complicate
315. complicated
316. compliment
317. compose
318. compromise
319. conceal
320. concentrate
321. concept
322. concern
323. concerned
324. conclude
325. conclusion
326. concrete
327. condition
328. conduct
329. conference
330. confess
331. confidence
332. confident
333. confine
334. confirm
335. conflict
336. conform
337. confront
338. confuse
339. congratulation
340. conquer
341. conscience
342. conscious
343. consent
344. consequence
345. conserve
346. consider
347. considerable
348. considerate
349. consist
350. consistent
351. constant
352. constantly
353. construct
354. construction
355. consult
356. consume
357. contact
358. contain
359. container
360. contemporary
361. content
362. context
363. continent
364. continue
365. continuous
366. contract
367. contrary
368. contrast
369. contribute
370. convenient
371. convention
372. conversation
373. convert
374. convey
375. convince
376. cooperate
377. cooperative
378. coordinate
379. corporation
380. correctly
381. costly
382. cotton
383. council
384. counsel
385. counselor
386. crack
387. craft
388. crash
389. crawl
390. crazy
391. creation
392. creature
393. credit
394. crime
395. criminal
396. crisis
397. critical
398. criticize
399. crop
400. crowd
401. crowded
402. crucial
403. cruel
404. crush
405. cultivate
406. cultural
407. cure
408. curiosity
409. curious
410. current
411. curve
412. custom
413. customer
414. cyber
415. cycle
416. damage
417. damp
418. dare
419. data
420. daytime
421. deadly
422. deal
423. dealer
424. debate
425. debt
426. decade
427. decay
428. deceive
429. decision
430. declare
431. decline
432. decorate
433. decoration
434. decrease
435. dedicate
436. dedication
437. defeat
438. defend
439. defense
440. define
441. definite
442. degree
443. delay
444. delicate
445. delight
446. deliver
447. delivery
448. demand
449. democracy
450. demonstrate
451. dense
452. deny
453. department
454. depend
455. depress
456. depressed
457. depth
458. derive
459. descend
460. describe
461. description
462. desert
463. deserve
464. desire
465. despair
466. desperate
467. despite
468. destination
469. destiny
470. destroy
471. destruction
472. detail
473. detect
474. detective
475. determine
476. develop
477. device
478. devise
479. devote
480. dew
481. diagnose
482. diet
483. dietary
484. differ
485. difference
486. difficulty
487. dig
488. digest
489. digestion
490. diligent
491. diminish
492. direction
493. disabled
494. disadvantage
495. disagree
496. disappear
497. disappoint
498. disappointed
499. disaster
500. discipline
501. discount
502. discourage
503. discrimination
504. discuss
505. discussion
506. disease
507. disgust
508. dislike
509. dismiss
510. display
511. dispose
512. distance
513. distant
514. distinct
515. distinguish
516. distract
517. distress
518. distribute
519. district
520. disturb
521. dive
522. diverse
523. divide
524. document
525. domain
526. domestic
527. dominant
528. donate
529. doubt
530. downtown
531. drag
532. dramatic
533. draw
534. drip
535. drown
536. due
537. durable
538. dust
539. duty
540. dynamic
541. dynasty
542. eager
543. earn
544. earthquake
545. ease
546. economic
547. economy
548. ecosystem
549. edit
550. editor
551. educate
552. education
553. effect
554. effective
555. efficient
556. effort
557. elaborate
558. elect
559. electric
560. electricity
561. electronic
562. element
563. eliminate
564. embarrass
565. embrace
566. emerge
567. emergence
568. emergency
569. emission
570. emotion
571. empathy
572. emphasize
573. empire
574. employ
575. enable
576. encounter
577. encourage
578. encouragement
579. endure
580. enforce
581. engage
582. engineer
583. enhance
584. enjoyable
585. enormous
586. enrich
587. enroll
588. ensure
589. entertain
590. enthusiasm
591. entire
592. entirely
593. entrance
594. envelope
595. environment
596. environmental
597. equal
598. equipment
599. equivalent
600. erase
601. escalate
602. escape
603. especially
604. essence
605. essential
606. establish

607. estimate
608. ethic
609. ethical
610. ethnic
611. evaluate
612. evaporate
613. eventually
614. evidence
615. evident
616. evil
617. evolve
618. exactly
619. exaggerate
620. examine
621. exceed
622. except
623. excess
624. exchange
625. excitement
626. exclude
627. exhaust
628. exhausted
629. exhibit
630. exhibition
631. exist
632. existence
633. exotic
634. expand
635. expect
636. expend
637. expense
638. experience
639. experiment
640. expert
641. explain
642. explode
643. explore
644. export
645. expose
646. express
647. expression
648. extend
649. extent
650. external
651. extinct
652. extra
653. extraordinary
654. extreme
655. fabric
656. facility
657. factor
658. fade
659. failure
660. faint
661. fair
662. faith
663. fake
664. fame
665. familiar
666. fancy
667. fantasy
668. fare
669. fascinate
670. fashionable
671. fasten
672. fate
673. fatigue
674. faucet
675. fault
676. favor
677. favorite
678. fear
679. feast
680. feather
681. feature
682. fee
683. feed
684. fellow
685. fiction
686. field
687. figure
688. filter
689. finance
690. financial
691. fine
692. firm
693. fit
694. flame
695. flash
696. flat
697. flavor
698. flesh
699. flexible
700. flight
701. float
702. flood
703. flourish
704. flow
705. fluid
706. fold
707. folk
708. following
709. forbid
710. force
711. forecast
712. foreign
713. foresee
714. forever
715. forget
716. forgive
717. formal
718. format
719. former
720. formula
721. fortunate
722. fortunately
723. fortune
724. found
725. fountain
726. fragile
727. frame
728. frankly
729. freedom
730. freezing
731. frequent
732. friendship
733. fright
734. frighten
735. frustrate
736. fuel
737. fulfill
738. function
739. fund
740. fundamental
741. furniture
742. further
743. furthermore
744. gap
745. garage
746. gender
747. general
748. generally
749. generate
750. generation
751. generous
752. genetic
753. genius
754. genuine
755. geography
756. gesture
757. glance
758. glory
759. glow
760. govern
761. government
762. grab
763. grade
764. gradual
765. gradually
766. graduate
767. graduation
768. grain
769. grammar
770. grant
771. grateful
772. grave
773. gravity
774. grip
775. grocery
776. growth
777. guarantee
778. guard
779. guest
780. guilty
781. habitat
782. haircut
783. handle
784. happen
785. hardly
786. harm
787. harvest
788. haste
789. hatch
790. heal
791. heaven
792. height
793. heritage
794. hesitate
795. hiccup
796. highlight
797. highly
798. hire
799. historic
800. historical
801. hollow
802. holy
803. honor
804. horizon
805. horizontal
806. horror
807. hospitality
808. host
809. hostility
810. household
811. humanity
812. humble
813. humiliate
814. hunger
815. hurricane
816. hybrid
817. hypothesis
818. ideal
819. identical
820. identify
821. identity
822. idiom
823. idle
824. ignore
825. illegal
826. illustrate
827. imaginary
828. imagination
829. imaginative
830. imagine
831. imitate
832. immediate
833. immediately
834. immigrate
835. immune
836. impact
837. impatient
838. imply
839. import
840. importance
841. impossible
842. impress
843. impressed
844. impression
845. impressive
846. improve
847. incident
848. incline
849. include
850. income
851. increase
852. incredible
853. indeed
854. independence
855. independent
856. index
857. indicate
858. indifferent
859. individual
860. indoor
861. industry
862. inevitable
863. infant
864. infect
865. infection
866. inferior
867. influence
868. inform
869. informal
870. information
871. ingredient
872. inhabit
873. inherent
874. inherit
875. initial
876. initiate
877. injure
878. injured
879. injury
880. injustice
881. inner
882. innocent
883. innovation
884. input
885. inquire
886. inquiry
887. insert
888. insight
889. insist
890. inspect
891. inspire
892. install
893. instance
894. instant
895. instead
896. instinct
897. institute
898. institution
899. instruct
900. instrument
901. insult
902. insurance
903. intake
904. intellectual
905. intelligence
906. intelligent
907. intend
908. intense
909. interaction
910. interest
911. interfere

912. interior
913. internal
914. international
915. interpret
916. interpreter
917. interrupt
918. interval
919. intonation
920. introduce
921. invade
922. invent
923. invest
924. investigate
925. invitation
926. involve
927. iron
928. irritate
929. isolate
930. issue
931. jail
932. jealous
933. joint
934. journey
935. judge
936. justice
937. justify
938. kindness
939. knit
940. knowledge
941. labor
942. laboratory
943. lack
944. ladder
945. landscape
946. lastly
947. latter
948. launch
949. lawyer
950. lay
951. layer
952. league
953. leak
954. lean
955. leap
956. lecture
957. legal
958. legend
959. lend
960. length
961. liberal
962. liberty
963. license
964. lid
965. lightning
966. likely
967. limit
968. linguistic
969. link
970. liquid
971. literal
972. literally
973. literate
974. literature
975. litter
976. load
977. loan
978. local
979. locate
980. location
981. locker
982. logic
983. logical
984. loose
985. loosen
986. loss
987. loyal
988. luxury
989. lyric
990. magnet
991. maintain
992. major
993. majority
994. manage
995. manipulate
996. manner
997. manual
998. manufacture
999. margin
1000. mass
1001. massive
1002. master
1003. masterpiece
1004. material
1005. mature
1006. maximum
1007. mayor
1008. meaning
1009. meanwhile
1010. measure
1011. mechanic
1012. mechanical
1013. medical
1014. meditate
1015. medium
1016. melt
1017. memorable
1018. memorial
1019. memory
1020. mend
1021. mental
1022. mention
1023. mentor
1024. merchant
1025. mercy
1026. merely
1027. merit
1028. merry
1029. mess
1030. messy
1031. metal
1032. metaphor
1033. method
1034. migrate
1035. military
1036. minimize
1037. minimum
1038. minor
1039. miserable
1040. mission
1041. mixture
1042. moderate
1043. modern
1044. modest
1045. modify
1046. monitor
1047. monster
1048. mood
1049. moonlight
1050. moral
1051. moreover
1052. mostly
1053. motion
1054. motivate
1055. motto
1056. mount
1057. movement
1058. mud
1059. multiple
1060. multiply
1061. murder
1062. muscle
1063. mutual
1064. mysterious
1065. myth
1066. narrator
1067. narrow
1068. native
1069. natural
1070. navigate
1071. navy
1072. nearby
1073. necessary
1074. necessity
1075. negative
1076. neglect
1077. negotiate
1078. neighborhood
1079. nerve
1080. nervous
1081. nest
1082. net
1083. neuron
1084. neutral
1085. nevertheless
1086. newborn
1087. noble
1088. norm
1089. normal
1090. normally
1091. northern
1092. notice
1093. novel
1094. nowadays
1095. nuclear
1096. numerous
1097. nutrient
1098. obey
1099. object
1100. objective
1101. observe
1102. obstacle
1103. obtain
1104. obvious
1105. occasion
1106. occupation
1107. occupy
1108. occur
1109. odd
1110. offend
1111. offer
1112. official
1113. omit
1114. operate
1115. operation
1116. operator
1117. opinion
1118. opponent
1119. opportunity
1120. oppose
1121. opposite
1122. optimist
1123. option
1124. order
1125. ordinary
1126. organ
1127. organic
1128. organization
1129. organize
1130. orient
1131. origin
1132. original
1133. originate
1134. otherwise
1135. outcome
1136. outline
1137. output
1138. outstanding
1139. overall
1140. overcome
1141. overlap
1142. overlook
1143. overseas
1144. overwhelm
1145. owe
1146. oxygen
1147. pale
1148. panic
1149. parade
1150. paragraph
1151. parallel
1152. paralyze
1153. pardon
1154. participate
1155. particle
1156. particular
1157. partner
1158. passage
1159. passenger
1160. passion
1161. passive
1162. paste
1163. path
1164. patient
1165. pattern
1166. pause
1167. pave
1168. peaceful
1169. pedestrian
1170. peer
1171. penalty
1172. per
1173. perceive
1174. perform
1175. performance
1176. perhaps
1177. period
1178. permanent
1179. permit
1180. persist
1181. personal
1182. personality
1183. personnel
1184. perspective
1185. persuade
1186. pesticide
1187. phase
1188. phenomenon
1189. philosophy
1190. photographer
1191. phrase
1192. physical
1193. physician
1194. physics
1195. pile
1196. pillow
1197. pioneer
1198. pipe
1199. pity
1200. plain
1201. planet
1202. pleasure
1203. plenty
1204. plot
1205. plural
1206. poet
1207. poetry
1208. poison
1209. polar
1210. pole
1211. policy
1212. polish
1213. political
1214. politics
1215. poll
1216. pollute

1217. pollution
1218. popularity
1219. population
1220. portion
1221. portrait
1222. pose
1223. position
1224. positive
1225. possess
1226. possible
1227. postpone
1228. posture
1229. potential
1230. poverty
1231. powder
1232. practical
1233. pray
1234. precious
1235. precise
1236. predator
1237. predict
1238. prefer
1239. pregnant
1240. prejudice
1241. prescribe
1242. present
1243. presentation
1244. preserve
1245. press
1246. pressure
1247. pretend
1248. prevent
1249. previous
1250. prey
1251. priceless
1252. pride
1253. priest
1254. primary
1255. prime
1256. primitive
1257. principal
1258. principle
1259. prior
1260. priority
1261. privacy
1262. private
1263. privilege
1264. probably
1265. procedure
1266. proceed
1267. process
1268. produce
1269. product
1270. productive
1271. profession
1272. professional
1273. professor
1274. profit
1275. profound
1276. progress
1277. prohibit
1278. promote
1279. pronounce
1280. pronunciation
1281. proof
1282. proper
1283. properly
1284. property
1285. proportion
1286. propose
1287. prospect
1288. protect
1289. protein
1290. protest
1291. prove
1292. proverb
1293. provide
1294. psychology
1295. public
1296. publication
1297. publish
1298. punctual
1299. punish
1300. pupil
1301. purchase
1302. pure
1303. purify
1304. purpose
1305. pursue
1306. qualify
1307. quality
1308. quantity
1309. quarrel
1310. quarter
1311. quit
1312. quote
1313. racial
1314. radical
1315. rainforest
1316. raise
1317. random
1318. range
1319. rank
1320. rapid
1321. rapidly
1322. rare
1323. rarely
1324. rate
1325. rather
1326. rational
1327. raw
1328. react
1329. realistic
1330. reality
1331. realize
1332. reap
1333. reason
1334. reasonable
1335. recall
1336. receipt
1337. recent
1338. recharge
1339. reckless
1340. recognize
1341. recommend
1342. recover
1343. recreate
1344. recruit
1345. recycle
1346. reduce
1347. refer
1348. reference
1349. refine
1350. reflect
1351. reform
1352. refresh
1353. refund
1354. refuse
1355. regard
1356. region
1357. register
1358. regret
1359. regular
1360. regulate
1361. reinforce
1362. reject
1363. relate
1364. related
1365. relationship
1366. relative
1367. release
1368. relevant
1369. relief
1370. relieve
1371. religion
1372. religious
1373. rely
1374. remain
1375. remark
1376. remarkable
1377. remember
1378. remind
1379. remote
1380. remove
1381. renew
1382. repair
1383. repeat
1384. repeatedly
1385. replace
1386. reply
1387. represent
1388. representative
1389. reproduce
1390. republic
1391. reputation
1392. request
1393. require
1394. rescue
1395. research
1396. resemble
1397. resent
1398. reserve
1399. resident
1400. resign
1401. resist
1402. resolution
1403. resolve
1404. resource
1405. respect
1406. respectable
1407. respectful
1408. respective
1409. respond
1410. response
1411. responsible
1412. restore
1413. restrict
1414. retire
1415. reveal
1416. reverse
1417. revise
1418. revive
1419. revolution
1420. reward
1421. rhythm
1422. rid
1423. riddle
1424. risk
1425. ritual
1426. rob
1427. root
1428. rotate
1429. route
1430. routine
1431. row
1432. royal
1433. rub
1434. rubber
1435. rude
1436. ruin
1437. rural
1438. rush
1439. rusty
1440. sacred
1441. sacrifice
1442. safety
1443. sail
1444. satellite
1445. satisfaction
1446. satisfied
1447. satisfy
1448. saving
1449. saw
1450. saying
1451. scale
1452. scatter
1453. schedule
1454. scholar
1455. scientific
1456. scold
1457. scratch
1458. scream
1459. screen
1460. script
1461. seal
1462. secretary
1463. section
1464. secure
1465. security
1466. seed
1467. seek
1468. seize
1469. seldom
1470. select
1471. selective
1472. selfish
1473. senior
1474. sense
1475. sensible
1476. sensitive
1477. separate
1478. sequence
1479. series
1480. servant
1481. serve
1482. session
1483. setting
1484. settle
1485. several
1486. severe
1487. sew
1488. shallow
1489. shame
1490. share
1491. shave
1492. shelter
1493. shift
1494. shock
1495. shoot
1496. shore
1497. shortage
1498. shot
1499. shut
1500. sigh
1501. sight
1502. sightseeing
1503. signal
1504. signature
1505. significant
1506. silence
1507. silly
1508. similar
1509. similarity
1510. simplify
1511. simultaneously
1512. since
1513. sincere
1514. sink
1515. site
1516. situation
1517. skillful
1518. slave
1519. slice
1520. slight
1521. slightly

1522. slip
1523. slope
1524. smoke
1525. smooth
1526. sneeze
1527. snore
1528. social
1529. soil
1530. soldier
1531. solid
1532. solution
1533. somehow
1534. somewhat
1535. somewhere
1536. sore
1537. sort
1538. soul
1539. source
1540. southern
1541. sow
1542. spare
1543. sparkle
1544. specialize
1545. species
1546. specific
1547. spill
1548. spin
1549. spine
1550. spirit
1551. splendid
1552. split
1553. spoil
1554. spontaneously
1555. spot
1556. spray
1557. spread
1558. square
1559. squeeze
1560. stable
1561. staff
1562. stain
1563. stamp
1564. standard
1565. stare
1566. state
1567. statement
1568. station
1569. statue
1570. status
1571. steady
1572. steal
1573. steel
1574. steep
1575. stem
1576. stereotype
1577. stick
1578. sticky
1579. stiff
1580. stimulate
1581. sting
1582. stir
1583. stock
1584. stomachache
1585. stove
1586. straighten
1587. stranger
1588. strategy
1589. stream
1590. strength
1591. stress
1592. stretch
1593. strict
1594. strike
1595. string
1596. strip
1597. stripe
1598. stroke
1599. structure
1600. struggle
1601. studio
1602. stuff
1603. subject
1604. subjective
1605. submit
1606. substance
1607. substitute
1608. suburb
1609. succeed
1610. success
1611. successful
1612. successive
1613. sudden
1614. suffer
1615. sufficient
1616. suggest
1617. suggestion
1618. suit
1619. suitable
1620. sum
1621. summarize
1622. summary
1623. superior
1624. supervise
1625. supper
1626. supply
1627. support
1628. suppose
1629. surface
1630. surgery
1631. surprisingly
1632. surround
1633. survey
1634. survive
1635. suspect
1636. suspend
1637. suspension
1638. sustainable
1639. swallow
1640. swear
1641. sweat
1642. sweep
1643. switch
1644. symbol
1645. sympathy
1646. symptom
1647. system
1648. tag
1649. tale
1650. talented
1651. tap
1652. target
1653. task
1654. tax
1655. tease
1656. technical
1657. technician
1658. technology
1659. temper
1660. temperature
1661. temporary
1662. tend
1663. tendency
1664. tender
1665. tense
1666. tension
1667. term
1668. terrible
1669. terribly
1670. terrific
1671. territory
1672. theme
1673. theory
1674. therapy
1675. therefore
1676. thirst
1677. thoughtful
1678. thread
1679. threat
1680. threaten
1681. thrilling
1682. throat
1683. tide
1684. tidy
1685. tight
1686. tissue
1687. tolerate
1688. tomb
1689. tone
1690. totally
1691. tough
1692. trace
1693. tragedy
1694. tragic
1695. trail
1696. trait
1697. transfer
1698. transform
1699. translate
1700. transmit
1701. transport
1702. transportation
1703. trap
1704. treasure
1705. treat
1706. treatment
1707. trend
1708. trial
1709. tribe
1710. trick
1711. trigger
1712. troop
1713. tropical
1714. truly
1715. trust
1716. tune
1717. twist
1718. typhoon
1719. typical
1720. ultimate
1721. unbelievable
1722. undergo
1723. underground
1724. underwater
1725. uneasy
1726. unexpected
1727. unfortunately
1728. unhealthy
1729. unify
1730. union
1731. unique
1732. unit
1733. unite
1734. universal
1735. universe
1736. university
1737. unreasonable
1738. unusual
1739. upset
1740. upward
1741. urban
1742. urge
1743. urgent
1744. utilize
1745. vacation
1746. valid
1747. valley
1748. valuable
1749. value
1750. variable
1751. variety
1752. various
1753. vary
1754. vast
1755. vehicle
1756. version
1757. vertical
1758. vet
1759. via
1760. victim
1761. victory
1762. violate
1763. violence
1764. violent
1765. virtual
1766. virtue
1767. visible
1768. vision
1769. visitor
1770. visual
1771. vital
1772. vivid
1773. vocation
1774. voluntary
1775. volunteer
1776. wage
1777. wander
1778. warn
1779. waterproof
1780. wavy
1781. wealth
1782. weapon
1783. weed
1784. weep
1785. weigh
1786. whisper
1787. whistle
1788. whole
1789. widespread
1790. wipe
1791. wisdom
1792. wisely
1793. withstand
1794. witness
1795. wonder
1796. worship
1797. worth
1798. wound
1799. wrap
1800. yield